AMERICA'S
TOP
GUNS

GALLERY BOOKS

An Imprint of W. H. Smith Publishers Inc.

112 Madison Avenue

New York City 10016

AMERICA'S
TOP
GUNS

© Aerospace Publishing 1990

First published in the United States in 1990 by Gallery Books,
an imprint of W. H. Smith Publishers, Inc.,
112 Madison Avenue, New York, New York 10016

Gallery Books are available for bulk purchase for sales
promotions and premium use. For details write or telephone
the Manager of Special Sales, W. H. Smith Publishers, Inc.,
112 Madison Avenue, New York, New York 10016. (212) 532-
6600

Printed in Hong Kong

ISBN: 0-8317-0359-8

Pictures were supplied by:

Robin Adshead, Bell Helicopters, Boeing, British Aerospace,
David Donald, Malcolm English, Peter R. Foster, Rene J.
Francillon, General Dynamics, Grumman, Grumman Aerospace
Corporation, Grumman History Center, Hughes, Paul A.
Jackson, Jon Lake, Robert L. Lawson Collection, Lockheed,
MacClancy Collection, McDonnell Douglas, Peter R. March, Bob
Munro, R. J. Pickett, Chris Pocock, John D. R. Rawlings,
Rockwell International, Terry Senior, Robbie Shaw, Sikorsky, US
Air Force, US Army, US Marine Corps, US Navy, R. L. Ward,
Roger P. Wasley

Special thanks to TRH Pictures

Production controller: Alastair Gourlay
Production editor: Chris Marshall
Jacket design: Simon Bleeze
Design: Brown Packaging

Previous page: A pair of McDonnell Douglas F-15 Eagles.

CONTENTS

Bell Model 209 (single-engine)/AH-1 HueyCobra

Greece Israel Japan Jordan Pakistan Turkey United States

Bell AH-1S HueyCobra of the Israeli air force (Heyl Ha'Avir).

When details were issued of the Army's AAFSS (Advanced Aerial Fire Support System) requirement to replace the failed Lockheed Cheyenne, Bell initiated crash development of a company-funded prototype derived from the Model 204; it had the powerplant, transmission and wide-chord rotor of the UH-1C but introduced a new fuselage seating the gunner in the nose and the pilot higher in the rear. The fuselage was very narrow, only 0.97 m (3 ft 2 in) at its widest point and this, coupled with a low silhouette, made the aircraft easy to conceal on the ground and a more difficult target in the air. Designated **Bell Model 209 Huey-Cobra,** the prototype (N209J) was flown for the first time on 7 September 1965. It began service tests in December 1965, and then gained an order for two pre-production **AH-1G** helicopters on 4 April 1966 and an initial contract for 110 production AH-1Gs nine days later; such was the degree of urgency. Initial production deliveries reached the US Army in June 1967 and within weeks the type had become operational in Vietnam. AH-1G production totalled 1,119 for the US Army, of which 38 were transferred to the US Marine

Corps for training; some US Army AH-1Gs were converted as **TH-1G** dual-control trainers. Later variants include 92 **AH-1Q** conversions from AH-1Gs to fire TOW missiles, and the **AH-1R** conversion with a 1342-kW (1,800-shp) T53-L-703 turboshaft and no TOW capability. The designation **Modified AH-1S** applies to 315 AH-1Gs retrofitted with a TOW system and the powerplant of the AH-1R, plus the 92 AH-1Qs brought up to this same standard. They were followed by 100 **Production AH-1S** which have improved avionics, uprated powerplant and transmission; 98 similar **Up-gun AH-1S** which introduce a universal 20/30-mm gun turret and other refinements; and the current **Modernised AH-1S.** This last incorporates the updates of the Production and Up-gun AH-1S, and improvements that include new air data, Doppler navigation and fire-control systems, and continuing programmes are under development to enhance the capability of the HueyCobra. In addition to the production of Modernised AH-1S Hueys for the US Army, others are in the process of manufacture and delivery for foreign air arms.

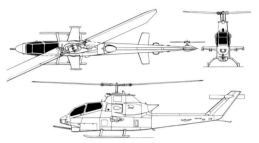

Bell AH-1S HueyCobra

Specification: Bell Modernised AH-1S
Origin: USA
Type: anti-armour attack helicopter
Powerplant: one 1342-kW (1,800-shp) Lycoming T53-L-703 turboshaft engine, flat-rated at 820 kW (1,100 shp)
Performance: maximum speed with TOW missiles 122 kts (227 km/h; 141 mph); initial rate of climb 1,620 ft (494 m) per minute; service ceiling 12,200 ft (3720 m); range with maximum fuel and reserves 507 km (315 miles) at sea level
Weights: empty 2939 kg (6,479 lb); maximum take-off 4536 kg (10,000 lb)
Dimensions: main rotor diameter 13.41 m (44 ft 0 in); length, rotors turning 16.14 m (52 ft 11.5 in); height 4.12 m (13 ft 6.25 in); main rotor disc area 141.26 m² (1,520.53 sq ft)
Armament: eight TOW missiles, one General Electric universal turret for 20-mm or 30-mm cannon, plus launcher pods for 2.75-in (69.85-mm) folding-fin rockets

Early AH-1Gs are still in service with the US Army National Guard. This example serves in Utah.

Aircraft of modernized AH-1S standard are now being supplied in some numbers to foreign users. The Pakistani army are to receive 20 for anti-armour duties, coming complete with TOW missiles.

Bell Model 209 (twin-engine)/AH-1J/T SeaCobra

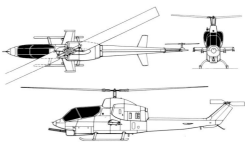

Bell AH-1J SeaCobra of the US Marine Corps.

US Marine Corps interest in a well-armed close-support helicopter was heightened by the US Army's procurement of the Bell AH-1G HueyCobra. Following USMC evaluation of the AH-1G it was decided to acquire this for service, but with the extra reliability of a twin-engine powerplant. In May 1968 the USMC ordered 49 **AH-1J SeaCobra** helicopters, and as an interim measure procured 38 AH-1G HueyCobras which were used for training and initial deployment until delivery of the SeaCobras during 1970-1. This initial AH-1J retained basically the same airframe as the AH-1G, with some detail changes to cater for the higher output of the Pratt & Whitney Canada T400-CP-400 powerplant, a revolutionary engine with two powerplants which ran for the first time in July 1968. Flat-rated at 820 kW (1,100 shp) and with a take-off and emergency power rating of 932 kW (1,250 shp), the T400 is a militarized version of Pratt & Whitney Canada's PT6T-3 Turbo Twin-Pac, incorporating aluminium instead of magnesium in its construction, which is essential for a maritime or seaboard environment. Bell was also to build for Iran 202 similar AH-1Js, but these incorporated TOW-capability.

An additional 20 AH-1Js were delivered to the USMC in 1974-5, the last two of this batch being modified subsequently to serve as prototypes for the **AH-1T Improved Sea-Cobra.** Retaining many features of the AH-1J airframe, these have a slightly lengthened fuselage (to increase fuel capacity), a lengthened tail boom, improved main and tail rotors as developed for the Bell Model 214, and an uprated transmission to handle the full rated power of the upgraded T400-WV-402 powerplant, developing 1469 kW (1,970 shp). The first of 57 AH-1Ts (59228) was flown on 20 May 1976 and delivered to the USMC on 15 October 1977. Of these, 51 have now been equipped to carry TOW missiles.

In 1980 Bell was loaned an AH-1T by the USMC, and demonstrated this machine with two General Electric T700-GE-700 turbo-shafts having a combined output of 2386 kW (3,200 shp). From this was planned an improved AH-1T which, in production form, will have T700-GE-401 turboshafts developing together 2424 kW (3,250 shp), a new combining gearbox and other improvements. Designated **AH-1T+ SuperCobra,** 44 have been ordered by the USMC with initial deliveries scheduled for March 1986.

Bell AH-1T SeaCobra

Sporting the new black markings, this AH-1J displays the far bulkier engine bay of the twin-engined version. These helicopters have recently had infra-red countermeasures fitted.

The Marine Corps Cobras are used for supporting ground operations, especially beach assaults. TOW missiles are used, and the new Rockwell Hellfire missile is also entering service.

Specification: Bell AH-1T SeaCobra

Origin: USA
Type: twin-turbine close-support/attack helicopter
Powerplant: one 1469-kW (1,970-shp) Pratt & Whitney Canada T400-WV-402 twin-turbine unit, which has a maximum continuous rating of 1248 kW (1,673 shp)
Performance: maximum speed 149 kts (277 km/h; 172 mph) at sea level; initial rate of climb 1,785 ft (544 m) per minute; service ceiling 7,400 ft (2255 m); range with maximum fuel 420 km (261 miles)
Weights: empty 3642 kg (8,030 lb); maximum take-off 6350 kg (14,000 lb)
Dimensions: main rotor diameter 14.63 m (48 ft 0 in); length, rotors turning 17.68 m (58 ft 0 in); height 4.32 m (14 ft 2 in); main rotor disc area 168.11 m² (1,809.56 sq ft)
Armament: chin turret housing a 20-mm M197 three-barrel cannon, plus underwing attachments for 2.75-in (69.85-mm) rocket pods, flare dispensers, grenade dispensers, parachute flares, Minigun pods, or alternative TOW or Hellfire missile installations

Role	
Fighter	
Close support	■
Counter-insurgency	
Tactical strike	
Strategic bomber	
Tactical reconnaissance	
Strategic reconnaissance	
Maritime patrol	
Anti-ship strike	
Anti-submarine warfare	
Search and rescue	
Assault transport	
Transport	
Liaison	
Trainer	
Inflight-refuelling tanker	
Specialized	
Performance	
All-weather capability	
Rough field capability	■
STOL capability	
VTOL capability	■
Airspeed 0-250 mph	■
Airspeed 250 mph-Mach 1	
Airspeed Mach 1 plus	
Ceiling 0-20,000 ft	■
Ceiling 20,000-40,000 ft	
Ceiling 40,000 ft plus	
Range 0-1,000 miles	■
Range 1,000-3,000 miles	
Range 3,000 miles plus	
Weapons	
Air-to-air missiles	
Air-to-surface missiles	■
Cruise missiles	
Cannon	■
Trainable guns	■
Naval weapons	
Nuclear-capable	
Rockets	■
'Smart' weapon kit	
Weapon load 0-4,000 lb	■
Weapon load 4,000-15,000 lb	
Weapon load 15,000 lb plus	
Avionics	
Electronic Counter Measures	
Electronic Support Measures	
Search radar	
Fire control radar	
Look-down/shoot-down	
Terrain-following radar	
Forward-looking infra-red	
Laser	
Television	

Iran   Israel   South Korea   United States

7

Bell Model 205/UH-1D/UH-1H Iroquois

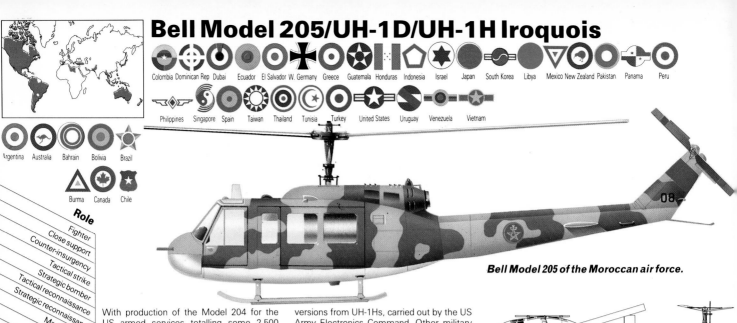

Colombia | Dominican Rep | Dubai | Ecuador | El Salvador | W. Germany | Greece | Guatemala | Honduras | Indonesia | Israel | Japan | South Korea | Libya | Mexico | New Zealand | Pakistan | Panama | Peru

Philippines | Singapore | Spain | Taiwan | Thailand | Tunisia | Turkey | United States | Uruguay | Venezuela | Vietnam

Argentina | Australia | Bahrain | Bolivia | Brazil

Burma | Canada | Chile

Bell Model 205 of the Moroccan air force.

With production of the Model 204 for the US armed services totalling some 2,500 examples, it is not surprising that an improved **Bell Model 205**, proposed in 1960, was of interest to the US Army; a contract followed in July 1960 for seven service test **YUH-1D** helicopters. These retained the Lycoming T53-L-11 turboshaft, but differed from the Model 204 by having a larger-diameter main rotor; a lengthened fuselage for a pilot and 12-14 troops, or six stretchers and a medical attendant, or 1814 kg (4,000 lb) of freight; and increased fuel capacity and provision for auxiliary fuel. The first was flown on 16 August 1961 and the type was ordered into production for the US Army under the designation **UH-1D**, the first being delivered on 9 August 1963. A total of 2,008 was built for the US Army, followed by the generally similar **UH-1H**, which differed by introducing the 1044-kW (1,400-shp) T53-L-13 turboshaft; final production of the UH-1H (40 for the Turkish army) is scheduled to end in 1986. Variants include three **EH-1H** ECM conversions from the UH-1H, with many more planned before the intended mission was taken over by the Sikorsky EH-60A, plus some 220 **UH-1V** medevac con-

versions from UH-1Hs, carried out by the US Army Electronics Command. Other military versions of the Model 205, generally similar to the UH-1H, have included 10 **CUH-1H** operational trainers for the Canadian Armed Forces (which designated them **CH-118**) and 30 **HH-1H** rescue helicopters for the USAF. Production of the UH-1H for the US Army totalled 3,573, and it is planned to retain some 2,700 in service into the 21st century. Under a product improvement programme these have gained new avionics and equipment, and new composite main rotor blades are to be introduced, as well as Doppler navigation and an improved cockpit. In addition to military exports by Bell, a multi-role utility helicopter for both civil and military use has been extensively licence-built by Agusta in Italy as the **Agusta-Bell AB.205**, with production continuing; Fuji in Japan is also building the Model 205 under the designation UH-1H. Dornier in Germany completed 352 equivalent to the UH-1D, which serve with the Luftwaffe and Heeresflieger-truppen, and in Taiwan AIDC built 118 similar to the UH-1H for the Chinese Nationalist army.

Bell Model 205 (UH-1D/H)

Fuji builds the Model 205 as the UH-1H for local use. This aircraft is typical of Japanese Hueys, which are used for general duties and search and rescue.

The US Army plans to retain masses of the UH-1H until the 21st century, despite widespread introduction of Sikorsky's Black Hawk. Many now serve with the National Guard.

Specification: Bell UH-1H
Origin: USA
Type: general-purpose helicopter
Powerplant: one 1044-kW (1,400-shp) Lycoming T53-L-13 turboshaft engine
Performance: maximum speed 110 kts (204 km/h; 127 mph); initial rate of climb 1,600 ft (488 m) per minute; service ceiling 12,600 ft (3840 m); range with maximum fuel 318 miles (512 km)
Weights: empty 2363 kg (5,210 lb); maximum take-off 4309 kg (9,500 lb)
Dimensions: main rotor diameter 14.63 m (48 ft 0 in); length, rotors turning 17.62 m (57 ft 9.7 in); height 4.41 m (14 ft 5.5 in); main rotor disc area 168.11 m² (1,809.56 sq ft)
Armament: none in this version

Bell Model 206 Army versions/OH-58 Kiowa

The US Army's competition for a Light Observation Helicopter (LOH), announced in 1960, appeared a reasonably uncomplicated problem. It was only when they read the 'small print' that prospective contenders realized that the term LOH covered a helicopter suitable not only for an observation role, but for missions that included also casevac, close support, photo-reconnaissance and light transport. This demanding challenge spurred interest, no fewer than 12 US manufacturers making design proposals for this four-seat helicopter, for which a payload of 181 kg (400 lb) and cruising speed of some 104 kts (193 km/h; 120 mph) was specified. Bell, Hiller and Hughes each gained contracts to build five prototypes for evaluation, the Hughes contender finally being chosen by the US Army. Nevertheless, convinced that its design had merit, Bell built a new five-seat prototype, the **Bell Model 206A JetRanger.** Flown on 10 January 1966 and certificated nine months later, the Model 206A was soon produced commercially and also built by Agusta in Italy.

In 1967 the US Army, worried by delivery rate and rising cost of the Hughes OH-6A reopened its LOH competition; on 8 March

1968 the Bell Model 206A was declared winner and ordered into production as the **OH-58A Kiowa.** Deliveries to the US Army began on 23 May 1969, and over five years a total of 2,200 were procured; the Canadian Armed Forces also acquired 74 as **COH-58A** (later **CH-136**) helicopters. On 30 June 1976 the US Army awarded Bell a development contract to convert one OH-58A to improved **OH-58C** standard; this introduced a flat glass canopy, uprated engine, and an installation for infra-red suppression, and two more OH-58C conversions followed before modification of 275 OH-58As to OH-58C standard began in March 1978.

In September 1981 the **Bell Model 406** proposal won the Army Helicopter Improvement Program (AHIP) to provide close combat reconnaissance and an ability to support attack helicopters and direct artillery fire. The Model 406 thus introduces a mast-mounted sight, specialized avionics and a cockpit control and display subsystem. The US Army expect that testing of five Model 406 prototypes, which ended in 1985, will result in the modification of 578 OH-58A Kiowas to this new AHIP standard under the designation **OH-58D.**

Specification: Bell OH-58C Kiowa
Origin: USA
Type: light observation helicopter
Powerplant: one 313-kW (420-shp) Allison T63-A-720 turboshaft engine
Performance: maximum speed 120 kts (222 km/h; 138 mph) at sea level; cruising speed 102 kts (188 km/h; 117 mph); initial rate of climb 1,780 ft (543 m) per minute; service ceiling 18,900 ft (5760 m); maximum range on armed scout mission at sea level with no reserves 491 km (305 miles)
Weights: empty 719 kg (1,585 lb); maximum take-off 1451 kg (3,200 lb)
Dimensions: main rotor diameter 10.77 m (35 ft 4 in); length, rotors turning 12.49 m (40 ft 11.75 in); height 2.91 m (9 ft 6.5 in); main rotor disc area 91.09 m² (980.56 sq ft)
Armament: the M27 armament kit incorporating a 7.62-mm (0.3-in) Minigun is standard

Bell OH-58A Kiowa of the 25th Aviation Company, US Army based in Germany.

Bell OH-58A Kiowa

Most early Kiowas are expected to be converted to OH-58D standard, featuring four-blade rotor and mast-mounted sight. Completely revised avionics will also be fitted.

The OH-58A serves in large numbers with the US Army, used in the spotting role. A six-barrel machine-gun provides suppressive fire whilst operating in hostile areas.

Role
Fighter
Close support
Counter-insurgency
Tactical strike
Strategic bomber
Tactical reconnaissance
Strategic reconnaissance
Maritime patrol
Anti-ship strike
Anti-submarine warfare
Search and rescue
Assault transport
Transport
Liaison
Trainer
Inflight-refuelling tanker
Specialized

Performance
All-weather capability
Rough field capability
STOL capability
VTOL capability
Airspeed 0-250 mph
Airspeed 250 mph-Mach 1
Airspeed Mach 1 plus
Ceiling 0-20,000 ft
Ceiling 20,000-40,000 ft
Ceiling 40,000ft plus
Range 0-1,000 miles
Range 1,000-3,000 miles
Range 3,000 miles plus

Weapons
Air-to-air missiles
Air-to-surface missiles
Cruise missiles
Cannon
Trainable guns
Naval weapons
Nuclear-capable
Rockets
'Smart' weapon kit
Weapon load 0-4,000 lb
Weapon load 4,000-15,000 lb
Weapon load 15,000 lb plus

Avionics
Electronic Counter Measures
Electronic Support Measures
Search radar
Fire control radar
Look-down/shoot-down
Terrain-following radar
Forward-looking infra-red
Laser
Television

Boeing B-52: the 'Buff' fights on

Boeing's monster bomber has carried the United States' airborne nuclear deterrent for over 30 years, and spent eight of those embroiled in the heaviest bombing campaign in history. The enormous range and bombload of these leviathans are still in demand in today's low-level, stand-off environment.

The B-52 is a cumbersome beast, especially on the ground, where large tow-trucks are required to manoeuvre them. The two blisters under the nose house the LLLTV and FLIR sensors for the electro-optical viewing system.

First flown in prototype form during April 1952, Boeing's mighty B-52 Stratofortress entered service with Strategic Air Command at the end of June 1955, the first examples of this massive eight-engined bomber joining that command's 93rd Bomb Wing at Castle Air Force Base, California. Today, over 30 years down the road, the Stratofortress is still easily the most numerous bomber type to be found in SAC's operational inventory, more than 250 examples of the B-52G and B-52H variants remaining active in late 1985.

Even more remarkable, however, is the fact that most of these great veterans are likely to remain in service until well into the 1990s, if not to the end of the present century, there being no plans to retire the type in the short term. When the last 'Buff' (Big ugly fat fella) is finally retired, Boeing's 'big stick' will have established a service longevity record that is second to none, and one that will clearly take some beating.

Originally conceived purely as a strategic bomber and initially armed solely with nuclear weapons, the B-52 has in more recent years demonstrated a surprising degree of versatility for so old a design. Although nuclear deterrence is still viewed as the primary responsibility of the dozen or so bomb wings which are presently equipped with the Stratofortress, the type can also be employed in a purely conventional role with free-fall 'iron' bombs or 'smart' weapons such as the EO-guided GBU-15 cruciform-wing glide bomb and AGM-109H Tomahawk non-nuclear Medium-Range ASM. Other missions which can be undertaken with near-equal facility are show-of-force, defence suppression, minelaying and long-range ocean surveillance, while the type frequently provides support to NATO exercises, simulating use in a conventional bombing role.

Short-tail survivors

Although the B-52 is still quite clearly a most important part of the US arsenal, only two of the eight basic production variants remain in service, the tall-tailed B-52A to B-52F models having all been retired and, in most cases, scrapped. Both the models which continue to operate with SAC feature the short vertical tail surface introduced on the B-52G, and it is this derivative which is by far the more numerous, approximately 165 of the 193 aircraft built still being in service. In addition, about 95 examples of the final production model, the B-52H, are still active, these being the survivors of the original production total of 102 aircraft.

While essentially similar in external appearance, there are significant differences between the B-52G and the B-52H. For a start, the B-52G is powered by a battery of eight Pratt & Whitney J57-P-43WB turbojet engines, each of which generates some 6237-kg (13,750-lb) static thrust with water-methanol injection. Conversely, the B-52H (colloquially known throughout SAC as 'the Cadillac', an allusion to the fact that it is rather quieter and therefore somewhat less fatiguing to fly) features eight 7711-kg (17,000-lb) static thrust Pratt & Whitney TF33-P-3 turbofan engines. Defensive armament also provides another distinguishing feature between the two versions: the older B-52G possesses a quartet of 0.5-in (12.7-mm) M3 machine-guns in its tail turret, while the B-52H is fitted with a single six-barrel 20-mm T171 Vulcan cannon, capable of spewing out shells at a rate of 6,000 rounds per minute.

The aircraft which now equip SAC's bomb wings are in fact very different from

The development of surface-to-air missiles has meant that the 'Buff' has had to take to the trees to perform its mission. Handling an aircraft of this size at low level makes for interesting flying, and many low-level flying aids have been added.

The mighty B-52 still forms an important third of the United States' nuclear deterrent triad and, even after wide-scale introduction of the Rockwell B-1, will soldier on in a nuclear role, albeit as back-up to the new bomber.

For many years, the B-52G force flew with three-tone upper surfaces and white undersides. Recently, aircraft have appeared with dark grey noses, whilst others now sport menacing two-tone dark grey and dark brown camouflage.

those which were delivered to the command between 13 February 1959, when the first B-52G joined the 5th Bomb Wing, and 26 October 1962, when the last B-52H was handed over to the 4136th Strategic Wing. In the intervening period, the aircraft have been subjected to numerous modification and updating programmes, all of which have been aimed at prolonging the Stratofortresses' operational careers. These objectives have been, and are still being, pursued along three broad fronts.

Specifically, these have involved extending fatigue life to a figure which is likely to approach three times the 5,000 hours originally projected; enhancing the type's chances of survival should it ever be required to penetrate Soviet airspace; and, finally, improving weapons capability in order that the type can inflict the maximum amount of damage in the event of being committed to combat. Updating the breed began as long ago as 1959 and has been an almost fabulously expensive process, resulting in the B-52 being subjected to modifications which, cumulatively, have cost far more than the aircraft actually did in the first place.

Space limitations preclude detailed examination of the many modification programmes accomplished during the past 25 years or so, but there are some recently concluded and on-going initiatives which merit fairly close attention by virtue of the fact that they have had a significant impact on the type's current capability.

Modifications aimed at improving fuselage and wing life were concluded on the B-52G and B-52H during the early 1970s, and these should ensure that the basic structure remains sound until the end of the present century, always assuming of course that utilization remains at existing levels. However, SAC has been looking into the possibility of using a variant of an existing executive jet as a kind of B-52 simulator, and acquisition of such a type

Full water-injection is needed to lift the giant off the runway, and this creates a dense smoke screen. A stream take-off by 'Buffs' leaves the airfield completely shrouded in smoke. Note the 'barn door' flaps.

would be doubly beneficial in that not only would it permit B-52 flying hours to be cut but it would also enable realistic training to be accomplished at much reduced cost.

A rather more visible update resulted in the appearance of the now-familiar blister fairings on the fuselage undersides beneath the nose radar, these housing sensors for the ASQ-151 EVS. Additional equipment associated with EVS takes the form of display screens and controls at the pilot, co-pilot and navigator stations, provision of this piece of kit significantly improving capability at low level.

Electronic eyes

Installed on all surviving B-52G and B-52H aircraft between 1971 and 1977 at a cost approaching $250 million, EVS basically comprises a Westinghouse AVQ-22 LLLTV camera on the port side and a Hughes AAQ-6 FLIR to starboard, each in a steerable turret, and these had an immediate impact in that the excellent quality of the resulting imagery raised crew confidence when operating in the potentially hazardous low-level flight regime. In addition, the EVS screens also feature alpha-numeric symbols displaying such data as radar altitude, indicated airspeed, time before weapons release, aircraft attitude and artificial horizon, all of which makes the task of flying the aircraft a great deal easier.

Running more or less concurrently with EVS was the Phase VI avionics update, which was rather less visible although it did result in numerous appendages sprouting at various strategic points on the airframe. This, too, encompassed both the B-52G and B-52H variants and was mainly aimed at enhancing ECM capability, which in turn would result in greater likelihood of survival in the event of penetration of enemy airspace. The Phase VI update was particularly complex in that it included installation of an ALQ-117 countermeasures set and an ALR-46 digital RWR, as well as provision of the ALQ-122 SNOE sensor/jammer package plus fitment of additional ALT-28 transmitters and ALE-20 flare launchers.

This, however, pales into insignificance when compared with the OAS which is now being installed on the B-52G and B-52H and which will eventually cost close to $2 billion by the time fleet-wide modification is completed in Fiscal Year 1989. First flown in prototype form in September 1980, the OAS update involves basically the replacement

Due to its exceptional range and large load-carrying capacity, the B-52 is ideal for maritime operations. Aerial sowing of mines is an important task for the B-52 fleet, as are long-range patrols. This G-model drops a mine in Korean waters.

of existing navigation and weapons management systems by an entirely new digital-based solid-state system which includes TERCOM guidance. Elements of OAS are hardened against EMP effects and comprise new processors, controls and displays as well as a new radar altimeter, an attitude and heading reference system, dual inertial navigation equipment and missile interface units, none of which comes cheap in these costly days.

Turning to weapons, the B-52's armoury has improved out of all recognition in comparison with that available when the type first entered service. Nevertheless, gravity weapons do still form a not-insignificant part of the US nuclear arsenal, but the North American AGM-28A/B Hound Dog missile which was deployed on both the B-52G and B-52H is long gone, having disappeared from the SAC inventory back in 1976.

Enter SRAM

Its place aboard the Stratofortress was taken by the Boeing AGM-69A SRAM which began to enter service with the 42nd Bomb Wing in March 1972, becoming operational on 4 August 1972. Each B-52 can carry up to 20 SRAMs, eight being housed internally on a rotary launcher plus six more on each of the two underwing hardpoints. Possessing a maximum range of the order of 160 km (100 miles), each SRAM has a single W-69 warhead with a yield of about 200 kilotons, and this weapon is still very much a part of SAC plans although it has been overshadowed rather more recently by the Boeing AGM-86B ALCM.

Initially deployed only by B-52G units,

Seen prior to the EVS fit, these B-52Gs are accompanied to the runway by Boeing KC-135s. The tankers are an important part of the nuclear bomber force, enabling aircraft to remain airborne in time of crisis, away from the vulnerable airfields.

ALCM has a range of about 2415 km (1,500 miles) and began to enter service with the 416th Bomb Wing in 1982, each ALCM aircraft being configured to carry 12 missiles underwing although the rotary launchers will eventually be modified to carry a further eight examples of this weapon. For the time being, though, B-52Gs operate with a mixture of ALCMs and SRAM missiles, or ALCMs and gravity bombs, being employed in a 'shoot and penetrate' mode, launching the AGM-86Bs from a position of relative safety before entering enemy airspace to deliver their remaining weapons. Although presently carried only by the B-52G, the ALCM is to be installed on the B-52H in a modification programme which was expected to begin in 1985 and which should more or less coincide with the entry into service of the Rockwell B-1B, this being the first entirely new bomber aircraft to join SAC since production of the B-52 and Convair B-58 Hustler terminated in 1962.

Despite the fact that all surviving examples of the Boeing B-52 Stratofortress are true veterans in that none are less than 23 years old, the trusty 'Buff' still features prominently in SAC's SIOP and it would undoubtedly be committed to action in the event of nuclear war. Quite how well

it would perform in such a conflict must remain a matter for conjecture, but there can be little doubt that the many and varied improvements incorporated in the basic design during the past two decades and more would provide the type with an excellent chance of performing its mission satisfactorily.

Paradoxically, if these features are ever put to the test in nuclear combat it will inevitably mean that both the B-52 and SAC have failed in their primary objective, for SAC still views its major function as being one of deterrence rather than of aggression. As it has been for the past 30 years, the Stratofortress is a key element in implementing such a policy.

Glossary
ALCM Air-Launched Cruise Missile
ASM Air-to-Surface Missile
ECM Electronic CounterMeasures
EMP Electro-Magnetic Pulse
EO Electro-Optical
EVS Electro-optical Viewing System
FLIR Forward-Looking Infra-Red
LLLTV Low-Light-Level TV
OAS Offensive Avionics System
RWR Radar Warning Receiver
SIOP Single Integrated Operational Plan
SNOE Smart Noise Operation Equipment
SRAM Short-Range Attack Missile
TERCOM TERrain COntour Matching

B-52 Stratofortress in service units and example aircraft

2nd Bomb Wing
Base: Barksdale AFB, Louisiana
Squadrons and aircraft:
62nd/596th BS (B-52G) 76506, 76512, 80219, 80251, 92586

5th Bomb Wing
Base: Minot AFB, North Dakota
Squadrons and aircraft:
23rd BS (B-52H) 00008, 00040, 10011, 10026, 10029

7th Bomb Wing
Base: Carswell AFB, Texas
Squadrons and aircraft:
9th/20th BS (B-52H) 00007, 00033, 00061, 10003, 10035

28th Bomb Wing
Base: Ellsworth AFB, South Dakota
Squadrons and aircraft:
77th BS (B-52H) 00026, 00030, 00054, 10004, 10017

42nd Bomb Wing
Base: Loring AFB, Maine
Squadrons and aircraft:
69th BS (B-52G) 76505, 76514, 80166, 80235, 92569

92nd Bomb Wing
Base: Fairchild AFB, Washington
Squadrons and aircraft:
325th BS (B-52G) 76475, 76499, 80168, 80227, 92593

93rd Bomb Wing
Base: Castle AFB, California
Squadrons and aircraft:
328th BS/4017th CCTS (B-52G) 76472, 76515, 80159, 80214, 92571

96th Bomb Wing
Base: Dyess AFB, Texas
Squadrons and aircraft:
337th BS (B-52H) recently relinquished its B-52s to become first B-1B unit

97th Bomb Wing
Base: Blytheville AFB, Arkansas
Squadrons and aircraft:
340th BS (B-52G) 76485, 76518, 80185, 80252, 92577

319th Bomb Wing
Base: Grand Forks AFB, North Dakota
Squadrons and aircraft:
46th BS (B-52G) no examples known

320th Bomb Wing
Base: Mather AFB, California
Squadrons and aircraft:
441st BS (B-52G) 76477, 76510, 80189, 80213, 92573

379th Bomb Wing
Base: Wurtsmith AFB, Michigan
Squadrons and aircraft:
524th BS (B-52G) 76474, 80165, 80217, 80244, 92589

410th Bomb Wing
Base: K.I. Sawyer AFB, Michigan
Squadrons and aircraft:
644th BS (B-52H) 00009, 00037, 00045, 10001, 10040

416th Bomb Wing
Base: Griffiss AFB, New York
Squadrons and aircraft:
668th BS (B-52G) 76487, 76501, 80160, 80231, 92602

Other Operators

43rd Strategic Wing
Base: Andersen AB, Guam
Squadrons and aircraft:
60th BS (B-52H) no examples known

NASA Dryden
Base: Edwards AFB, California
Aircraft: (NB-52B) 20008

Air Force Flight Test Center, 6512th Test Squadron
Base: Edwards AFB, California
Aircraft: (B-52G) 80245

13

B-52 recognition points

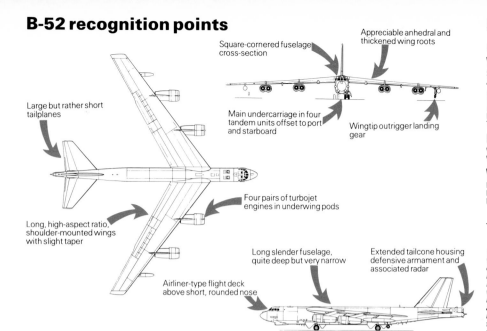

Square-cornered fuselage cross-section

Appreciable anhedral and thickened wing roots

Large but rather short tailplanes

Main undercarriage in four tandem units offset to port and starboard

Wingtip outrigger landing gear

Four pairs of turbojet engines in underwing pods

Long, high-aspect ratio, shoulder-mounted wings with slight taper

Long slender fuselage, quite deep but very narrow

Extended tailcone housing defensive armament and associated radar

Airliner-type flight deck above short, rounded nose

Specification:

Boeing B-52H Stratofortress

Wings
Span	56.39 m	(185 ft 0 in
Area	371.60 m²	(4,000.0 sq

Fuselage and tail unit
Length overall	49.04 m	(160 ft 10.
Height overall	12.40 m	(40 ft 8 in)
Tailplane span	16.95 m	(55 ft 7.5 in

Landing gear
Wheelbase	15.32 m	(50 ft 3 in)
Wheel track, over outer wheels	3.88 m	(12 ft 8.75

Weight
Maximum take-off exceeds	221353 kg	(488,000 lt
Maximum internal fuel	135821 kg	(299,434 lt
Maximum external fuel	4134 kg	(9,114 lb)

The immense size of the B-52 makes it difficult to confuse with any other Western warplane. The size and swept-win design show a similarity to the large Soviet bombers, the Myasishchev M-4 'Bison' and Tupolev Tu-142 'Bear'. The latter features turboprop engines mounted in slim nacelles whereas the 'Bison' has its engines buried in the wing root. Most B-52 confusion arises from the Boeing family of airliners (and, to some extent, the Douglas DC-8). The Boeing 707 and KC-135 are smaller but have a similar slim fuselage, whereas the much larger Boeing 747 features a wide fuselage. In plan view, the B-52 has much larger wing and tailplane areas in relation to the fuselage than do the airliners.

Boeing B-52 variants

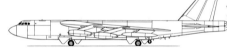

B-52A to B-52F
The early variants of the B-52 all featured tall vertical tail surfaces and a manned gun turret in the tail; J57 engines were standard throughout these versions. All have now been retired from USAF service, having seen much service throughout the Vietnam war. Illustrated is a B-52D, the most common early variant.

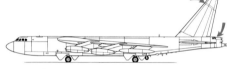

B-52G (early)
The B-52G introduced a number of improvements. The most notable of these were an integral tank, 'wet' wing housing an enormously increased fuel capacity, and a short vertical tail. The gunner was moved from his tail turret to sit in the cockpit alongside the electronic warfare officer, aiming the four 50-cal guns by radar. The version was used widely in Vietnam.

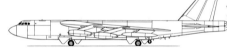

B-52G (contemporary)
The B-52 fleet has undergone many improvement programmes over the years. Current B-52Gs have a greatly increased ECM capability, which has resulted in the addition of more aerials and chaff dispensers. The change in role from high-level to low-level bombing resulted in the Electro-optical Visual Sensor (EVS) fit, with characteristic blisters for the Low-light Level TV (LLLTV) and Forward-looking Infra-red (FLIR) sensors under the chin. More ECM aerials are also housed on the side and front of the nose, and a further blister is now being incorporated on the side of the fin. Cruise-missile carrying B-52Gs have a distinctive wing root fairing for visual identification by the Soviets.

B-52H (early)
The B-52H introduced turbofans with far better fuel economy; both improvements resulted in a corresponding increase in range. The four rear guns are replaced by a six-barrel 20-mm Vulcan rotary cannon, with greater rate of fire. This is controlled from the cockpit.

B-52H (contemporary)
The B-52H fleet has received all the improvements over the years, including the EVS fit. Those due to be converted for cruise-missile carriage will have an internal rotary launcher as well as the G-model's wing pylon attachments.

Boeing B-52G Stratofortress cutaway drawing key

1 Nose radome
2 ALT-28 ECM antenna
3 Electronic countermeasures (ECM) equipment bay
4 Front pressure bulkhead
5 Electronic cooling air intake
6 Bombing radar
7 Low-light television scanner turret (EVS system), infra-red on starboard side
8 Television camera unit
9 ALQ-117 radar warning antenna
10 Underfloor control runs
11 Control column
12 Rudder pedals
13 Windscreen wipers
14 Instrument panel shroud
15 Windscreen panels
16 Cockpit eyebrow windows
17 Cockpit roof escape/ejection hatches
18 Co-pilot's ejection seat
19 Drogue chute container
20 Pilot's ejection seat
21 Flight deck floor level
22 Navigator's instrument console
23 Ventral escape/ejection hatch, port and starboard
24 Radar navigator's downward ejection seat, navigator to starboard
25 Access ladder and hatch to flight deck
26 EWO instructor's folding seat
27 Electronics equipment rack
28 In-flight refuelling receptacle, open
29 Refuelling delivery line
30 Electronic warfare officer's (EWO) ejection seat
31 Rear crew members escape/ejection hatches
32 EWO's instrument panel
33 Gunner's remote control panel
34 Gunner's ejection seat
35 Navigation instructor's folding seat
36 Radio and electronics ra
37 Ventral entry hatch and ladder
38 Lower deck rear pressur bulkhead
39 ECM aerials
40 ECM equipment bay
41 Cooling air ducting
42 Upper deck rear pressur bulkhead
43 Water injection tank, capacity 1,200 US gal (45 litres)
44 Fuselage upper longeror
45 Astro navigation antenna
46 Tank access hatches
47 Leading edge 'strakelets fitted to identify cruise missile carriers
48 Forward fuselage fuel ta
49 Air conditioning plant
50 Forward starboard main undercarriage bogie
51 Landing lamp
52 Forward port main undercarriage bogie
53 Torque scissor links
54 Steering jacks
55 Main undercarriage door
56 Main undercarriage leg strut
57 Wing front spar/fuselage main undercarriage attachment frame

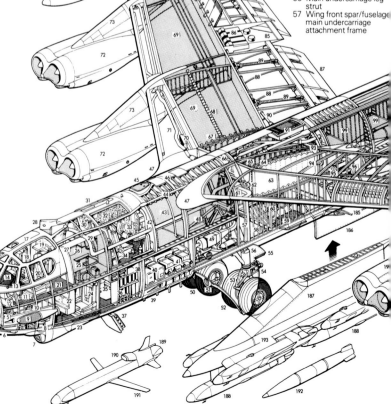

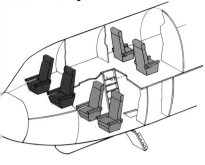

...ove: The B-52 crew is divided into three teams. In the ...ward cabin, the flight crew (blue) of pilot (port) and co-...ot (starboard) handle the flying of the aircraft. Behind ...m, facing backwards, sit the defensive team (red), ...mprising gunner (port) and electronic warfare officer ...arboard). On the lower deck, facing forward, sit the ...ensive team (green), consisting of the navigator ...arboard) and the radar navigator/bombardier (port).

...ght: The 'office' of the B-52 is dominated by the eight ...lumns of engine dials and the huge bunch of throttle ...ndles. On each side of the engine instruments are the two ...eens for the EV system (forward-looking infra-red and low ...ht-level TV). Basic flight instruments are duplicated on ...th the aircraft commander's (left) and co-pilot's (right) ...de. The co-pilot has most of the communications controls ...his side, whilst the secondary flight instruments are on the ...ot's side. On the left-hand side of the throttle bank is the ...ge elevator trim wheel.

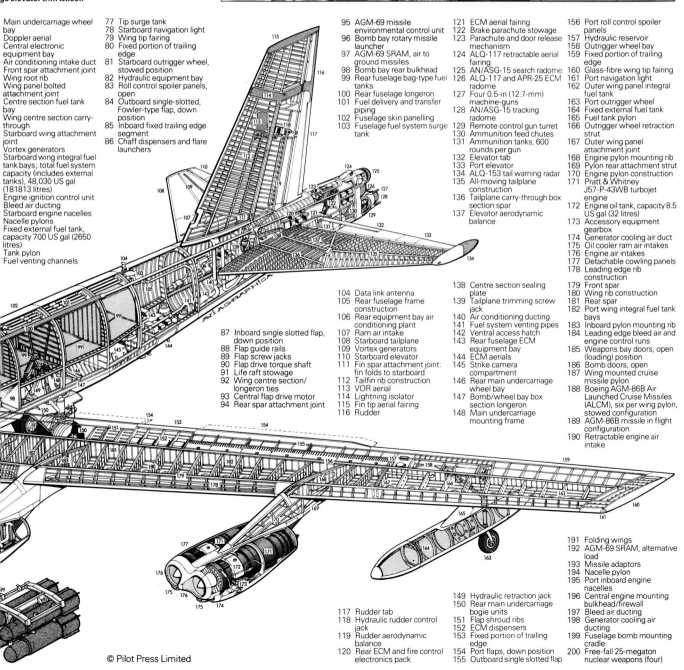

Main undercarriage wheel bay
Doppler aerial
Central electronic equipment bay
Air conditioning intake duct
Front spar attachment joint
Wing root rib
Wing panel bolted attachment joint
Centre section fuel tank bay
Wing centre section carry-through
Starboard wing attachment joint
Vortex generators
Starboard wing integral fuel tank bays; total fuel system capacity (includes external tanks), 48,030 US gal (181813 litres)
Engine ignition control unit
Bleed air ducting
Starboard engine nacelles
Nacelle pylons
Fixed external fuel tank, capacity 700 US gal (2650 litres)
Tank pylon
Fuel venting channels

77 Tip surge tank
78 Starboard navigation light
79 Wing tip fairing
80 Fixed portion of trailing edge
81 Starboard outrigger wheel, stowed position
82 Hydraulic equipment bay
83 Roll control spoiler panels, open
84 Outboard single-slotted, Fowler-type flap, down position
85 Inboard fixed trailing edge segment
86 Chaff dispensers and flare launchers

87 Inboard single slotted flap, down position
88 Flap guide rails
89 Flap screw jacks
90 Flap drive torque shaft
91 Life raft stowage
92 Wing centre section/ longeron ties
93 Central flap drive motor
94 Rear spar attachment joint

95 AGM-69 missile environmental control unit
96 Bomb bay rotary missile launcher
97 AGM-69 SRAM, air to ground missiles
98 Bomb bay rear bulkhead
99 Rear fuselage bag-type fuel tanks
100 Rear fuselage longeron
101 Fuel delivery and transfer piping
102 Fuselage skin panelling
103 Fuselage fuel system surge tank

104 Data link antenna
105 Rear fuselage frame construction
106 Rear equipment bay air conditioning plant
107 Ram air intake
108 Starboard tailplane
109 Vortex generators
110 Starboard elevator
111 Fin spar attachment joint: fin folds to starboard
112 Tailfin rib construction
113 VOR aerial
114 Lightning isolator
115 Fin tip aerial fairing
116 Rudder

117 Rudder tab
118 Hydraulic rudder control jack
119 Rudder aerodynamic balance
120 Rear ECM and fire control electronics pack

121 ECM aerial fairing
122 Brake parachute stowage
123 Parachute and door release mechanism
124 ALQ-117 retractable aerial fairing
125 AN/ASG-15 search radome
126 ALQ-117 and APR-25 ECM radome
127 Four 0.5-in (12.7-mm) machine-guns
128 AN/ASG-15 tracking radome
129 Remote control gun turret
130 Ammunition feed chutes
131 Ammunition tanks, 600 rounds per gun
132 Elevator tab
133 Port elevator
134 ALQ-153 tail warning radar
135 All-moving tailplane construction
136 Tailplane carry-through box section spar
137 Elevator aerodynamic balance

138 Centre section sealing plate
139 Tailplane trimming screw jack
140 Air conditioning ducting
141 Fuel system venting pipes
142 Ventral access hatch
143 Rear fuselage ECM equipment bay
144 ECM aerials
145 Strike camera compartment
146 Rear main undercarriage wheel bay
147 Bomb/wheel bay box section longeron
148 Main undercarriage mounting frame

149 Hydraulic retraction jack
150 Rear main undercarriage bogie units
151 Flap shroud ribs
152 ECM dispensers
153 Fixed portion of trailing edge
154 Port flaps, down position
155 Outboard single slotted flap

156 Port roll control spoiler panels
157 Hydraulic reservoir
158 Outrigger wheel bay
159 Fixed portion of trailing edge
160 Glass-fibre wing tip fairing
161 Port navigation light
162 Outer wing panel integral fuel tank
163 Port outrigger wheel
164 Fixed external fuel tank
165 Fuel tank pylon
166 Outrigger wheel retraction strut
167 Outer wing panel attachment joint
168 Engine pylon mounting rib
169 Pylon rear attachment strut
170 Engine pylon construction
171 Pratt & Whitney J57-P-43WB turbojet engine
172 Engine oil tank, capacity 8.5 US gal (32 litres)
173 Accessory equipment gearbox
174 Generator cooling air duct
175 Oil cooler ram air intakes
176 Engine air intakes
177 Detachable cowling panels
178 Leading edge rib construction
179 Front spar
180 Wing rib construction
181 Rear spar
182 Port wing integral fuel tank bays
183 Inboard pylon mounting rib
184 Leading edge bleed air and engine control runs
185 Weapons bay doors, open (loading) position
186 Bomb doors, open
187 Wing mounted cruise missile pylon
188 Boeing AGM-86B Air Launched Cruise Missiles (ALCM), six per wing pylon, stowed configuration
189 AGM-86B missile in flight configuration
190 Retractable engine air intake

191 Folding wings
192 AGM-69 SRAM, alternative load
193 Missile adaptors
194 Nacelle pylon
195 Port inboard engine nacelles
196 Central engine mounting bulkhead/firewall
197 Bleed air ducting
198 Generator cooling air ducting
199 Fuselage bomb mounting cradle
200 Free-fall 25-megaton nuclear weapons (four)

© Pilot Press Limited

Boeing B-52 warload

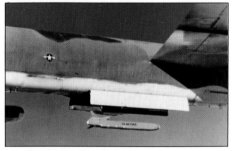

B-52Gs are configured to carry six AGM-86 air-launched cruise missiles on each pylon, with other weaponry, usually the SRAM, carried internally.

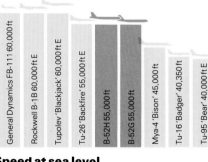

Cruise missiles will be carried on rotary launchers in the weapons bay of the B-52H. Eight rounds will be carried. This ALCM is seen falling from a test aircraft, just prior to the wings unfolding.

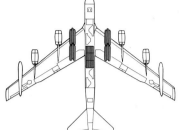

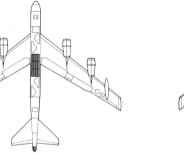

Maritime support
(B-52G)

■ 4×12.7-mm (0.5-in) remotely operated machine-guns with ASG-15 fire-control system
12×AGM-84 Harpoon anti-ship missiles on underwing pylons

Those B-52Gs not modified to CMC configuration are being converted to replace the B-52D in the maritime support role, with the ability to carry out anti-shipping search and strike missions over a wide operational radius in the sea-control role. The sea control B-52G is supported by 'Outlaw Shark' Boeing E-3 AWACS platforms, which provide OTH (over the horizon) targeting. Maritime B-52s can also be used in the minelaying role.

Cruise missile carrier (B-52G and B-52H)

■ 4×12.7-mm (0.5-in) remotely operated machine-guns with ASG-15 fire-control system (B-52G) or
1×20-mm T171 cannon (B-52H)
8×Boeing AGM-69 SRAM short-range attack missiles on rotary launcher in the bomb bay
12×AGM-86 air-launched cruise missiles on inboard underwing pylons

Full-scale development of the B-52 as a cruise missile carrier began in 1978, and 99 B-52Gs plus 96 B-52Hs are being modified to carry 12 AGM-86s externally with SRAMs and other weapons internally. The B-52Hs will later be modified to carry 8×AGM-86s internally on a rotary launcher. Cruise missile carrying B-52Gs are fitted with distinctive wing root fairings in accordance with the SALT 2 agreement.

Defence suppression
(B-52G and B-52H)

■ 4×12.7-mm (0.5-in) remotely controlled machine-guns with ASG-15 fire-control system (B-52G), or
1×20-mm T171 cannon with Mod ASG-15 fire-control system (B-52H)
8×AGM-69 SRAM air-to-surface missiles on internally-carried rotary launcher
12×AGM-69 SRAM air-to-surface missiles on wing pylons

In this mission SRAM supersonic attack missiles, whose short-range designation belies their actual range (in excess of 161 km/100 miles), are individually targeted on known hostile defence complexes such as airfields, major radar sites and surface-to-air missile complexes.

Freefall nuclear bombing
(B-52G and B-52H)

■ 4×12.7-mm (0.5-in) remotely operated machine-guns with ASG-15 fire-control system
8×B28 or B43, or
12×B61 or B83 bombs carried internally

This freefall nuclear payload can be combined with SRAM defence-suppression missiles on the wing pylons, and can be carried by the B-52G and B-52H models over the maximum mission radius of the two variants.

Freefall conventional bombing
(B-52H modified)

■ 1×20-mm T171 cannon with Mod ASG-15 fire-control system
84×Mk 82 500-lb (227-kg) GP iron bombs carried internally, and
24×Mk 82 500-lb (227-kg) GP iron bombs carried on underwing Multiple Ejector Racks (MERs)

The conventional limit for a B-52G in the same role is 12701 kg (28,000 lb), all carried internally.

Performance

Maximum speed above 36,090 ft (11000 m)	517 kts	Mach 0.90 or 958 km/h	(595 mph)
Cruising speed above 36,090 ft (11000 m)	442 kts	Mach 0.77 819 km/h	(509 mph)
Penetration speed at low altitude between and	352 kts 365 kts	652 km/h 676 km/h	(405 mph) (420 mph)
Service ceiling	55,000 ft		(16764 m)
Range with maximum fuel but no inflight refuelling	16093 km		(10,000 miles)

Service ceiling

- General Dynamics FB-111 60,000 ft
- Rockwell B-1B 60,000 ft E
- Tupolev 'Blackjack' 60,000 ft E
- Tu-26 'Backfire' 55,000 ft E
- B-52H 55,000 ft
- B-52G 55,000 ft
- Mya-4 'Bison' 45,000 ft
- Tu-16 'Badger' 40,350 ft
- Tu-95 'Bear' 40,000 ft E

Unfuelled range

- 16093 km B-52H
- 14600 km E Tupolev 'Blackjack'
- 12550 km Tu-95 'Bear'
- 12070 km B-52G
- 12000 km Rockwell B-1B
- 9650 km E Tu-26 'Backfire'
- 8000 km Mya-4 'Bison'
- 4800 km Tu-16 'Badger'
- 4707 km General Dynamics FB-111

Speed at high altitude

- Mach 2.5 General Dynamics FB-111
- Mach 2.1 E Tupolev 'Blackjack'
- Mach 1.92 Tu-26 'Backfire'
- Mach 1.25 Rockwell B-1B
- 538 kt Mya-4 'Bison'
- 535 kt Tu-16 'Badger'
- 516 kt B-52H
- 516 kt B-52G
- 500 kt Tu-95 'Bear'

Speed at sea level

- General Dynamics FB-111 Mach 1.2
- Tu-26 'Backfire' Mach 0.9
- Rockwell B-1B 521 kt
- Tu-95 'Bear' 450 kt E
- B-52H 365 kt
- B-52G 365 kt

Weapons load

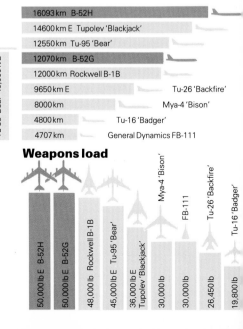

- 50,000 lb E B-52H
- 50,000 lb E B-52G
- 48,000 lb Rockwell B-1B
- 45,000 lb E Tu-95 'Bear'
- 36,000 lb E Tupolev 'Blackjack'
- 30,000 lb Mya-4 'Bison'
- 30,000 lb FB-111
- 26,450 lb Tu-26 'Backfire'
- 19,800 lb Tu-16 'Badger'

A Boeing KC-135R

Boeing C-135/KC-135

On 15 July 1954 Boeing flew its private-venture Model 367-80 prototype for the first time. For the company it represented an enormous gamble, one that depended on winning orders from the US Air Force. In consequence the 'Dash-80' prototype, as it soon became known, was initially a military demonstrator equipped with a Boeing-developed inflight-refuelling boom. This boom, controlled by an operator, was thought to be more practical than the 'probe-and-drogue' system developed in the UK, and its effective demonstration in the 'Dash-80' convinced the USAF that not only was Boeing's rigid 'flying boom' an efficient re-fuelling system, but that the aircraft had important potential as a tanker/transport. In August 1954, a few weeks after the maiden flight of the 'Dash-80', the USAF placed its first contract for the Model 717 as the **Boeing KC-135A Stratotanker**; the first (55-3118) was flown on 31 August 1956 and initial deliveries, to Castle AFB, California, began on 28 June 1957; production totalled 724.

Generally similar to the 'Dash-80', but smaller than even the first Boeing Model 707 developed from it, the KC-135A was powered by four J57 turbojets. In the tanker role fuel system capacity was 118105 litres (31,200 US gal), but the cabin could be used alternatively to carry cargo, loaded via a large door

in the port forward fuselage, or up to 80 passengers or a mixture of freight and passengers; with reduced fuel a maximum of 160 troops could be airlifted. Variants include a small number of KC-135As rebuilt for special duties as **JC-135A** and **JKC-135A**, subsequently becoming **NC-135A** and **NKC-135A** which was the designation of some 20 rebuilds for test and research programmes; 17 new-build **KC-135B** tankers had improved equipment, increased fuel capacity, TF33-5 turbofan engines and provisions for use as airborne command posts; and 56 conversions of KC-135As to transfer JP-7 fuel to Lockheed SR-71 'Blackbirds' were redesignated **KC-135Q**. The Model 717 airframe was adopted also as a cargo/troop transport for MATS (later MAC) as the **C-135A Stratolifter** accommodating 126 troops or 44 stretchers and 54 seated casualties. The C-135A (18 built) was followed by the **C-135B** (30 with TF33-5 engines), but the **C-135F** was a tanker/transport of which 12 were built for France. Seven **VC-135A** staff transports were conversions of C/KC-135A aircraft, two of them retaining tanker capability; five **VC-135B** staff transports were conversions of C-135Bs, as were 11 **WC-135B** weather reconnaissance aircraft, three of which later became reconverted as **C-135C** freighters.

Specification: Boeing KC-135A
Origin: USA
Type: inflight-refuelling tanker/cargo/transport aircraft
Powerplant: four 6237-kg (13,750-lb) thrust Pratt & Whitney J57-59W turbojet engines
Performance: average cruising speed 460 kts (853 km/h; 530 mph) between 30,500 and 40,000 ft (9300 and 12190 m); initial rate of climb 1,290 ft (393 m) per minute; time to climb to 30,500 ft (9300 m) 27 minutes; transfer radius with 3040-kg (6,702-lb) reserve fuel 1850 km (1,150 miles)
Weight: empty 44663 kg (98,466 lb); maximum take-off 136078 kg (300,000 lb); maximum fuel load 86047 kg (189,702 lb)
Dimensions: span 39.88 m (130 ft 10 in); length 41.53 m (136 ft 3 in); height, short fin 11.68 m (38 ft 4 in); wing area 226.03 m² (2,433.0 sq ft)
Armament: none

Boeing KC-135A Stratotanker of the 145th Air Refueling Squadron, 160th ARG, Ohio National Guard.

Boeing KC-135A Stratotanker

A dozen tankers were built for France under the designation C-135F. Eleven survive, and these are shortly to be re-engined with the CFM 56 turbofan.

This is typical of the many KC-135As in service with SAC. Most report to the strategic bomber force, being based with the B-52s and B-1s. This aircraft is from the 92nd BW at Fairchild.

Boeing EC-135

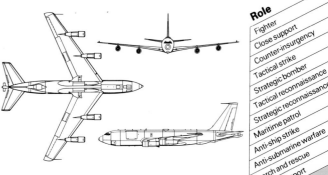

Boeing EC-135H assigned to the 6th ACCS, 1st Tactical Fighter Wing.

In the early days of KC-135A production, the USAF's Strategic Air Command identified the requirement for an airborne command post (ABCP). The idea was for an aircraft equipped for this role to be airborne at all times so that, in the event of a devastating strike against SAC's fixed-position ground control centres, it would be possible to maintain command of its strategic retaliatory force from a command post that was on the move and high above the ground. Accordingly the 17 T33-engined KC-135B tankers delivered to the command also had comprehensive communications systems, were equipped to receive fuel in flight, and had work areas and living quarters laid out within the large cabin area. By 1964 the fact that these aircraft were dedicated ABCPs was recognized by redesignation as the **Boeing EC-135C**, and in mid-1985 13 of the original 17 remained in service in this role.

Over the years the number of EC-135 variants has grown, the EC-135C being joined first by six conversions from J57-engined KC-135A tankers to provide communications relay aircraft able to double in the ABCP role; designated **EC-135A**, five of these aircraft are still operating as relay aircraft. Other variants are in use, although the numbers

quoted have been altered by subsequent further conversions. The **EC-135G** (three converted from KC-135A) serve as airborne control centres for ballistic missile launch but can double for communications relay. Five advanced airborne national command posts (ABNCP) have the designation **EC-135H** (from four KC-135As and one VC-135A) and other ABNCPs include the **EC-135J** (four upgraded from EC-135C). There were originally three **EC-135K** ABNCP conversions from KC-135As for Tactical Air Command, but one was later taken to serve as a zero-gravity astronaut trainer; two **EC-135P** ABNCP conversions now with the Pacific Air Forces are similar but have changes in communications equipment for use in that theatre. Also in current service are five **EC-135L** radio relay aircraft which have reverse refuelling capability to allow for extended missions. Another known variant is the **EC-135N**, of which eight were equipped for satellite tracking and other space projects. At least four **EC-135B ARIA** (Advanced Range Instrumentation Aircraft) each with a steerable antenna in a bulbous nose were derived as conversions of the C-135B.

Boeing EC-135C

This collection of EC-135B and EC-135N ARIA aircraft was brought together for Apollo space missions. The large antenna in the bulbous nose is for tracking missiles and rockets.

The EC-135J is a rebuild of the EC-135C for airborne command post duties. These are typical of the ABNCP EC-135s and are active with the 9th ACCS, 15th ABW.

Specification: Boeing EC-135A
Origin: USA
Type: communications relay aircraft
Powerplant: four 6237-kg (13,750-lb) thrust Pratt & Whitney J57-59W turbojet engines
Performance: maximum speed 508 kts (941 km/h; 585 mph) at 30,000 (9145 m); average cruising speed 460 kts (853 km/h; 430 mph) between 30,500 and 40,000 ft (9300 and 12190 m); initial rate of climb 2,000 ft (610 m) per minute; service ceiling 50,000 ft (15240 m)
Weights: empty 46633 kg (98,466 lb); maximum take-off 134717 kg (297,000 lb)
Dimensions: span 39.88 m (130 ft 10 in); length 41.53 m (136 ft 3 in); height 12.70 m (41 ft 8 in); wing area 226.03 m² (2,433.0 sq ft)
Armament: none

Role
Fighter
Close support
Counter-insurgency
Tactical strike
Strategic bomber
Tactical reconnaissance
Strategic reconnaissance
Maritime patrol
Anti-ship strike
Anti-submarine warfare
Search and rescue
Assault transport
Transport
Liaison
Trainer
Inflight-refuelling tanker
Specialized

Performance
All-weather capability
Rough field capability
STOL capability
VTOL capability
Airspeed 0-250 mph
Airspeed 250 mph-Mach 1
Airspeed Mach 1 plus
Ceiling 0-20,000 ft
Ceiling 20,000-40,000 ft
Ceiling 40,000ft plus
Range 0-1,000 miles
Range 1,000-3,000 miles
Range 3,000 miles plus

Weapons
Air-to-air missiles
Air-to-surface missiles
Cruise missiles
Cannon
Trainable guns
Naval weapons
Nuclear-capable
Rockets
'Smart' weapon kit
Weapon load 0-4,000 lb
Weapon load 4,000-15,000 lb
Weapon load 15,000 lb plus

Avionics
Electronic Counter Measures
Electronic Support Measures
Search radar
Fire control radar
Look-down/shoot-down
Terrain-following radar
Forward-looking infra-red
Laser
Television

Boeing KC-135E and KC-135R

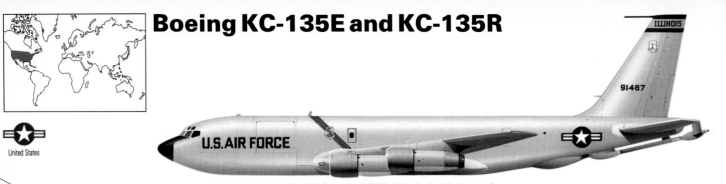

Boeing KC-135E Stratotanker of the 108th ARS, 126th ARW, Illinois Air National Guard.

Modern performance requirements for fighter/interceptor aircraft are an antithesis to range, yet the policy of major air forces to react quickly when needed in a far distant policing role demands unprecedented range. It is a constantly growing demand, one which makes the requirement for inflight-refuelling tankers increase by leaps and bounds, and it is important for an air arm to get the maximum utilization from its existing fleet.

When production of Boeing KC-135 tankers for the US Air Force ended a total of 724 had been built, of which about 650 remain in use. It was decided to ensure they would remain operational into the next century, the major requirement being replacement of the underwing skin. This task, started in 1975, has progressed steadily and by mid-1985 more than 500 KC-135s had benefited from this modification which should extend service life by some 27,000 hours. It was followed by a programme to re-engine Air National Guard and Air Force Reserve KC-135s with JT3D engines (civil equivalent of the TF33). These powerplants were removed and refurbished from ex-commercial Boeing 707s acquired by the USAF, and at the same time the KC-135s gain also tail units, engines pylons and cowlings

from the Model 707s. Simultaneously new brakes and anti-skid units are installed and, upon completion of the work, the aircraft are redesignated **KC-135E**.

Far more comprehensive is the programme to update the main tanker fleet with the 9979-kg (22,000-lb) thrust CFM International F108-CF-100 turbofan (equivalent to the civil CFM56-2B-1), existing contracts covering 108 conversions. With this powerplant revision comes also an APU to give self-start capability; more advanced autopilot, avionics, controls and displays on the flight deck; strengthened main landing gear incorporating anti-skid units; revised hydraulic/pneumatic systems; and an enlarged tailplane. Redesignated **KC-135R** on completion of this update, the first example was redelivered to SAC's 384th Air Refueling Wing at McConnell AFB, Wichita in July 1984. Improved capability enables the KC-135R to operate from shorter runways (civil airports if necessary) and to transfer more fuel, to an extent that two can cover the workload of three KC-135A tankers. In addition to KC-135R conversions for the USAF, Boeing received a contract to modify seven of the 11 remaining French C-135F tankers to this same standard.

Specification: Boeing KC-135R
Origin: USA
Type: inflight-refuelling tanker/cargo/transport aircraft
Powerplant: four 9979-kg (22,000-lb) thrust CFM International F108-CF-100 turbofan engines
Performance: average cruising speed 460 kts (853 km/h; 530 mph) between 30,500 and 40,000 ft (9300 and 12190 m); able to transfer 150 per cent more fuel than the KC-135A at a radius of 4627 km (2,875 miles)
Weight: maximum take-off 146284 kg (322,500 lb); maximum fuel-load 92210 kg (203,288 lb)
Dimensions: span 39.88 m (130 ft 10 in); length 41.53 m (136 ft 3 in); height 12.70 m (41 ft 8 in); wing area 226.03 m² (2,433.0 sq ft)
Armament: none

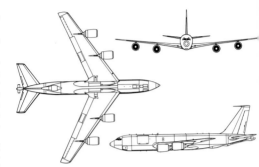

Boeing KC-135R Stratotanker

An early KC-135R shows the large high-bypass ratio CFM F108 turbofans which have replaced the thirsty J57s. Fuel receiving capability has also been added.

The whole first-line KC-135 fleet will eventually be re-engined, giving a planned service life into the 21st century. This example is from the 384th ARW at McConnell AFB.

Boeing EC-137D/E-3 Sentry

One of the most vital roles fulfilled by the Model 707 airframe is that of the USAF's and NATO's Airborne Warning And Control System (AWACS) aircraft, which carries the designation **Boeing E-3 Sentry**. It is, in effect, an airborne radar station serving also as a command, control and communications (C³) centre. Operating in three dimensions it is regarded as survivable under wartime conditions, as it is highly resistant to jamming, and in addition to the C³ function provides long-range surveillance over all terrains.

On 23 July 1970 the Boeing Aerospace Company, previously concerned only with missiles and space, became prime contractor/integrator for the AWAC System, proposing the Model 707-320B as its carrier and recommending that the aircraft be powered by eight TF34 engines, a choice later changed back to four TF33 turbofans to save cost. Under the designation **EC-137D**, two prototypes evaluated competing radar systems proposed by Hughes Aircraft and Westinghouse, the latter finally being named winner. The most notable external feature of these aircraft is the 9.14-m (30-ft) diameter rotodome pylon-mounted above the rear fuselage, which streamlines the back-to-back antennas for the radar and IFF. In January 1973 the USAF authorized development of the AWACS, designating these aircraft E-3 and later naming them Sentry. The first USAF **E-3A** was delivered to TAC's 552nd AWAC

Wing on 24 March 1977, and the force of 34 was completed in 1985. NATO's 18 Luxemburg-registered multi-national crew E-3As were delivered from 22 January 1982 to 25 April 1985.

The USAF's first 24 Sentries were equipped to **Core E-3A** standard, which provides pulse-Doppler radar, a CC-1 computer, nine situation display consoles (SDCs), two auxiliary display units (ADUs) and 13 communication links. These 24 aircraft are in the process of updating to **E-3B** standard with the secure Joint Tactical Information Distribution System (JTIDS), faster CC-2 computer, some maritime reconnaissance capability and other equipment. The remaining 10 USAF and 18 NATO aircraft, designated **Standard E-3A**, have maritime (overwater) reconnaissance capability plus the JTIDS and CC-2 computer. Under modifications started in 1984 the 10 USAF Standard E-3As are being updated to **E-3C** configuration, gaining five more SDCs, additional UHF radios and provision for 'Have Quick' anti-jamming improvements.

Five **E-3A/Saudi** AWACS have been contracted for the Royal Saudi Air Force, with initial deliveries planned for 1986; like the tanker/transports on order for this air arm under the designation KE-3A, they are powered by 9979-kg (22,000-lb) thrust CFM International CFM56-2 turbofan engines.

Boeing E-3A Sentry of the NATO Airborne Early Warning Force, based at Geilenkirchen, West Germany.

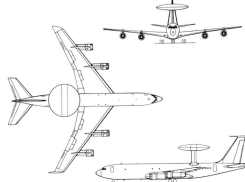

Boeing E-3A Sentry

Specification: Boeing E-3 Sentry
Origin: USA
Type: airborne early-warning and C³ aircraft
Powerplant: four 9525-kg (21,000-lb) thrust Pratt & Whitney TF33-100/100A turbofan engines
Performance: maximum speed 460 kts (853 km/h; 530 mph); operating ceiling 29,000 ft (8840 m); loiter time on station 1609 km (1,000 miles) from base 6 hours; maximum endurance on internal fuel 11 hours
Weights: maximum take-off 147418 kg (325,000 lb)
Dimensions: span 44.42 m (145 ft 9 in); length 46.61 m (152 ft 11 in); height 12.73 m (41 ft 9 in); wing area 283.35 m² (3,050.0 sq ft)
Armament: none

The carriage of the large rotodome is clearly seen here, on each side of the scanning radar and the IFF antenna. The E-3 design was based upon the Model 707 airframe.

E-3s now serve in some numbers, most in USAF service having been updated to E-3B or E-3C standard as better equipment has become available to the AWACS force.

Role	
Fighter	
Close support	
Counter-insurgency	
Tactical strike	
Strategic bomber	
Tactical reconnaissance	
Strategic reconnaissance	
Maritime patrol	
Anti-ship strike	
Anti-submarine warfare	
Search and rescue	
Assault transport	
Transport	
Liaison	
Trainer	
Inflight-refuelling tanker	
Specialized	
Performance	
All-weather capability	
Rough field capability	
STOL capability	
VTOL capability	
Airspeed 0-250 mph	
Airspeed 250 mph-Mach 1	
Airspeed Mach 1 plus	
Ceiling 0-20,000 ft	
Ceiling 20,000-40,000 ft	
Ceiling 40,000ft plus	
Range 0-1,000 miles	
Range 1,000-3,000 miles	
Range 3,000 miles plus	
Weapons	
Air-to-air missiles	
Air-to-surface missiles	
Cruise missiles	
Cannon	
Trainable guns	
Naval weapons	
Nuclear-capable	
Rockets	
'Smart' weapon kit	
Weapon load 0-4,000 lb	
Weapon load 4,000-15,000 lb	
Weapon load 15,000 lb plus	
Avionics	
Electronic Counter Measures	
Electronic Support Measures	
Search radar	
Fire control radar	
Look-down/shoot-down	
Terrain-following radar	
Forward-looking infra-red	
Laser	
Television	

Primary capability
Secondary capability

Thunderbolt II: rough, tough, slow and low

Looking more like an escapee from a wartime German drawing board than a modern combat aircraft, the Fairchild Republic A-10A has earned the respect of both its pilots and adversaries. Questions abound over its survivability in the battlezone, yet the strength and firepower of the Warthog will play an enormous part in any future land battle.

Judged solely on aesthetic grounds, the Fairchild Republic A-10A Thunderbolt II has to be one of the least attractive aircraft to have appeared in recent years. Standing high above the ground on its gawky landing gear, with engines which look as if they have been added almost as an afterthought, the A-10A gives a first impression that is almost invariably unflattering, and the type's generally angular appearance undoubtedly played a major part in it being dubbed 'Warthog' by pilots of the US Air Force.

On the ground it may appear grotesque. In the air, although the type still looks

The harsh, snowy wastes of Alaska would be ideal for the tough Soviet troops and equipment, and would provide a good hold on the American mainland. The USAF has consequently stationed A-10s here to counter any attempted armoured drive across the territory.

decidedly odd, it soon became clear that in the hands of a skilled pilot the A-10A is a remarkable performer and one that is well suited for its primary mission of battlefield interdiction. Possessing almost unparalleled agility and man-oeuvrability at low level, the Thunderbolt II also has the ability to carry a most impressive array of ordnance, and these two factors conspire to make it a weapon to be at once feared and respected, although there are many who hold the opinion that its low speed would render it vulnerable to enemy defences when operating over a hotly contested battle-field.

While not quite as versatile as the Douglas A-1 Skyraider, the A-10A might with some justification lay claim to the mantle of 'Skyraider of the 1970s' and, indeed, it is in many ways similar to the classic 'Spad', being exceedingly tough

Inflight-refuelling is not an important part of the A-10's combat operations, but does enable it to deploy quickly to global hotspots as part of America's rapid reaction forces. This 81st TFW 'Boar' receives a faceful as the KC-135's boom is retracted.

yet simple to maintain, fairly easy to fly and, perhaps most important of all, able to loiter within the vicinity of the battle-field with a quite respectable weapons load for prolonged periods. 'Handsome is as handsome does' they often say, and on this basis the Thunderbolt II can be described only as a beautiful aircraft. Nevertheless, the quantity produced for service with the USAF is relatively modest when compared with the products of other contemporary programmes such as the McDonnell Douglas F-15 and General Dynamics F-16 for, with the two proto-

types and six pre-production examples taken into account, the total number of A-10s built was just 721, the last example of which was handed over to the USAF on 20 March 1984.

The low-cost philosophy which was an inherent aspect of the entire project means that although the A-10A is an unusual design, it possesses few innovative features. Construction is largely conventional, the fuselage consisting of three major sub-assemblies, namely front, centre and rear with four continuous longerons and multiple frames providing the basic structure. Aluminium alloy is predominant, although extensive use is made of titanium armour plating in and around the cockpit where it protects the pilot and vulnerable items such as control column linkages. The wing is a triple-spar structure made up of a one-piece centre section with integrally strengthened skinning and two outer panels based on conventional rib, stringer and skin methods of construction, as are the vertical and horizontal tail surfaces. The offset nosewheel and main landing gear units all retract forwards, the mainwheels being housed in fairings located on the extreme leading edge of the wing centre section. This rather unusual arrangement permits a greater amount of wing area to be set aside for the carriage of weaponry.

Hidden power

Motive power is furnished by two General Electric TF34-GE-100 high-bypass-ratio turbofan engines. Each is rated at 4112-kg (9,065-lb) static thrust, and the engines are positioned high up on the aft fuselage side, where the hot gases are partially masked by the wing, thus reducing the type's infra-red signature from below and making it less vulnerable to heat-seeking missiles.

Total integral fuel capacity is of the order of 4853 kg (10,700 lb), this being contained in four self-sealing cells, two surmounting the wing box directly aft of the cockpit and two more located in the wing centre section. Additional fuel may be carried in auxiliary drop tanks, the Thunderbolt II having no less than 11 stores stations which permit it to carry a maximum external payload of 7257 kg (16,000 lb). However, with a full weapons payload internal fuel capacity is limited. As far as weaponry is concerned, the A-10A is able to operate with most of the items of conventional ordnance now found in the US arsenal, these including AGM-65 Maverick air-to-surface missiles, Rockeye cluster bomb units, 'Paveway' laser-guided bombs, 'Hobos' electro-optically guided bombs, Mk 84 2,000-lb (907-kg) bombs, Mk 82 500-lb (227-kg) bombs and napalm.

In addition there is the quite fearsome integral General Electric GAU-8/A Avenger seven-barrelled 30-mm Gatling-type rotary cannon around which the A-10A was more or less built. A truly massive weapon, this is some 6.71 m (22 ft)

The A-10 concept stemmed from the need for a counter-insurgency aircraft for use in the jungles of South East Asia. Like its Central Front heliborne partner, the Bell AH-1 Cobra, the role quickly changed to dedicated anti-armour following the end of the war in Vietnam.

long, tips the scales at an impressive 1856 kg (4,091 lb) and fires shells which weigh slightly more than 0.91 kg (2 lb), the associated ammunition drum being able to accommodate a total of 1,174 rounds of either high explosive or armour-piercing incendiary shells. High explosive rounds are intended mainly for use against what are euphemistically described as 'soft' targets such as vehicles or supply dumps, while armour-piercing ammunition is more normally employed against 'hard' targets such as tanks and armoured personnel carriers. Ammunition is fed to the firing chambers by a double-ended linkless system driven by dual hydraulic motors operating off the Thunderbolt II's hydraulic systems. Two rates of fire (2,100 rpm or 4,200 rpm) are available, only a single motor being used when the lower rate is selected. Almost inevitably, the remarkable rate of fire has led to some restrictions being imposed to avoid the possibility of overheating, and the design firing duration is 10 2-second bursts with a 60-second cooling period between each burst.

Although the A-10 is compatible with a variety of hardware, the most commonly used mix employed in the tank-busting role would be four to six Maverick air-to-surface missiles backed up by the GAU-8/A gun, this enabling targets to be engaged at short range as well as in a sort of 'stand-off' mode in instances where the threat from enemy anti-aircraft weapons (such as the ZSU-23-4 Shilka multi-barrelled mobile 23-mm cannon system, the SA-8 'Gecko' mobile surface-to-air missile system and the SA-13 SAM) are considered to be high. Operating tactics will, of course, play an important part in any battle, and these are continually be-

ing refined in the light of developing Soviet capability. Basically, though, it appears that the A-10's remarkable manoeuvrability will be a key factor in ensuring its survival for, when flying at normal cruise speed at ultra low level, it can take full advantage of all available cover while looking for targets, only emerging into the high-threat area for sufficient time to permit a target to be engaged, thereafter getting back down 'amongst the weeds' as soon as possible. In this way, the time available for enemy anti-aircraft systems visually to acquire and lock-on to the A-10 is kept to the barest minimum. Detailed studies of West Germany's Fulda Gap (long viewed as a likely area for combat) have resulted in the finding that the hilly terrain would significantly impair the capability of the ZSU-23-4 if the target kept below an altitude of 90 m (300 ft). One additional benefit of such low-level operations is that it limits the risk of destruction by enemy fighter aircraft for, although Soviet forces do have some 'look-down/shoot-down' capability, this is unlikely to be able to deal effectively with a slow-moving machine like the Thunderbolt II which has a very low infra-red signature.

With regard to performance, sheer speed was never a key factor in design, with the result that the A-10's maximum speed with weapons is rather on the low side, being just 368 kts (682 km/h; 424 mph) in level flight while it can cruise at about 336 kts (623 km/h; 387 mph) with maximum payload at an altitude of 1525 m (5,000 ft). However, since the A-10 is expected to spend much of its time at altitudes of the order of 15-30 m (50-100 ft) over the battlefield, manoeuvrability was clearly of paramount import-

The incredible GAU-8/A Avenger cannon forms the heart of the A-10; the aircraft was more or less designed round it. Armament is housed in a titanium box for protection (as is the pilot). Both armour-piercing (for tanks) and high-explosive (for trucks and buildings) rounds are carried, each round weighing about 0.91 kg (2 lb).

The official name for the A-10 is Thunderbolt II, but it is universally known in service as the Warthog, a more appropriate epithet for this immensely strong yet ungainly aircraft. The gun is restricted to short bursts as the weight of fire can cause the aircraft to slow down dramatically.

ance and there can be few who would question the A-10's ability in this area, the aircraft possessing a quite remarkable turn radius. In addition, the A-10 is no slouch when it comes to field performance, being able to lift a respectable payload even when flying from forward strips of just 305-m (1,000-ft) length, while at maximum gross weight it unsticks in 1220 m (4,000 ft).

The first full production A-10A made its maiden flight on 21 October 1975, deliveries to Tactical Air Command beginning just a few months later (in February 1976) when the 355th Tactical Fighter Training Wing at Davis-Monthan AFB, Arizona, received its first example. As its designation implies, the 355th TFTW was selected to serve as the principal training unit, the honour of being the first fully combat-capable A-10 wing falling to the

354th Tactical Fighter Wing at Myrtle Beach AFB, South Carolina, which began to convert from the Vought A-7D Corsair in July 1977 and which has since been joined by the 23rd TFW at England AFB, Louisiana. One other TAC component which also operates the 'Warthog' is the 57th Fighter Weapons Wing at Nellis AFB, Nevada, this important unit being principally concerned with formulating operational doctrine, conceiving and evaluating tactics, and assessing new weapons: consequently, it operates some examples of most of the types presently found in the front-line TAC inventory.

In addition to these US-based units, the Thunderbolt II has been deployed overseas in fairly substantial numbers, examples of the type now equipping one European-based wing as well as elements of the Alaskan Air Command and the Pacific Air Forces. Second-line squadrons of the Air National Guard and the Air Force Reserve have also taken delivery of the A-10A, this marking a welcome continuation of the trend towards giving reserve forces equipment comparable with that of their front-line counterparts, and there is no doubt that the advent of the Thunderbolt II has significantly enhanced the capability of these elements.

Detachment to the front

One of the key aspects of operational doctrine (and one which was largely proven by the UK-based 81st TFW) entails the use of the so-called FOL (Forward Operating Location). Essentially, this means that the parent wing routinely

detaches a portion of its overall complement to other bases where this portion operates on a semi-autonomous basis, dispersal of the force in this way increasing the chances of a substantial part of the unit's strength surviving in the event of a surprise counter-airfield attack. In the case of the 81st TFW, six such FOLs apparently exist (the only four that have been publicly identified being Ahlhorn, Leipheim, Norvenich and Sembach) in West Germany, which is perceived as being the most likely battlefield in the event of a major conventional conflict. Each FOL normally serves as home for about eight to 10 Thunderbolt IIs, the support infrastructure concentrating on meeting operational and tactical requirements in the event of war rather than routine peacetime considerations. Thus, the FOLs are relatively austere, possessing little in the way of sophisticated support equipment, aircraft being rotated regularly from the wing's main bases at Bentwaters and Woodbridge where 'deep' maintenance is performed.

A company proposal to produce a two-seat night/adverse-weather version of the Thunderbolt II resulted in the first of the six pre-production machines being modified to serve as a prototype, this making a successful maiden flight on 4 May 1979. In the event USAF plans to acquire a limited number of a variant known as the A-10B were not implemented and the project was eventually abandoned. Nevertheless, despite the fact that production for the USAF ceased in 1984, Fairchild Republic continues to promote single- and two-seat variants of the Thunderbolt II on the export market, and it is not beyond the realms of possibility that the type could one day be reinstated in production for an overseas customer.

The AGM-65 Maverick TV-guided missile provides the A-10 with stand-off ability, enabling it to destroy tanks without getting too close to areas of intense ground-fire. In the future, infra-red and laser-guided versions should be available, allowing the A-10 to make fire-and-forget attacks.

A-10A Thunderbolt II in service units and example aircraft

23rd TFW (code letters 'EL')
Base: England AFB, Louisiana
Squadrons and aircraft:
74th TFS 90180, 90207, 00210

75th TFS 90202, 00152, 20662
76th TFS 90179, 00166, 20653

74th TFS

75th TFS

Shark's-mouth markings applied to 23rd TFW A-10As are a fearsome addition around the nose-mounted multi-barrel cannon.

51st TFW (code letters 'OS')
Base: Suwon AB, South Korea
Squadrons and aircraft:
25th TFS 00252, 00282, 10973

25th TFS

81st TFW (code letters 'WR')
Base: RAF Bentwaters/RAF Woodbridge, England
Squadrons and aircraft:
78th TFS 00235, 10960, 10982
91st TFS 90225, 00234, 10983
92nd TFS 00191, 00281, 10992
509th TFS 00219, 10939, 10988
510th TFS 00215, 00228, 10980
511th TFS 90219, 10967, 20647

78th TFS (red)
91st TFS (blue)
92nd TFS (yellow)
509th TFS (grey)
510th TFS (purple)
511th TFS (black)

343rd CW (code letters 'AK')
Base: Eielson AFB, Alaska
Squadrons and aircraft:
18th TFS 00222, 10997

18th TFS

354th TFW (code letters 'MB')
Base: Myrtle Beach AFB, South Carolina

Squadrons and aircraft:
353rd TFS 70183, 80600, 90118
355th TFS 80591, 80672,

90139
356th TFS 80595, 80725, 90157

355th TFS

356th TFS

355th TTW (code letters 'DM')
Base: Davis-Monthan AFB, Arizona
Squadrons and aircraft:
333rd TFTS 50264, 50289, 70187
357th TFTS 50267, 60549, 70201
358th TFTS 50279, 60516, 70222

357th TFTS

358th TFTS

57th FWW (code letters 'WA')
Base: Nellis AFB, Nevada
Squadrons and aircraft:
A-10 FWS 90169, 00225, 10958

Air National Guard Units

The A-10 has provided a major step forward in the equipment operated by ANG and AFRes units in recent years, with responsibilities including the reinforcement of front-line units.

176th TFS/128th TFW (code letters 'WI')
Base: Truax Field, Wisconsin
Aircraft: 70250, 70263

138th TFS/174th TFW (code letters 'NY')
Base: Syracuse, New York
Aircraft: 80653, 80711

138th TFS/174th TFG

138th TFS/174th TF

118th TFS/103rd TFG (code letters 'CT')
Base: Bradley Field, Connecticut
Aircraft: 80586, 90103

131st TFS/104th TFG (code letters 'MA')
Base: Barnes Airport, Westfield, Maine
Aircraft: 80611, 80644

104th TFS/175th TFG (code letters 'MD')
Base: Martin Airport, Baltimore, Maryland
Aircraft: 80627, 90088

118th TFS/103rd TFG

131st TFS/104th TFG

131st TFS/104th TFG

104th TFS/175th TF

Air Force Reserve Units

434th TFW (code letters 'IN')
Base: Grissom AFB, Indiana
Squadrons and aircraft:
45th TFS 70192, 70234

442nd TFG (code letters 'KC')
Base: Richards-Gebaur AFB, Missouri
Squadrons and aircraft:
303rd TFS 80605, 90114

917th TFG (code letters 'BD')
Base: Barksdale AFB, Louisiana
Squadrons and aircraft:
46th TFTS 80696, 90106
47th TFS 90094, 90156

926th TFG (code letters 'NO')
Base: New Orleans NAS, Louisiana
Squadrons and aircraft:
706th TFS 60540, 70273

45th TFS

47th TFTS

46th TFS

Fairchild A-10A Thunderbolt II cutaway drawing key

1 Cannon muzzles
2 Nose cap
3 ILS aerial
4 Air-to-air refuelling receptacle (open)
5 Nosewheel bay (offset to starboard)
6 Cannon barrels
7 Rotary cannon barrel bearing
8 Gun compartment ventilating intake
9 L-band radar warning aerial
10 Electrical system relay switches
11 Windscreen rain dispersal air duct
12 Pave Penny laser receiver and tracking pod
13 Windscreen panel
14 Head-up display symbol generator
15 Pilot's head-up display screen
16 Instrument panel shroud
17 Air-to-air refuelling pipe
18 Titanium armour cockpit enclosure
19 Rudder pedals
20 Battery
21 General Electric GAU-8/A 30-mm seven-barrelled rotary cannon
22 Ammunition feed ducts
23 Steering cylinder
24 Nose undercarriage leg strut
25 Nosewheel
26 Nosewheel scissor links
27 Retractable boarding ladder
28 Ventilating air outlets
29 Ladder stowage box
30 Pilot's side console panel

31 Engine throttles
32 Control column
33 McDonnell Douglas ACES 2 ejection seat
34 Headrest canopy breakers
35 Cockpit canopy cover
36 Canopy hinge mechanism
37 Space provision for additional avionics
38 Angle-of-attack probe
39 Emergency canopy release handle
40 Ventral access panels to gun compartment
41 Ammunition drum (1,174 rounds)
42 Ammunition drum armour plating
43 Electrical system servicing panel
44 Ventral fin
45 Spent cartridge-case return chute
46 Control cable runs
47 Avionics compartments
48 Forward/centre fuselage joint bulkhead
49 Aerial selector switches
50 IFF aerial
51 Anti-collision light
52 UHF/TACAN aerial
53 Starboard wing integral fuel tank
54 Wing skin plating
55 Outer wing panel attachment joint strap
56 Starboard fixed wing pylons
57 ALE-37A chaff dispenser pod
58 ALQ-119 electronic countermeasures pod
59 Pitot tube

60 Starboard drooped wing tip fairing
61 Split aileron/deceleron mass balance
62 Deceleron open position
63 Starboard aileron/deceleron
64 Deceleron hydraulic jack
65 Aileron hydraulic jack
66 Control linkages
67 Aileron tab
68 Tab balance weight
69 Slotted trailing edge flaps
70 Outboard flap jack
71 Flap synchronizing shafts
72 Fuselage self-sealing fuel cells (maximum internal fuel capacity 10,700 lb/ 4853 kg)
73 Fuselage main longeron
74 Longitudinal control and services duct
75 Air conditioning supply duct
76 Wing attachment fuselage main frames
77 Gravity fuel filler caps
78 Engine pylon fairing
79 Pylon attachment joint
80 Starboard intake
81 Intake centre cone
82 Engine fan blades
83 Night/adverse weather two-seater variant
84 Radar pod (forward looking infra-red in starboard pod)
85 Engine mounting struts
86 Nacelle construction
87 Oil tank
88 General Electric TF34-GE-100 turbofan
89 Rear engine mounting
90 Pylon trailing edge fillet
91 Engine exhaust duct

92 Fan air duct
93 Rudder hydraulic jack
94 Starboard tail fin
95 X-band aerial
96 Rudder mass balance weight
97 Starboard rudder
98 Elevator tab
99 Tab control rod
100 Starboard elevator
101 Starboard tailplane
102 Tailplane attachment frames
103 Elevator hydraulic jacks
104 Tailcone
105 Tail navigation light
106 Rear radar warning receiver aerial
107 Honeycomb elevator construction
108 Port vertical tailfin construction
109 Honeycomb rudder panel
110 Rudder hydraulic jack
111 Formation light
112 Vertical fin ventral fairing
113 Tailplane construction
114 Tailplane control links
115 Port engine exhaust duct
116 Tailboom frame construction
117 VHF/AM aerial
118 Fuel jettison
119 VHF/FM aerial
120 Fuel jettison duct
121 Hydraulic reservoir
122 Port engine nacelle attachment joint
123 Cooling system intake and exhaust duct
124 Engine bleed air ducting
125 Auxiliary power unit
126 APU exhaust
127 Engine nacelle access door

128 Air conditioning plant
129 Port engine intake
130 Trailing edge wing root fillet
131 Fuselage bomb rack
132 Inboard slotted flap
133 Flap guide rails
134 Rear spar
135 Flap shroud structure
136 Honeycomb trailing edge panel
137 Outboard slotted flap
138 Port deceleron open position
139 Aileron tab
140 Aileron hinges
141 Port split aileron/deceleron
142 Drooped wing tip fairing construction
143 Port navigation light
144 Honeycomb leading edge panels
145 Wing rib construction
146 Centre spar
147 Leading edge spar
148 Two outer fixed pylons (1,000-lb/453.6-kg capacity)
149 ALQ-119 electronic countermeasures pod
150 ALE-37A chaff dispenser
151 Port mainwheel
152 2,500-lb (1134-kg) capacity stores pylon
153 Main undercarriage leg strut
154 Undercarriage leg doors
155 Main undercarriage leg pivot fixing
156 Port mainwheel semi-recessed housing
157 Pressure refuelling point
158 Undercarriage pod fairing

airchild A-10A warload

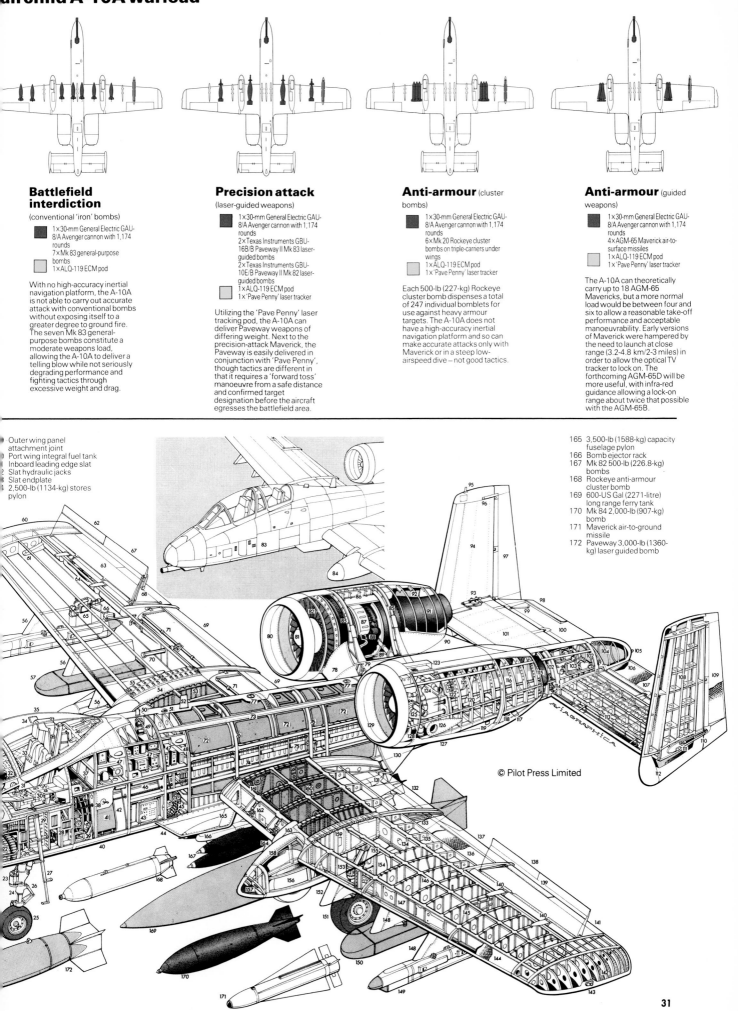

Battlefield interdiction
(conventional 'iron' bombs)

- 1 × 30-mm General Electric GAU-8/A Avenger cannon with 1,174 rounds
- 7 × Mk 83 general-purpose bombs
- 1 × ALQ-119 ECM pod

With no high-accuracy inertial navigation platform, the A-10A is not able to carry out accurate attack with conventional bombs without exposing itself to a greater degree to ground fire. The seven Mk 83 general-purpose bombs constitute a moderate weapons load, allowing the A-10A to deliver a telling blow while not seriously degrading performance and fighting tactics through excessive weight and drag.

Precision attack
(laser-guided weapons)

- 1 × 30-mm General Electric GAU-8/A Avenger cannon with 1,174 rounds
- 2 × Texas Instruments GBU-16B/B Paveway II Mk 83 laser-guided bombs
- 2 × Texas Instruments GBU-10E/B Paveway II Mk 82 laser-guided bombs
- 1 × ALQ-119 ECM pod
- 1 × 'Pave Penny' laser tracker

Utilizing the 'Pave Penny' laser tracking pod, the A-10A can deliver Paveway weapons of differing weight. Next to the precision-attack Maverick, the Paveway is easily delivered in conjunction with 'Pave Penny', though tactics are different in that it requires a 'forward toss' manoeuvre from a safe distance and confirmed target designation before the aircraft egresses the battlefield area.

Anti-armour (cluster bombs)

- 1 × 30-mm General Electric GAU-8/A Avenger cannon with 1,174 rounds
- 6 × Mk 20 Rockeye cluster bombs on triple-carriers under wings
- 1 × ALQ-119 ECM pod
- 1 × 'Pave Penny' laser tracker

Each 500-lb (227-kg) Rockeye cluster bomb dispenses a total of 247 individual bomblets for use against heavy armour targets. The A-10A does not have a high-accuracy inertial navigation platform and so can make accurate attacks only with Maverick or in a steep low-airspeed dive – not good tactics.

Anti-armour (guided weapons)

- 1 × 30-mm General Electric GAU-8/A Avenger cannon with 1,174 rounds
- 4 × AGM-65 Maverick air-to-surface missiles
- 1 × ALQ-119 ECM pod
- 1 × 'Pave Penny' laser tracker

The A-10A can theoretically carry up to 18 AGM-65 Mavericks, but a more normal load would be between four and six to allow a reasonable take-off performance and acceptable manoeuvrability. Early versions of Maverick were hampered by the need to launch at close range (3.2-4.8 km/2-3 miles) in order to allow the optical TV tracker to lock on. The forthcoming AGM-65D will be more useful, with infra-red guidance allowing a lock-on range about twice that possible with the AGM-65B.

- Outer wing panel attachment joint
- Port wing integral fuel tank
- Inboard leading edge slat
- Slat hydraulic jacks
- Slat endplate
- 2,500-lb (1134-kg) stores pylon

165 3,500-lb (1588-kg) capacity fuselage pylon
166 Bomb ejector rack
167 Mk 82 500-lb (226.8-kg) bombs
168 Rockeye anti-armour cluster bomb
169 600-US Gal (2271-litre) long range ferry tank
170 Mk 84 2,000-lb (907-kg) bomb
171 Maverick air-to-ground missile
172 Paveway 3,000-lb (1360-kg) laser guided bomb

© Pilot Press Limited

31

Specification:

Fairchild A-10A Thunderbolt II

Wings
Span	17.53 m	(57 ft 6 in)
Chord, at root	3.04 m	(9 ft 11.5 in)
at tip	1.99 m	(6 ft 6.4 in)
Area	47.01 m²	(506.0 sq ft)

Fuselage and tail unit
Length overall	16.26 m	(53 ft 4 in)
Height overall	4.47 m	(14 ft 8 in)

Landing gear
Wheelbase	5.40 m	(17 ft 8.75 in)
Wheel track	5.25 m	(17 ft 2.5 in)

Weights
Empty	11321 kg	(24,959 lb)
Take-off, operating from forward airstrip with four Mk 82 bombs, 750 rounds of ammunition and 2041 kg (4,500 lb) of fuel	14865 kg	(32,771 lb)
Maximum take-off	22680 kg	(50,000 lb)
Maximum internal fuel	4853 kg	(10,700 lb)
Maximum auxiliary fuel in drop tanks	2410 kg	(5,314 lb)
Maximum weapon load	7257 kg	(16,000 lb)
Maximum weapon load with full internal fuel	6505 kg	(14,341 lb)

Fairchild Republic A-10A Thunderbolt II recognition points

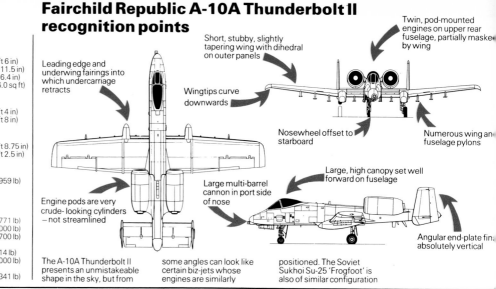

Leading edge and underwing fairings into which undercarriage retracts

Short, stubby, slightly tapering wing with dihedral on outer panels

Wingtips curve downwards

Twin, pod-mounted engines on upper rear fuselage, partially masked by wing

Numerous wing and fuselage pylons

Nosewheel offset to starboard

Engine pods are very crude-looking cylinders – not streamlined

Large multi-barrel cannon in port side of nose

Large, high canopy set well forward on fuselage

Angular end-plate fins, absolutely vertical

The A-10A Thunderbolt II presents an unmistakeable shape in the sky, but from some angles can look like certain biz-jets whose engines are similarly positioned. The Soviet Sukhoi Su-25 'Frogfoot' is also of similar configuration

Performance:

Maximum speed, 'clean' at sea level	381 kts	707 km/h	(439 mph)
Cruising speed at sea level	300 kts	555 km/h	(345 mph)
Combat speed, with six Mk 82 bombs at 5,000 ft (1524 m)	380 kts	705 km/h	(438 mph)
Cruising speed at 5,000 ft (1524 m)	336 kts	623 km/h	(387 mph)
Initial rate of climb per minute	1829 m	(6,000 ft)	
Combat radius with 20-minute fuel reserves:			
close air support, 1.7 hours loiter	463 km	(288 miles)	
deep strike	998 km	(620 miles)	
Ferry range	3949 km	(2,454 miles)	

Weapon load

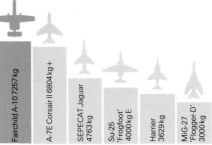

- Fairchild A-10 7257 kg
- A-7E Corsair II 6804 kg+
- SEPECAT Jaguar 4763 kg
- Su-25 'Frogfoot' 4000 kg E
- Harrier 3629 kg
- MiG-27 'Flogger-D' 3000 kg

Time on station 185 km from base

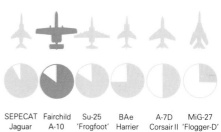

SEPECAT Jaguar	Fairchild A-10	Su-25 'Frogfoot'	BAe Harrier	A-7D Corsair II	MiG-27 'Flogger-D'
110 min E	102 min	100 min	90 min	60 min	30 min E

Speed at sea level

- SEPECAT Jaguar 729 kts
- MiG-27 'Flogger-D' 725 kts E
- Harrier 635 kts
- A-7E Corsair II 600 kts
- Su-25 'Frogfoot' 475 kts E
- Fairchild A-10 381 kts

Take-off run

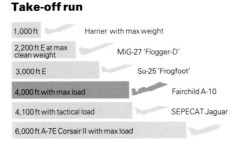

- 1,000 ft — Harrier with max weight
- 2,200 ft E at max clean weight — MiG-27 'Flogger-D'
- 3,000 ft E — Su-25 'Frogfoot'
- 4,000 ft with max load — Fairchild A-10
- 4,100 ft with tactical load — SEPECAT Jaguar
- 6,000 ft A-7E Corsair II with max load

Combat radius lo-lo-lo

- SEPECAT Jaguar 917 km with external fuel
- A-7D Corsair II 885 km
- Fairchild A-10 463 km with 20 min reserve
- MiG-27 'Flogger-D' 390 km E with 2900-kg load
- Harrier 370 km
- Su-25 'Frogfoot' 300 km E

Fairchild A-10
Thunderbolt II variants

YA-10A: designation of two prototypes (71-1369/1370) for evaluation against the competing Northrop YA-9A

A-10A: sole production version of which 739 were planned, but funding was terminated in 1984 after 713 had been completed (including the six D, T & E pre-production aircraft)

N/AW A-10: company-funded night/all-weather derivative of the A-10A, produced as a conversion of the first of the six D, T & E aircraft (73-1664) leased from the USAF; basic dimensions unchanged but height of vertical tail surfaces increased by 0.51 m (1 ft 8 in) and empty weight increased by 948 kg (2,091 lb); role equipment included General Electric LLTV (low-light TV) sensors, Texas Instruments AAR-42 FLIR (forward-looking infra-red) and Westinghouse WX-50 terrain-avoidance radar; no production

A-10B: planned two-seat trainer version using structure of N/AW A-10 and retaining full operational capability; procurement of 30 was intended for Air National Guard and US Air Force Reserve but was ultimately not funded

Right: Avionics in the A-10A have been kept to a minimum. The instrument panel has fuel gauges at extreme right and a panel of 12 dials covering engine and APU operation. Immediately above these are the altimeter and variometer, with the large video display screen for use in Maverick missile launches to their right. The centre panel is occupied by the artificial horizon and direction indicator. The left-hand area has weapons select and release panels, with the dials above including airspeed indicator, angle of attack and stand-by artificial horizon. On top of the instrument panel is the head-up display (HUD) unit, which displays information such as vertical speed and flight angle, distance and time to pre-programmed waypoints and navigation details, linked to the inertial navigation system.

Below: The A-10B night/adverse weather development has a two-seat enlarged cockpit, increased fin height and two avionic subsystem pods on underfuselage pylons. These avionics were to be incorporated in the wing leading-edge and landing gear fairings for the intended production A-10B.

A Fairchild Republic A-10A Thunderbolt II

General Dynamics F-16 Fighting Falcon

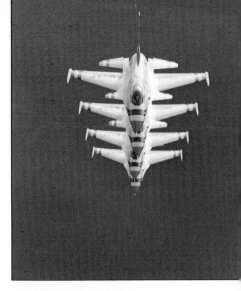

Spearheading United States air power capabilities worldwide, the F-16 Fighting Falcon is a highly versatile bird of prey, ready to pounce on the enemy and bring its formidable weapons load to bear while outflying almost every other warplane.

Now well established in operational service with several major subordinate commands of the US Air Force as well as a number of overseas air arms, the General Dynamics F-16 Fighting Falcon is clearly one of the most important fighter aircraft to have made its debut in recent years.

With the dollar purchasing less and less hardware during the early 1970s, those responsible for ensuring that the USA obtained the best value from its admittedly large defence budget were naturally concerned about the seemingly ever-spiralling costs, and it was therefore hardly surprising that they greeted the idea of a low-cost lightweight fighter with some warmth. In the opposite corner, however, sat the US Air Force which, ultimately, would have to operate any new type and which was, somewhat understandably, concerned that the acquisition of another fighter would seriously compromise overall capability by limiting the number of McDonnell Douglas F-15 Eagles that could be purchased.

What eventually emerged was the General Dynamics YF-16, which made an unscheduled maiden flight on 20 January 1974, this arising from a problem experienced during a high-speed taxi trial which prompted pilot Phil Oestricher to take-off for a six-minute sortie ending in an uneventful landing. In contrast the second flight, made on 2 February, was wholly intentional, Oestricher being airborne for some 90 minutes. The second YF-16 took to the air for the first time on 9 May, whilst the maiden flight of the opposition aircraft, Northrop's YF-17, did not take place until June.

The resulting evaluation revealed that on most counts the YF-16 was significantly superior, and this aircraft was announced as the winner in mid-January 1975, by which time it had been revealed by the Department of Defense that no less than 650 examples of a much-improved version known as the Air Combat Fighter would be obtained for service with the USAF.

Development aircraft

As part of the process of bringing the type to operational service a small number of Full-Scale Development aircraft was ordered in early 1975, this batch comprising 11 single-seat F-16As and four two-seat F-16B trainers, although, in the event, the number of aircraft involved was quickly cut to just eight, the revised quantity being made up of six F-16As and two F-16Bs.

Testing of the first of these got under way shortly before the end of 1976, and was accomplished largely at Edwards AFB, California, although portions of the programme entailed visits to other test centres. Moreover, since the type had also been selected to replace the Lockheed F-104G with four NATO air arms, part of the Multi-National Operational Test and Evaluation programme was undertaken in Europe.

This eventually resulted in the F-16A being cleared for service with Tactical Air Command, and the first example was duly handed over at Hill AFB, Utah on 6 January 1979. The recipient unit was the 388th Tactical Fighter Wing. Initial Operational Capability was achieved in October 1980, and since then the Fighting Falcon has entered service with several other TAC units as well as elements of PACAF and USAFE. Although initial deliveries were made to front-line combat echelons, the F-16 has now also found its way into service with second-line elements of the Air National Guard and

Flying the flag for the US Air Force with the General Dynamics F-16A as their mount, the 'Thunderbirds' display team make full use of this nimble aircraft's extreme agility and 9g airframe tolerance during their precision aerobatics displays.

The glow of full afterburner as an F-16A gets airborne for another sortie. The one-piece bubble canopy affords excellent all-round visibility to the pilot – an essential factor when the F-16 operates in the air superiority role.

the Air Force Reserve, this process beginning in the spring of 1983 when the South Carolina Air National Guard's 157th Tactical Fighter Squadron began to convert from the Vought A-7D Corsair II at McEntire ANGB.

Although initially conceived as a lightweight air superiority fighter, the evolutionary process resulted in a significant shift in role, the F-16A which entered service in 1979 being designed mainly for use on air-to-ground tasks such as close air support and tactical strike. As a result, whilst still a most potent opponent in the air-to-air regime, the F-16A was somewhat limited by the fact that it lacked the facility to operate with radar-guided missiles such as the AIM-7F Sparrow. Nevertheless, heat-seeking AIM-9 Sidewinders did (and indeed still do) provide a measure of self-defence capability, and the F-16A also features an M61 Vulcan 20-mm cannon for close-in air-to-air combat, this weapon being an almost obligatory feature of the modern fighter aircraft.

Improvement programme

The variants now in quantity production for the US Air Force are the single-seat F-16C and the two-seat F-16D, these resulting from a Multi-Stage Improvement Program which has greatly enhanced Fighting Falcon capability. At the heart of the update initiative, the APG-68 radar offers increased detection range as well as TWS capability and a high-resolution ground-mapping mode. In addition, the cockpit instrumentation has been much improved, pilots benefiting from incorporation of two multi-function CRT displays as well as a wide-angle HUD, the HOTAS design philosophy playing some part in cockpit redesign. This, by enabling the pilot to keep his head 'out of the cockpit', greatly enhances his tactical awareness and increases his probability of survival in a high-threat environment such as that likely to be encountered in any future European conflict.

Operational deployment of the F-16C and F-16D models of the Fighting Falcon

began during the summer of 1984, initial deliveries being made to elements of TAC and PACAF, and it seems reasonable to assume that these variants will also find their way into the USAFE inventory in due course, initially with the Ramstein-based 86th Tactical Fighter Wing which is expected to complete transition to the General Dynamics machine between 1985-7.

Missile fits

Looking ahead a couple of years, further improvements to be adopted by the F-16C/D series as part of the MSIP package include the Lantirn night nav/attack pod system and the AIM-120 AMRAAM. Both of these are due to make their debut during the course of 1987, although the extent of their use seems likely to vary considerably, the Lantirn pod which is intended to be employed in conjunction with the AGM-65D infra-red imaging anti-armour variant of the highly successful Maverick air-to-surface missile not being scheduled for fleet-wide introduction. AMRAAM, however, will almost certainly be deployed much more extensively and, by virtue of the fact that it is a fire-and-forget beyond-visual-range weapon, will do much to enhance

Supreme in the art of air-to-air combat, the F-16 is a highly potent addition to US forces deployed around the world. Regular exercises and deployments overseas help prepare Fighting Falcon units to strike hard if called upon to defend Western interests.

the capability of the Fighting Falcon in the secondary air-to-air role assigned to this fighter.

Although production for the USAF now centres around the new F-16C/D versions, the original F-16A and F-16B models are still available for export customers. However, in view of past experience with the F-16/79 (a less sophisticated model powered by the General Electric J79 turbojet engine and optimized for the air-defence role, but which has thus far failed to secure any orders) it is unlikely that they will find too many takers, most overseas buyers being insistent on receiving the latest variant available.

In the primary air-to-ground role, the Fighting Falcon is a most capable performer, being able to accommodate up to

An 8th TFW 'Wolf Pack' F-16A reveals the distinctive lines of this lightweight fighter. The ejection seat is reclined 30° to offer better pilot g tolerance, essential because of the aircraft's excellent manoeuvring.

6895 kg (15,200 lb) of ordnance on no less than nine external stores stations, although this configuration limits the amount of fuel which may be carried. Alternatively, with full internal fuel, payload is reduced somewhat but, at 4627 kg (10,200 lb) is still nevertheless quite respectable. Conventional free-fall weapons such as the Mk 83 1,000-lb (454-kg) bomb may be employed, but the Fighting Falcon can also operate with electro-optically guided weapons (such as the Maverick air-to-surface missile) or with laser-guided devices. In addition, in a high-threat environment, ECM pods may be fitted in place of some weapons in order to provide a measure of jamming capability. Auxiliary fuel tanks can also be carried if greater combat radius is required. As noted elsewhere, AIM-9L Sidewinder heat-seeking air-to-air missiles provide a measure of defensive capability, whilst the forthcoming AIM-120 radar-guided weapon will be a welcome addition to the F-16's arsenal.

As far as the USAF is concerned, from its very tentative beginnings the F-16 has become a cornerstone of this air arm and present planning anticipates the eventual procurement of no less than 2,795 examples. Refinement of the aircraft has resulted in the appearance of the F-16C model and its two-seat counterpart, the F-16D, but General Dynamics continues to work on improving the Fighting Falcon, and it is not inconceivable that the arrow-winged F-16XL may eventually also find widespread acceptance, this being a potential contender for the USAF's existing close air support requirement.

XL failure

Although it might seem that the Fighting Falcon has gone from strength to strength in recent years, the story has not been entirely one of success, for the F-16XL has thus far failed to secure any orders, having been outpointed by the McDonnell Douglas F-15E Strike Eagle in its attempt to satisfy the USAF's requirement for 392 all-weather interdictor/strike aircraft. Initiated as a private venture, the F-16XL (or F-16E as it is known by the USAF) introduced an entirely new double-delta wing planform which was instrumental in enhancing performance by a great degree. Some idea of the benefits gained can be understood when one realizes that combat radius has risen by some 45 per cent even when operating with twice the payload of the original F-16A, whilst field performance is significantly better, the arrow-winged aircraft being able to take-off and land in only two-thirds of the distance required by the F-16A. In addition, air-to-air combat potential is expanded, the 9g manoeuvre envelope being double that of the F-16A, and low-level penetration speed has increased slightly.

The F-16XL was first flown in single-seat form during July 1982, and a second F-16XL conversion made its debut in October of the same year, this two-seater being powered by the General Electric F110 engine which is to be installed in the majority of F-16C/D aircraft earmarked for purchase with FY 85 funding. Extensively evaluated by the USAF for the dual-role fighter contract which was eventu-

ally awarded to the F-15E Strike Eagle in March 1984, the F-16XL is still under consideration and this particularly attractive machine may yet take its place in the USAF's combat inventory.

US Navy purchase

Another important new customer for the Fighting Falcon is the US Navy which recently revealed plans to acquire a modest number of a variant (known by the parent company as the F-16N) for use as adversary aircraft by aggressor training units. Although these will not form part of the front-line inventory and will not be carrier compatible, they will nevertheless play a vital role in enhancing overall Navy capability by honing the skills of pilots in the demanding air combat arena. Present planning calls for a total of 26 examples of the Fighting Falcon to be purchased by the Navy.

Whether or not the arrow-winged F-16E progresses from prototype to production status, there can be little doubt that the General Dynamics Fighting Falcon is assured of a bright future, and that it will remain in production for many years to come. With orders currently approaching the 4,000 mark for all customers the F-16 has clearly vindicated the faith of its early

With state-of-the-art avionics and weapons delivery capability, the new-generation F-16C is a formidable addition to the US Air Force. Allocation to front-line units is under way, ensuring that the F-16 will stay ahead of its potential adversaries for many years.

proponents, even if the evolutionary process has led to it becoming rather more than the fairly unsophisticated and relatively inexpensive day air-superiority fighter that was originally demanded.

Glossary

AFB Air Force Base
AMRAAM Advanced Medium-Range Air-to-Air Missile
CRT Cathode Ray Tube
ECM Electronic CounterMeasures
HOTAS Hands On Throttle And Stick
HUD Head-Up Display
MSIP Multi-Stage Improvement Program
TWS Track-While-Scan

Several F-16 variants have flown, but none are quite so radical as the F-16XL with its futuristic 'cranked arrow' wing and lengthened fuselage. Though it is undoubtedly superior to the standard F-16 in terms of combat radius and payload, it has yet to win production orders.

F-16 Fighting Falcon in service units and example aircraft

Tactical Air Command

56th TTW (code letters 'MC')

Base: MacDill AFB, Florida
Squadrons and aircraft:
61st TFTS (F-16A) 80061, 90331; (F-16B) 80111
62nd TFTS (F-16A) 80062, 90364; (F-16B) 90425
63rd TFTS (F-16A) 80063,
90332; (F-16B) 90416
72nd TFTS (F-16A) 80053, 90297; (F-16B) 00631

58th TTW (code letters 'LF')

Base: Luke AFB, Arizona
Squadrons and aircraft:
310th TFTS (F-16A) 80001, 80014; (F-16B) 80088
311th TFTS (F-16A) 80020, 90307; (F-16B) 80101
312th TFTS (F-16C) 31118, 31121; (F-16D) 31175

363rd TFW (code letters 'SW')

Base: Shaw AFB, South Carolina
Squadrons and aircraft:
17th TFS (F-16A) 21017, 31078; (F-16B) 31170
19th TFS (F-16A) 21016, 31076; (F-16B) 21049
30th TFS (F-16C/D) no data known

388th TFW (code letters 'HL')

Base: Hill AFB, Utah
Squadrons and aircraft:
4th TFS (F-16A) 10762, 10781; (F-16B) 21039
16th TFS (F-16A) 10778, 20915; (F-16B) 21038
34th TFS (F-16A) 20953,
21000; (F-16B) 21042
421st TFS (F-16A) 10751, 10763; (F-16B) 21044

474th TFW (code letters 'NA')

Base: Nellis AFB, Nevada
Squadrons and aircraft:
428th TFS (F-16A) 90369, 90371; (F-16B) 90428
429th TFS (F-16A) 90404, 00488; (F-16B) 90429
430th TFS (F-16A) 00517, 00535; (F-16B) 90430

57th FWW (code letters 'WA')

Base: Nellis AFB, Nevada
Squadrons and aircraft:
F-16 FWS (F-16A) 10811, 20940; (F-16B) 21003; (F-16C) 31122

In a relatively short time-span, the F-16 has become a major front-line service aircraft in the US Air Force. Nine wings are now fully operational on the Fighting Falcon, in addition to AFRes, ANG and testing units. The 86th TFW at Ramstein AB, West Germany, has begun to receive its first F-16C/Ds and, as a prelude to further re-equipment plans this F-16A has been adorned with the squadron and wing crests and tail code letters of the 31st TFW, due to relinquish its F-4D Phantom IIs in 1986/7.

United States Air Forces in Europe

50th TFW (code letters 'HR')

Base: Hahn AB, West Germany
Squadrons and aircraft:
10th TFS (F-16A) 00559, 10699; (F-16B) 21035
313th TFS (F-16A) 00574, 10671; (F-16B) 00636
496th TFS (F-16A) 00604, 10707; (F-16B) 10820

86th TFW (code letters 'RS')

Base: Ramstein AB, West Germany
Squadrons and aircraft:
417th TFS (F-16C) 41238, 41239; (F-16D) 41323
512th TFS re-equipping in 1986
526th TFS re-equipping in 1986

401st TFW (code letters 'TJ')

Base: Torrejon AB, Spain
Squadrons and aircraft:
612th TFS (F-16A) 10788, 31066; (F-16B) 31169
613th TFS (F-16A) 20964, 20980; (F-16B) 31167
614th TFS (F-16A) 20911, 20999; (F-16B) 21047

Pacific Air Forces

8th TFW (code letters 'WP')

Base: Kunsan AB, South Korea
Squadrons and aircraft:
35th TFS/80th TFS (F-16A) 00486, 00492, 00501, 00514, 00579

432nd TFW (code letters 'MJ')

Base: Misawa AB, Japan
Squadrons and aircraft:
13th TFS (F-16A) 31101; (F-16B) 31172

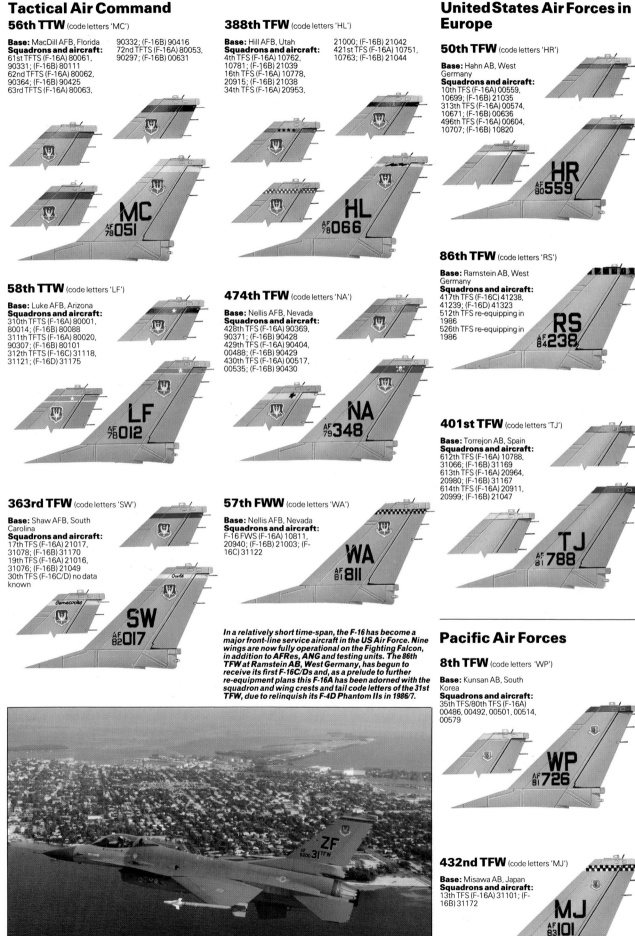

Air Force Reserve

466th TFS (code letters 'HI')

Base: Hill AFB, Utah
Aircraft: (F-16A) 80041, 88075; (F-16B) 90419

Non-operational units

3246th TW/AFAD (code letters 'AD')

Base: Eglin AFB, Florida
Aircraft: (F-16A) 80055

6512th TS/AFFTC (code letters 'ED')

Base: Edwards AFB, California
Aircraft: (F-16A/B/C/D)

Air National Guard

157th TFS (code letters 'SC')

Base: McEntire ANGB, South Carolina
Aircraft: (F-16A) 90304, 90320; (F-16B) 90410

4485th TS (code letters 'OT')

Base: Eglin AFB, Florida
Aircraft: (F-16A) 90326

Ogden ALC

Base: Hill AFB, Utah
Aircraft: (F-16A) 90402

F-16 variants

YF-16: two prototypes used in the fly-off programme with the Northrop YF-17 for the USAF's Light-Weight Fighter requirement; both aircraft had the original smaller nose radome, wing and horizontal tailplane areas; following success in the fly-offs, the YF-16 undertook further test and evaluation programmes

FSD YF-16A: six Full-Scale Development single-seaters used for overall F-16 flight qualification trials; slightly larger in most dimensions (e.g. horizontal tailplanes enlarged by 15 per cent) and enlarged nose radome; structural strengthening enabled full exploration of F-16 manoeuvrability, and external stores carriage capability increased

FSD YF-16B: two dual-control trainer derivatives of the YF-16A also used in the F-16 'shakedown' programme, including weapons-delivery trials

F-16A: first full-scale production model, first flown 7 August 1978; powered by a 10818-kg (23,850-lb) Pratt & Whitney F100 turbofan; combat-ready status achieved in October 1980; aircraft from production blocks 15 and 20 are receiving Multi-National Stage Improvement Programme 1 (MSIP 1) modifications enabling new systems, weapons and sensors to be carried, along with a drag chute in the fin base fairing, and enlarged horizontal tailplanes of lighter construction

F-16B: two-seat trainer derivative of the F-16A; overall dimensions unchanged but internal fuel capacity reduced to 2620 kg (5,775 lb)

F-16/79: company-funded project for a lower-cost export fighter; powerplant was a General Electric J79-GE-17X (later -119) afterburning turbojet offering an increased maximum speed of Mach 2.1; modifications (of an F-16B) included a 45.7-cm (18-in) fuselage extension and revised exhaust nozzle to accommodate the J79, and fitment of a fixed-compression ramp air inlet

F-16/101: the first FSD YF-16A fitted with a General Electric F101 DFE (Derivative Fighter Engine) for research into alternative powerplant compatability with the F-16 airframe; externally distinguishable by a shortened exhaust nozzle; as a result of flight tests by the aircraft, the F101 is now in production as an alternative F-16 turbofan powerplant

YF-16/CCV: for research into optimum handling characteristics for future fighter development, the first YF-16 was modified into a Control Configured Vehicle (CCV), this including the fitting of nose canards with pronounced anhedral; internal modifications included fly-by-wire control system computers for research into optimum flight-control modes

F-16/AFTI: research into Advanced Fighter Technology Integration (AFTI) saw the canards from the F-16/CCV fitted to the seventh FSD YF-16A, along with the addition of a faired dorsal spine housing flight test equipment; internal modifications include an advanced flight-control system

F-16C: major upgrading and expansion of avionics and weapon capabilities under MSIPs 2 and 3 has led to the new F-16C designation for aircraft from production blocks 20 and 25 onwards; external differences from the F-16A are restricted to an extended fin leading edge to house the ASJP jamming system

F-16D: two-seat dual-control derivative of F-16C, externally distinguishable from the earlier F-16B two-seat trainer by the same fin leading edge extension as the F-16C

F-16XL: company-funded project with an F-16A and F-16B fitted with a 'cranked arrow' wing with 50°/70° compound leading-edge sweep doubling the wing surface area of the F-16A; the fuselage has been lengthened by 1.42 m (4 ft 8 in), and wing span reduced to 9.88 m (32 ft 4.8 in), and internal fuel capacity has been increased by 82 per cent; first flown 3 July 1982 (single-seat prototype) with research development continuing

General Dynamics F-16 cutaway drawing key

1 Pitot tube
2 Glassfibre radome
3 Planar radar scanner
4 ILS glideslope aerial
5 Scanner drive units
6 Radar mounting bulkhead
7 ADF aerial
8 Forward electronics equipment bay
9 Westinghouse AN/APG-66 digital pulse Doppler radar electronics
10 Forward identification light, Danish and Norwegian aircraft only
11 Radar warning antenna
12 Cockpit front pressure bulkhead
13 Instrument panel shroud
14 Weapons systems fire control electronics
15 Fuselage forebody strake fairing
16 Marconi-Elliot wide-angle raster-video head-up display (WARHUD)
17 Side stick controller (fly-by-wire control system)
18 Cockpit floor
19 Frameless bubble canopy
20 Canopy fairing
21 McDonnell-Douglas ACES II zero-zero ejection seat
22 Pilot's safety harness
23 Engine throttle
24 Side console panel
25 Cockpit frame construction
26 Rear pressure bulkhead
27 Ejection seat headrest
28 Seat arming safety lever
29 Cockpit sealing frame
30 Canopy hinge point
31 Ejection seat launch rails
32 Rear electronics equipment bay (growth area)
33 Boundary layer splitter plate
34 Fixed geometry engine air intake
35 Lower UHF/IFF aerial
36 Aft retracting nosewheel
37 Shock absorber scissor links
38 Retraction strut
39 Nosewheel door
40 Forward position light
41 Intake trunking
42 Cooling air louvres
43 Gun gas suppression nozzle
44 Air conditioning system piping
45 Forward fuselage fuel tank, total system capacity 1,072.5 US gal (4060 litres)
46 Canopy aft glazing
47 Starboard 370 US gal external fuel tank (1400 litres)
48 Forebody blended wing root
49 Upper position light and flight refuelling floodlight
50 Fuel tank bay access panel
51 Rotary cannon barrels
52 Forebody frame construction
53 M-61 Vulcan, 20-mm rotary cannon
54 Ammunition feed and link return chutes
55 Ammunition drum, 515-rounds
56 Ammunition drum flexible drive shaft
57 Hydraulic gun drive motor
58 Leading-edge flap control shaft
59 Hydraulic equipment service bay
60 Primary system hydraulic reservoir
61 Leading-edge manoeuvre flap drive motor
62 TACAN aerial
63 No. 2 hydraulic system reservoir
64 Leading-edge flap control shaft
65 Inboard pylon
66 Pylon fixing
67 Wing centre pylon
68 Triple ejector bomb rack
69 MK 82 500-lb (227-kg) bombs
70 Oldelft Orpheus reconnaissance pod, Netherlands aircraft only
71 Infra-red linescan
72 Camera ports
73 Reconnaissance pod pylon adaptor, centre line fixing
74 SUU-25E/A flare launcher
75 AN/ASQ aircraft instrumentation system data link transmitter
76 Outboard wing pylon
77 Missile launch shoe

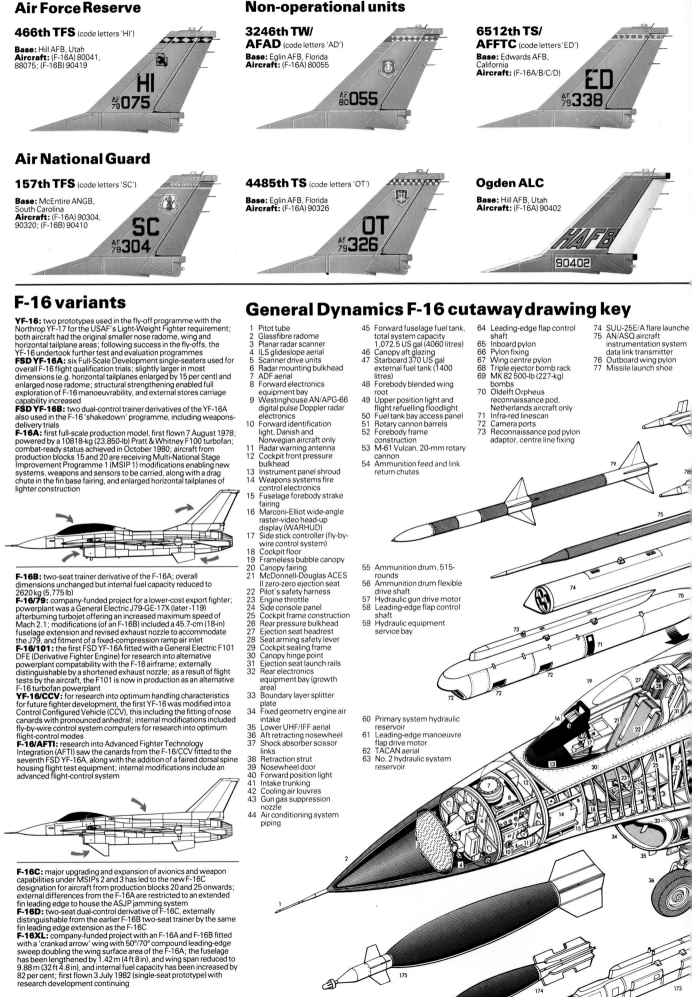

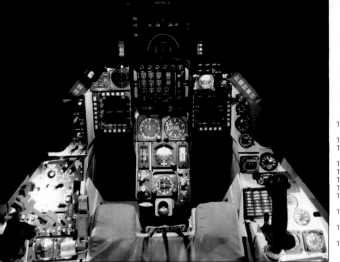

excellent and essential visibility afforded by the one-piece canopy is complemented by ...ckpit design and arrangement that allows the pilot to concentrate on visually scanning ...skies for targets. Most noticeable is the lack of a conventional centrally-mounted control ...umn, this being replaced by the side-stick controller on the right. This allows more ...cise control of the aircraft through slight amounts of hand pressure. In the upper centre is ...HUD information panel which incorporates flight data, FLIR and weapons release ...abilities. The square screens on each side of the central instrument block are dual ...rchangeable multi-function displays, allowing the pilot to monitor his weapons status. In ...lower central set of instruments, features include angle of attack, airspeed Mach no. and ...tude director indicators. Constant updates and improvements are being introduced into ...F-16 cockpit, making configurational changes almost inevitable.

93 Engine compressor face
94 Pratt & Whitney F100-PW-100(3) afterburning turbofan engine
95 Jet fuel starter
96 Engine accessory gearbox, airframe mounted
97 Gearbox drive shaft
98 Ground pressure refuelling receptacle
99 Flaperon servo actuator
100 Rear fuselage frame construction
101 Rear integral fuel tank
102 Main engine mounting suspension link
103 Upper UHF/IFF aerial
104 Fuselage skin plating
105 Starboard side-body fairing
106 Fin root fillet
107 Flight control system hydraulic accumulators
108 Anti-collision light power supply unit
109 Starboard tailplane (increased area 'big tail')
110 Tailplane surfaces interchangeable port and starboard
111 Graphite-epoxy skin panels
112 Fin construction
113 Aluminium honeycomb leading-edge panel
114 Steel leading-edge strip
115 VHF communications aerial
116 Anti-collision light
117 Tail radar warning antennae
118 Aluminium honeycomb rudder construction
119 Rudder servo actuator
120 Radar warning power supply
121 Brake parachute housing, Norwegian aircraft only
122 Tail navigation light
123 Electronic countermeasures (ECM) aerials, port and starboard

124 Fully variable exhaust nozzle
125 Nozzle flaps
126 Split trailing edge airbrake, upper and lower surfaces
127 Airbrake hydraulic jack
128 Port tailplane (increased area 'big tail')
129 Static dischargers
130 Graphite-epoxy tailplane skin panels
131 Corrugated aluminium sub-structure
132 Hinge pivot fixing
133 Tailplane servo actuator
134 Nozzle sealing fairing
135 Fueldraulic nozzle actuators
136 Afterburner tailpipe
137 Rear fuselage bulkheads
138 Rear engine mounting
139 Aft position light
140 Port side-body fairing
141 Runway arrester hook
142 Ventral fin, port and starboard
143 Port flaperon
144 Flaperon hinges
145 Aluminium honeycomb flaperon construction
146 Static dischargers
147 Fixed trailing edge section
148 Port AIM-9L Sidewinder air-to-air missiles

149 Missile launcher shoe
150 Wing tip launcher fixing
151 Port navigation light
152 Outboard pylon fixing rib
153 Multi-spar wing construction
154 Centre pylon attachment rib
155 Wing centre pylon
156 MK 84 2,000-lb (908-kg) low-drag bomb
157 Leading-edge manoeuvre flap
158 Leading-edge flap rotary actuators
159 Integral wing fuel tank
160 Inboard pylon fixing
161 Wing attachment fishplates
162 Landing/taxiing lamp
163 Main undercarriage shock absorber strut
164 Mainwheel leg strut
165 Retraction strut
166 Mainwheel door
167 Forward retracting mainwheel
168 Port underwing fuel tank, 370 US gal (1401 litres)

78 AIM-9J Sidewinder air-to-air missile
79 Advanced medium range air-to-air missile (AMRAAM)
80 Aluminium honeycomb leading-edge flap construction
81 Starboard navigation light
82 Static dischargers
83 Fixed trailing edge section
84 Multi-spar wing construction
85 Integral wing fuel tank
86 Starboard flaperon
87 Fuel system piping
88 Access panels
89 Centre fuel tank bay access panel
90 Intake ducting
91 Wing mounting bulkheads
92 Universal air refuelling receptacle (UARSSI)

169 Centre line external fuel tank, 300 US gal (1136 litres)
170 Electro-optical forward looking infra-red pod (EO-FLIR)
171 Laser target designator pod (LAST)
172 LAU-3/A rocket launcher, 19×2.75-in (6.98-cm) ground attack rockets

173 Westinghouse AN/ALQ119-1 electronic suppression system radar jamming pod (ESM)
174 Snakeye, 500-lb (227-kg) retarded bomb
175 GBU-10C/B 2,000-lb (908-kg) laser guided bomb

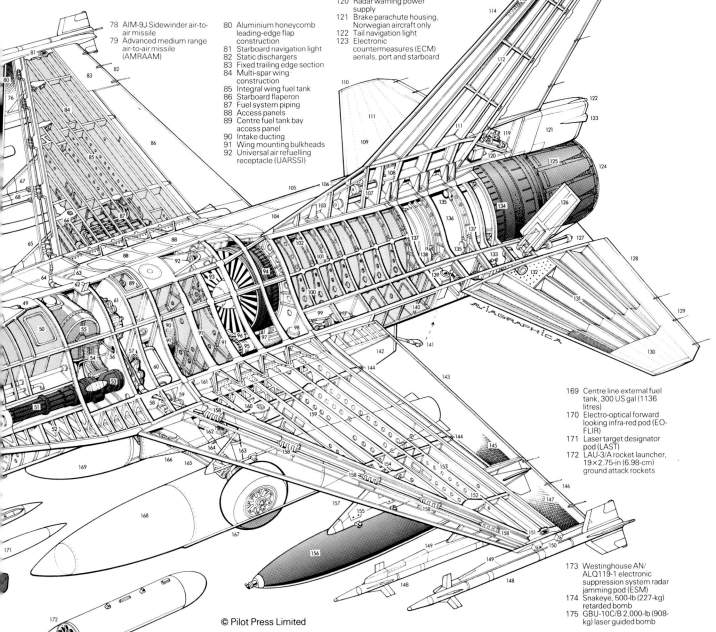

F-16 warload

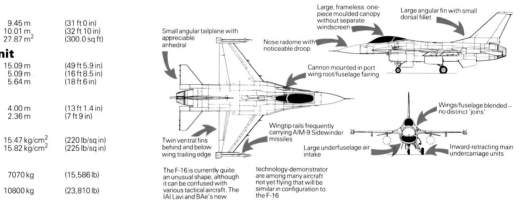

- ■ 2×AIM-9L Sidewinder close-range AAMs on wingtip launcher rails
  1×internal 20-mm M61 cannon with 515 rounds

- ■ 2×AIM-9L Sidewinder close-range AAMs on wingtip launcher rails
  1×internal 20-mm M61 cannon with 515 rounds
  2×AIM-7 Sparrow or AIM-120A AMRAAM medium-range AAMs underwing
  ■ 1×1136-litre (300-US gal) fuel tank on centreline
  2×Sargent-Fletcher 1400-litre (370-US gal) drop tanks on inboard underwing stations

- ■ 2×Mk 83 1,000-lb (907-kg) bombs on mid-wing pylons (nuclear weapons can also be carried)
  2×AIM-9L Sidewinder close-range AAMs on wingtip launcher rails
  1×internal 20-mm M61 cannon with 515 rounds

- ■ 4×Mk 82 Snakeye 500-lb (227-kg) retarded bombs on twin-carriers on mid-wing pylons
  2×AIM-9L Sidewinder close-range AAMs on wingtip launcher rails
  1×internal 20-mm M61 cannon with 515 rounds
  ■ 2×Sargent-Fletcher 1400-litre (370-US gal) drop tanks on inboard underwing stations

- ■ 2×AGM-78 Standard anti-radar missiles on mid-wing pylons
  2×AIM-9L Sidewinder close-range AAMs on wingtip launcher rails
  1×internal 20-mm M61 cannon with 515 rounds

- ■ 2×Paveway laser-guided bombs on mid-wing pylons
  2×AIM-9L Sidewinder close-range AAMs on wingtip launcher rails
  1×internal 20-mm M61 cannon with 515 rounds
  ■ 1×1136-litre (300-US gal) fuel tank on centreline

Dogfighter

The majority of USAF F-16s carry only a very small warload with two Sidewinders on the wingtip launchers which do not restrict the aircraft's phenomenal ability to withstand prolonged 9g manoeuvres. Whether or not the missiles can be launched throughout the entire flight envelope has not been revealed, but the AAMs are backed up by an internal gun for use in a high energy close-in environment.

Long-range interception

USAF F-16s can frequently be seen carrying only their wingtip Sidewinders, but they do back these up with other weapons, even in the air-to-air role. The AIM-7 is the most common such 'extra', although it is being replaced by the newer AMRAAM.

Strike

The F-16 is quite a potent attack machine, able to carry a sizeable weapon load. The penalties are such that to retain manoeuvrability, attack-configured F-16s generally carry far fewer stores than they are capable of lifting. The B-43 nuclear weapon is the 'nuke' most likely to be carried.

Ground attack

F-16s seldom operate in the attack role during peace, but they can do so, and have turned in some impressive results during bombing and air-to-ground gunnery competitions. The retarded Snakeye is a particularly effective weapon.

Wild Weasel

The F-16 could perform as a dedicated Wild Weasel aircraft with Standard ARMs, Shrikes or HARMs, and the USAF has been considering the acquisition of such a variant. The standard F-16 might well carry one or two defence-suppression missiles in addition to a normal attack payload.

Precision attack

Paveways could be replaced by Hobo guided bombs, or by TV-o laser-guided AGM-65 Maverick missiles, but without a dedicated air-to-ground radar and nav/attack system there are limits to what can be achieved.

Specification:

General Dynamics F-16A Fighting Falcon

Wings
Span, over wingtip missile launchers	9.45 m	(31 ft 0 in)
over wingtip missiles	10.01 m	(32 ft 10 in)
Area	27.87 m²	(300.0 sq ft)

Fuselage and tail unit
Length overall	15.09 m	(49 ft 5.9 in)
Height overall	5.09 m	(16 ft 8.5 in)
Tailplane span	5.64 m	(18 ft 6 in)

Landing gear
Wheelbase	4.00 m	(13 ft 1.4 in)
Wheel track	2.36 m	(7 ft 9 in)
Tyre pressures at AUW below 11340 kg (25,000 lb),		
mainwheels	15.47 kg/cm²	(220 lb/sq in)
nosewheel	15.82 kg/cm²	(225 lb/sq in)

Weights
Empty	7070 kg	(15,586 lb)
Maximum take-off, air combat with no external tanks	10800 kg	(23,810 lb)
Maximum take-off with external load	16057 kg	(35,400 lb)
Maximum internal fuel	3162 kg	(6,972 lb)

General Dynamics F-16 Fighting Falcon recognition points

Small angular tailplane with appreciable anhedral

Nose radome with noticeable droop

Large, frameless, one-piece moulded canopy without separate windscreen

Large angular fin with small dorsal fillet

Cannon mounted in port wing root/fuselage fairing

Twin ventral fins behind and below wing trailing edge

Wingtip rails frequently carrying AIM-9 Sidewinder missiles

Wings/fuselage blended – no distinct 'joins'

Large underfuselage air intake

Inward-retracting main undercarriage units

The F-16 is currently quite an unusual shape, although it can be confused with various tactical aircraft. The IAI Lavi and BAe's new technology-demonstrator are among many aircraft not yet flying that will be similar in configuration to the F-16

Performance:

Maximum speed 'clean' more than 1,146 kts	Mach 2.0+ or 2124 km/h	(1,320 mph)
Service ceiling more than	50,000 ft	(15240 m)
Tactical radius more than	925 km	(575 miles)
Ferry radius, with drop tanks more than	3887 km	(2,415 miles)

Weapons load

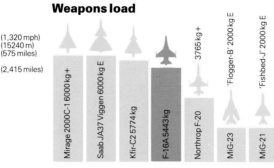

- Mirage 2000C-1 6000 kg+
- Saab JA37 Viggen 6000 kg E
- Kfir-C2 5774 kg
- F-16A 5443 kg
- Northrop F-20 3765 kg+
- 'Flogger-B' 2000 kg E
- 'Fishbed-J' 2000 kg E

Service ceiling

- MiG-23 'Flogger-B' 61,000 ft E
- Saab JA37 Viggen 60,000 ft
- Mirage 2000C-1 59,000 ft
- Kfir-C2 58,000 ft
- Northrop F-20 56,800 ft
- F-16A 50,000 ft+
- MiG-21 'Fishbed-J' 50,000 ft

Speed at high altitude

- MiG-23 'Flogger-B' Mach 2.35 E
- Kfir-C2 Mach 2.3+
- Mirage 2000C-1 Mach 2.3+
- Saab JA37 Viggen Mach 2.1
- MiG-21 'Fishbed-J' Mach 2.02
- F-16A Mach 2+
- Northrop F-20 Mach 2+

Speed at low altitude

- Mirage 2000C-1 Mach 1.2 E 'clean'
- MiG-23 'Flogger-B' Mach 1.2 E
- Saab JA37 Viggen Mach 1.2
- Kfir-C2 Mach 1.1 'clean'
- MiG-21 'Fishbed-J' Mach 1.06
- F-16A Mach 1
- Northrop F-20 Mach 1 E

Take-off run

- F-16A 1,200 ft E
- Saab JA37 Viggen 1,310 ft E
- Mirage 2000C-1 1,500 ft E
- MiG-21 'Fishbed-J' 2,625 ft
- MiG-23 'Flogger-B' 2,950 ft E
- Northrop F-20 at max weight 3,550 ft
- Kfir-C2 at max weight 4,750 ft

General Dynamics F-16 Fighting Falcons

F-111: Tripoli Troubleshooter

The history of the F-111 has been chequered to say the least, but through it all the 'Aardvark' has emerged as an extremely potent weapons platform with commendable mission versatility. Specializing in bad-weather operations, the F-111 has earned the respect it deserves from friend and foe alike.

Colloquially known as the 'Aardvark', the General Dynamics F-111 is assured of a place in aviation history by virtue of the fact that it was the first variable-geometry or 'swing-wing' aircraft to attain quantity production for any air arm in the world. Today, of course, VG is a commonplace feature of modern combat aircraft, types such as the Panavia Tornado, Grumman F-14 Tomcat and Mikoyan-Gurevich MiG-23/27 'Flogger' all using such wings to achieve satisfactory low-speed handling qualities, good range/payload characteristics and superior field performance without compromising capability at the other end of the speed scale.

The design and manufacturing teams for these later aircraft seem to have encountered few serious development problems. But the same was most certainly not true of the F-111, General Dynamics running into great difficulty during the course of development. Even after the type attained operational service it continued to fall victim to a succession of problems, being grounded on several occasions as a result of accidents, whilst the fact that it was something of a political 'hot potato' added fuel to the fires of controversy which raged around the F-111 for several years. Like most innovative types, it took time to develop fixes, but once these had been incorporated the F-111 began to show definite signs of living up to its early promise. Indeed, it

has now matured into a most effective warplane and one which occupies a unique slot in the USAF inventory, for it is the only attack aircraft with that service possessing the ability to operate at low level by day or night in all weather conditions.

Development of what eventually evolved into the F-111 can be traced back to July 1960, when Specific Operational Requirement No. 183 was issued by the USAF: in essence this called for a new fighter capable of fulfilling such disparate missions as air superiority, conventional and nuclear strike, and reconnaissance. One of the key aspects of SOR183 concerned the VG wing, the USAF being of the opinion that this represented the most suitable line of approach whilst also expressing the view that a turbofan engine would be worthy of consideration. Had the Air Force been allowed to proceed independently the F-111's subsequent history might have been less chequered, but the fact that the US Navy was also engaged in the preliminary stages of the search for a new fighter to replace the McDonnell Douglas F-4 Phantom prompted Secretary of Defense Robert McNamara to recommend that the two requirements be combined into a single programme known by the acronym TFX. Not surprisingly, this recommendation met considerable opposition within the two armed forces, but McNamara

Lurking in its lair, an F-111F sits in silence, awaiting its next demanding mission. A pioneer in getting down low in the worst of weather, locating the target and blasting it with a deadly array of weapons, the F-111 is a valuable warrior.

stuck to his guns, a new request for proposals being issued at the end of September 1961. In the event, nine responses were received during December of that year, the same month in which the designation F-111 was allocated to the new fighter.

Competition victory

Study of these submissions revealed that none was acceptable in its original form, but Boeing and General Dynamics were invited to refine their concepts further and the next few months witnessed considerable in-fighting as the services sought to reconcile their requirements in the face of McNamara's continuing intransigence. Eventually, after extensive redesign and despite Air Force recommendation of the Boeing contender, the General Dynamics submission emerged victorious, initial procurement of 23 development aircraft (18 USAF F-

This view shows an F-111E roaring off after a commendably short take-off run, clearly illustrating the full-span trailing edge, double-slotted flaps which help provide excellent low-speed handling as well as the all-moving slab-like stabilators.

United States Air F[orce]
Tactical Air Comma[nd]

The largest USAF Command in terms of nu[mbers] operated has two Tactical Fighter Wings e[quipped with] different models of the F-111, both forming [part of the] Air Force. The 366th TFW gave up its F-mo[del] 10 years ago to the 48th TFW within USAF[E. The 474th] TFW remains the sole operator of the F-111[A and is] each equipped with a training squadron for [crew conversion] while the 57th FWW is engaged in ongoing [evaluation] and training in operational tactics. Aircraft f[rom these units] detached to the two TFW bases for training [purposes of] crews and their aircraft.

366th Tactical
Fighter Wing   391st[

Base: Mountain Home AFB, Idaho
Squadrons and fin-tip colours: 389th TFTS (yellow); 391st TFS (blue)
Tailcode letters: 'MO'
Equipment: F-111A
Example aircraft: 70046, 70067; 70095, 70108

389th[

United States Air F[orce]

Examples of the F-111 have been based in t[he United] Kingdom since late 1970 when the first F-11[1E joined the] 20th TFW at RAF Upper Heyford. Today, thi[s unit]

20th Tactical
Fighter Wing

Base: RAF Upper Heyford, Oxfordshire
Squadrons and fin-tip colours: 55th TFS (blue/white checks); 77th TFS (red); 79th TFS (tiger stripes)
Tailcode letters: 'UH'
Equipment: F-111E
Example aircraft: 80006, 80036; 80017, 80077; 70123, 80050

55th T[

79th T[

United States Air F[orce]
Strategic Air Comm[and]

The two Bomb Wings which operate the FB[-111A form] part of the 8th Air Force, and are part of the [US nuclear] deterrent force. Some 60 examples of this [type] are currently in service, though plans for any [further] development of the type seem highly unlike[ly now that the] Rockwell B-1B is in service. Aircraft are har[dly ever seen] outside the continental USA, though obviou[sly their] operations in times of real tension would m[ean strikes] against overseas targets. The force is likely [to adopt a new] colour scheme in the near future as part of t[he change from] dark grey/dark green camouflage to the SAC[?]

380th Bomb   509th
Wing   Wing

Base: Plattsburgh AFB, New York
Squadrons: 528th BS, 529th BS and 4007th Combat Crew Training Squadron
Equipment: FB-111A
Example aircraft: 80240, 80246, 80255, 80257, 80284, 96507

Base: Pea[se AFB, New] Hampshire
Squadro[ns:
BS
Equipme[nt:
Example [aircraft:
80255, 80[?
96503

United States Air F[orce]

The F-111 continues to serve with test and [evaluation] agencies as part of ongoing programmes to [further] enhance the aircraft and its associated syst[ems, and to] act as a test vehicle for technology which m[ay be used] in future aircraft designs. Prominent among[st these] programmes is the use of an F-111A fitted w[ith a Mission] Adaptive Wing (MAW). This joint USAF/NA[SA programme] uses the F-111 as part of the broader Advan[ced Fighter] Technology Integration project, with opera[tions conducted] from Edwards AFB. The ADTC in Florida use[s the F-111 for] development and testing of non-nuclear we[apons for tactical] and strategic forces.

Control of F-111 overhaul and moderniza[tion rests with] the Sacramento Air Logistics Center at McC[lellan AFB,] California, this being part of Air Force Logist[ics Command.] Aircraft from the various F-111 units pass th[rough here] on a regular basis, though much of the work[on RAF aircraft] is carried out in the United Kingdom.

In addition to front-line opera[tional]
service, the F-111 is engaged [in various]
research projects. This mach[ine is fitted]
with a mission-adaptive wing[, a device]
incorporating variable cambe[r...]

111As and five USN F-111Bs) being authorized. Manufacture of the USAF examples was entrusted to General Dynamics' Fort Worth factory, whilst the Navy aircraft was the responsibility primarily of Grumman at Bethpage. The two variants made their first flights on 21 December 1964 and 18 May 1965 from Carswell AFB and Calverton respectively.

Flight testing soon began to reveal problems, but the F-111A model did eventually attain operational status almost three years later when the first production examples began to join the 474th Tactical Fighter Wing at Cannon AFB, New Mexico in mid-October 1967, this unit moving to Nellis AFB, Nevada early in 1968.

Like most types then in or about to enter USAF service, the F-111 was introduced to combat at the earliest possible date, 'Combat Lancer' being the code name assigned to the deployment of six F-111As from Nellis to Takhli, Thailand in March 1968. This initial exposure to the hazards of combat proved to be most inauspicious, two F-111As being lost during the course of the first 55 missions against targets in North Vietnam. Replacements were despatched from Nellis, but before they arrived another F-111A was reported missing on 22 April, this effectively marking the end of the Aardvark's combat debut, although it was not until November that the surviving aircraft returned to the USA.

Several years elapsed before the F-111 returned to the rigours of war during the final stages of the Vietnam conflict. This time, two entire squadrons with a combined strength of about 50 aircraft were committed to action at the end of September 1972, and despite several losses the aircraft performed well, logging more than 3,000 missions before 'Linebacker II' prompted the North Vietnamese to return to the negotiating table in earnest.

Often operating alone or in small 'packages', the Aardvark repeatedly flew when other types were grounded by poor weather, this period effectively signalling that the F-111 was at last maturing into a most effective warplane. Nevertheless,

there were still many problems to be overcome.

Although the Air Force eventually succeeded in getting the aircraft it had originally wanted, the same claim could not be made for the Navy which had never been particularly enthusiastic about the F-111B. Eventually, unacceptable weight growth coupled with a serious performance shortfall resulted in a production hold order being placed on the type during July 1968. By that time, the five development F-111Bs has been joined in the flight test programme by the first two production examples, which eventually proved to be the last F-111Bs completed, funding for 30 more of the latter being blocked by the Senate and the House Armed Services Committee. This effectively killed the F-111B, but it was not until August 1968 that the F-111B programme was officially cancelled, a further blow to General Dynamics which was still recovering from the British decision to abandon plans to acquire 50 examples of a variant designated F-111K.

Further models

As far as the initial model was concerned, only 17 RDT&E F-111As were completed, the 18th and last example being employed as the FB-111A prototype. These initial aircraft were followed by 141 production machines, the last of which was delivered to the USAF at the

end of August 1969. By then, the first example of the second production version (rather confusingly designated F-111E) had flown, this being the forerunner of 94 aircraft and it initially entered service with the 27th TFW at Cannon AFB, New Mexico in the autumn of the same year although most of these aircraft were subsequently deployed overseas with the 20th TFW at RAF Upper Heyford, England. There followed some 96 examples of the considerably more capable F-111D, which featured much revised avionics, this variant also making its debut with the 27th TFW. Production of tactical fighter models for the USAF terminated with 106 copies of the F-111F. Introducing a considerably more powerful version of the TF30 turbofan engine, the F-111F was first assigned to the 347th TFW at Mountain Home AFB, Idaho but, following a complex realignment exercise involving the

Piercing the sky on a low-level, high-speed run, an F-111F illustrates the maximum wing sweepback of 72.5° – giving the aircraft an almost delta-wing appearance. The twin TF30 afterburning turbofans give the aircraft very impressive high speeds.

One of the contemporary weapons configurations of the F-111F includes laser-guided bombs, air defence missiles, laser designating equipment and an ECM pod – a lethal combination which no enemy would want to receive, night or day.

F-111A, F-111D and
too is now also in Eu
squadrons of the
Lakenheath.

The remaining
veloped for service
the FB-111A, which
Strategic Air Comm
the north-eastern
Optimized for strate
cal missions, the
(originally laid down
F-111A) flew for the
of July 1967 and was
by the first produ
under a year later. F
until mid-October 19
SAC began, this com
ceiving 75 of the 7
mens built, one bein
delivery accident. V
the FB-111A is esse
the F-111D fuselag
larger wing of the F
tures stronger land
different variant of t

Limited exports

On the export fr
achieved modest su
chasing two dozen e
known as the F-111C
replace the vetera
Canberra light bomb
Squadrons at RA
Australians had to w
years before deliverie
extensive modificati
part in bringing abou
unit cost to the emba
ties. So serious was t
ing availability of t
was eventually prov
Phantoms on a loan b
until 1972-3 when
turned to the USA.
attrition has claimed
the decade or so tha
been in service, bu
fleet was topped u
handful of surplus U
delivered. Most of th
have been subjected

This view of the F-111D forward instrument panel clearly shows the prominent terrain-following radar scope panel at top. At bottom right is the attack radar scope panel, its range being indicated.

44 UHF recovery
45 ECM antennas (port and starboard)
46 Forward fuselage fuel bay
47 Ground refuelling receptacle
48 Weapons bay
49 Module pitch flaps (port and starboard)
50 Aft flotation bag stowage
51 Aerial refuelling receptacle
52 Primary heat-exchanger (air-to-water)
53 Ram air inlet

54 Rate gyros
55 Rotating glove
56 Inlet variable spike
57 Port intake
58 Air brake/landing gear
59 Auxiliary inlet blow-in doors
60 Rotating glove pivot po
61 Inlet vortex generators
62 Wing sweep pivot
63 Wing centre-box asser
64 Wing sweep actuator
65 Wing sweep feedback
66 Control runs
67 Rotating glove drive se
68 Inboard pivot pylons (2
69 Auxiliary drop tanks (60 US gal/2271 litres)
70 Outboard fixed pylons(subsonic/jettisonable
71 Slat drive set
72 Wing fuel tank (389.2 U gal/1473 litres)
73 Leading-edge slat
74 Starboard navigation li
75 Flap drive set
76 Outboard spoiler actua
77 Starboard spoilers
78 Inboard spoiler actuato
79 Flaps
80 Wing swept position
81 Auxiliary flap
82 Auxiliary flap actuator
83 Nuclear weapons and weapon control equip package

F-111 variants

F-111A: initial production model for service with US Air Force; development batch of 17 RD&E aircraft followed by 141 production examples; production aircraft powered by 8392-kg (18,500-lb) thrust TF30-P-3s, armament comprising one M61 Vulcan 20-mm cannon and one 750-lb (340-kg) nuclear free-fall B43 bomb or two 750-lb bombs housed internally plus up to 13608 kg (30,000 lb) of external stores on six underwing hardpoints; flown for first time on 21 December 1964

F-111B: navalized derivative intended for service with US Navy in fleet fighter role; five RDT&E aircraft and two production specimens completed before project cancelled in July 1968; would have used six AIM-54A Phoenix air-to-air missiles as primary armament; unacceptable weight growth principal factor in cancellation; first flight on 18 May 1965 by TF30-P-3 powered aircraft, but production model would have used TF30-P-12 engines

F-111C: export model for Royal Australian Air Force, which ordered 24 aircraft to replace Canberra light bomber; basically similar to F-111A but features eight underwing pylons; eventually entered service with RAAF in 1973 and still operational

F-111D: vastly improved variant with Mk II avionics and more powerful TF30-P-9 engines; first flown on 15 May 1970, and total of 96 built for service with TAC

F-111E: improved F-111A with modified air inlets and detail changes; powered by TF30-P-3 engine and first flown on 20 August 1969; total of 94 built, initially for service with TAC but deployed to UK from 1970 onwards, equipping USAFE's 20th TFW at RAF Upper Heyford

F-111F: simplified version of F-111D, employing considerably more powerful TF30-P-100 engines and less complex avionics fit; has since been retrofitted with 'Pave Tack' sensor package to improve night/all-weather capability; joined TAC inventory in 1971 but later transferred to USAFE, joining 48th TFW at RAF Lakenheath; F-111 production ceased with delivery of 106th example

FB-111B: proposed improved strategic bomber model with General Electric F101 or similar engines and SRAM armament; original study advocated conversion of existing FB-111As and F-111Ds, but not proceeded with

FB-111H: proposed advanced strategic bomber version with General Electric F101 engines, advanced avionics and with an enlarged internal weapons bay; did not progress beyond study phase

The rear end of the F-111 is dominated by the huge variable-area exhaust nozzles. The large side fairings contain ECM equipment.

General Dynamics F-111D cutaway drawing key

1 Hinged nose cone
2 Attack radar
3 Terrain-following radar
4 Nose hinges (2)
5 Radar mounting
6 Nose lock
7 Angle-of-sideslip probe
8 Homing antenna (high)
9 Forward warning antenna
10 Homing antenna (low and mid)
11 ALR-41 antenna
12 Flight control computers
13 Feel and trim assembly
14 Forward avionics bay (Advanced Mk II digital computer)
15 Angle-of-attack probe
16 UHF Comm/Tacan No. 2
17 Module forward bulkhead and stabilization flaps (2)
18 Twin nosewheels

19 Shock strut
20 Underfloor impact attenuation bag stowage (4)
21 Nosewheel well
22 LOX converter
23 Rudder pedals
24 Control column
25 LOX heat exchanger
26 Auxiliary flotation bag pressure bottle
27 Weapons sight
28 Forward parachute bridle line
29 De-fog nozzle
30 Windscreen
31 Starboard console
32 Emergency oxygen bottles
33 Crew seats
34 Bulkhead console
35 Wing sweep control handle

36 Recovery chute catapult
37 Provision/survival pack
38 Attenuation bags pressure bottle
39 Recovery chute
40 Aft parachute bridle line
41 UHF data link/AG IFF No. 1 (see 123)
42 Stabilization-brake chute
43 Self-righting bag

84 Wing sweep/Hi Lift co box
85 Flap, slat and glove dri mechanism
86 Starboard engine bay
87 Yaw feel spring
88 Roll feel spring
89 Yaw trim actuator
90 Yaw damper servo
91 Roll stick position transducer
92 Pitch trim actuator (manual)

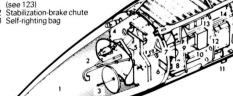

© Pilot Press Ltd

Specification General Dynamics F-111F

Wings

..n, fully spread	19.20 m	(63 ft 0 in)
.. fully swept	9.74 m	(31 ft 11.5 in)
.. fully swept	61.07 m²	(657.3 sq ft)
..ep, fully spread	16°	
.. fully swept	72°30'	

..selage and tail unit

..ommodation   pilot and electronic warfare officer in
a McDonnell Douglas rocket-
powered escape capsule

..gth overall	22.40 m	(73 ft 6 in)
..ht overall	5.22 m	(17 ft 1.5 in)

..nding gear

..raulically retractable tricycle landing gear with giant single main
..els

..eights

..ty	21398 kg	(47,175 lb)
..imum take-off	45360 kg	(100,000 lb)
..imum external load	13608 kg	(30,000 lb)

..werplant

.. Pratt & Whitney TF30-P-100 afterburning turbofans
..ic thrust with afterburning,
..ch   11385 kg   (25,100 lb)

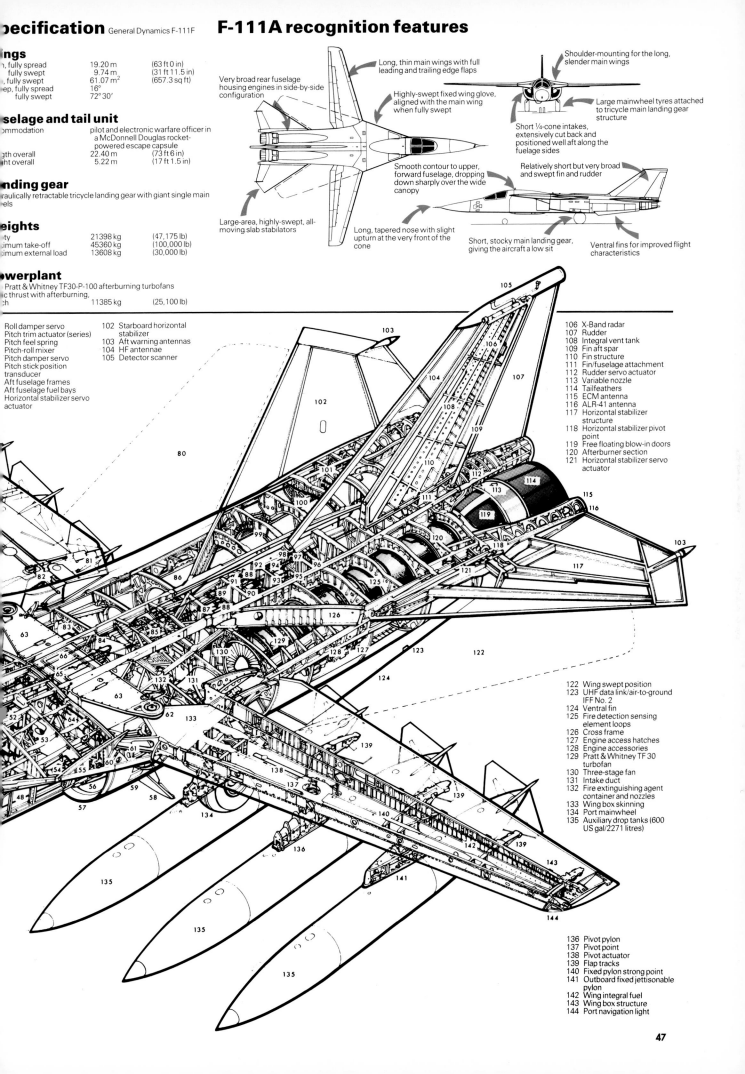

Very broad rear fuselage housing engines in side-by-side configuration

Long, thin main wings with full leading and trailing edge flaps

Highly-swept fixed wing glove, aligned with the main wing when fully swept

Shoulder-mounting for the long, slender main wings

Large mainwheel tyres attached to tricycle main landing gear structure

Short ¼-cone intakes, extensively cut back and positioned well aft along the fuselage sides

Large-area, highly-swept, all-moving slab stabilators

Smooth contour to upper, forward fuselage, dropping down sharply over the wide canopy

Relatively short but very broad and swept fin and rudder

Long, tapered nose with slight upturn at the very front of the cone

Short, stocky main landing gear, giving the aircraft a low sit

Ventral fins for improved flight characteristics

.. Roll damper servo	102 Starboard horizontal
.. Pitch trim actuator (series)	stabilizer
.. Pitch feel spring	103 Aft warning antennas
.. Pitch-roll mixer	104 HF antennae
.. Pitch damper servo	105 Detector scanner
.. Pitch stick position	
transducer	
.. Aft fuselage frames	
.. Aft fuselage fuel bays	
.. Horizontal stabilizer servo	
actuator	

106 X-Band radar
107 Rudder
108 Integral vent tank
109 Fin aft spar
110 Fin structure
111 Fin/fuselage attachment
112 Rudder servo actuator
113 Variable nozzle
114 Tailfeathers
115 ECM antenna
116 ALR-41 antenna
117 Horizontal stabilizer structure
118 Horizontal stabilizer pivot point
119 Free floating blow-in doors
120 Afterburner section
121 Horizontal stabilizer servo actuator

122 Wing swept position
123 UHF data link/air-to-ground IFF No. 2
124 Ventral fin
125 Fire detection sensing element loops
126 Cross frame
127 Engine access hatches
128 Engine accessories
129 Pratt & Whitney TF 30 turbofan
130 Three-stage fan
131 Intake duct
132 Fire extinguishing agent container and nozzles
133 Wing box skinning
134 Port mainwheel
135 Auxiliary drop tanks (600 US gal/2271 litres)

136 Pivot pylon
137 Pivot point
138 Pivot actuator
139 Flap tracks
140 Fixed pylon strong point
141 Outboard fixed jettisonable pylon
142 Wing integral fuel
143 Wing box structure
144 Port navigation light

F-111 warload

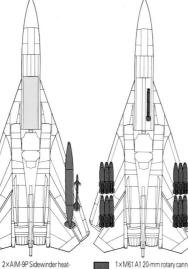

■ 4×AGM-84A Harpoon air-to-surface missiles, one per underwing pylon

■ 2×AIM-9P Sidewinder heat-seeking air-to-air missiles, one shoulder-mounted on each of the outer section of the pylons carrying the fuel tanks
■ 2×2273-litre (500-Imp gal) auxiliary fuel tanks, one per outer underwing pylon

■ 1×M61 A1 20-mm rotary cannon in the right-hand section of the internal weapons bay with 2,084 rounds of ammunition
■ 12×Mk 82 227-kg (500-lb) Snakeye low-drag retarded 'iron' bombs, carried in tandem triplets on two multiple ejector racks (MERs), one per outer underwing pylon

■ 4×B61 thermonuclear tactical free-fall bombs, two side-by-side in the internal weapons bay and one on each of the inner underwing pylons
■ 2×AIM-9P heat-seeking air-to-air missiles, one shoulder-mounted on each of the outer section of the pylons carrying the fuel tanks
■ 2×2273-litre (500-Imp gal) auxiliary fuel tanks, one per outer underwing pylon

■ 2×GBU-15 Cruciform Wing Weapon (CWW) electro-optical 'smart' bombs, one per outer wing pylon
■ 1×AN/AVQ-26 Pave Tack laser designator pod semi-recessed in the internal weapons bay
1×AN/AXQ-14 two-way data-link weapon control and guidance pod under the rear fuselage

■ 2×AGM-69A short-range attack missiles (SRAMs), side-by-side in the internal weapons bay
■ 4×2273-litre (500-Imp gal) auxiliary fuel tanks on underwing pylons

F-111C anti-shipping strike
Current munitions available to the RAAF F-111C force include items such as the Snakeye 'smart' bomb and the Pave Tack laser designator pod, but the warload above will represent a major boost to the F-111 strike capability. The configuration is currently undergoing evaluation, tactics including the saturation of a seaborne target with all four missiles being fired consecutively on a single approach. For longer-range missions and/or increased target area loiter, two missiles could be replaced by auxiliary fuel tanks. Current plans call for the Harpoon to enter RAAF front-line service by 1988/89.

RF-111C reconnaissance
Various combinations of low/medium-altitude panoramic cameras and electronic sensors can be fitted in the reconnaissance package now occupying the internal weapons bay. Cameras include vertical and oblique format for general and post-strike reconnaissance. The sensor equipment includes infra-red linescan.
The sole operational version of the F-111 configured for dedicated reconnaissance duties, the small force of RAAF RF-111Cs has the entire internal weapons bay fitted with photographic and electronic sensor equipment, though the underwing panels can still be used for both auxiliary fuel and a variety of weapons. Exact details of the reconnaissance equipment are unavailable, though the standard form of such pallets is related above, no doubt including a configuration allowing for overwater reconnaissance around the vast coastline of Australia.

F-111D low-level bombing
Use of the M61 A1 cannon has never been made by F-111 models other than the F-111D. The bomb load illustrated is by no means the maximum weapons load that can be carried, rather a realistic configuration if aircraft performance is not to be seriously degraded, particularly as this mission will take the aircraft down as low as 100 ft (30 m) over the battlefield. Full use will be made of the excellent terrain-following radar, the aircraft hugging the contours of the land with minimum clearance in an attempt to avoid detection by enemy radar.

F-111E tactical nuclear strike
On the tactical models of the F-111, the internal weapons bay is used exclusively for carriage of nuclear bombs and not conventional free-fall munitions. The bombs carried can have their explosive yield varied depending on mission requirements, the number of weapons carried also varying from two to six. The two air-to-air missiles provide a degree of self-defence, the attack radar supplying range information to the pilot's lead-computing optical sight (LCOS).

F-111F tactical precision attack
An important element in the overall updating of F-111 weapons and the associated delivery systems, the GBU-15 units can be fitted to the standard 907-kg (2,000-lb) bomb and the CBU-75 cluster munitions dispenser. The nose area includes an electro-optical unit, this relaying images to the cockpit visual display via the data-link pod carried under the rear fuselage. This latter item also guides the GBU-15 by emitting signals from its phased-array aerial system. Pave Tack acts as a laser designator pod, providing range information on a tracked target to the aircrew via a cockpit display, thus allowing for precision delivery of the weapons. The pod can then swivel aft to scan for target damage information, this being taped if necessary.

FB-111A stand-off attack
An important element within Strategic Air Command, the FB-111A force can carry a variety of nuclear bombs and air-launched cruise missiles. A maximum of two can be carried internally, though the external underwing pylons could each carry the weapon. The fuel tanks are almost mandatory if the FB-111A is to perform anything like a long-range mission, six tanks (an additional pair on outside, unswivelling pylons) providing an intercontinental mission capability, though these would have to be jettisoned if the wings were to be swept further than 26°.

Performance

Sustained speed at
35,000 ft (10670 m) Mach 2.2; 1267 kts; 2348 km/h (1,459 mph)
Speed at low level   Mach 1.2; 793 kts; 1469 km/h (913 mph)
Service ceiling in clean condition   60,000 ft (18290 m)
Maximum range with internal/external
fuel more than   4707 km (2,925 miles)
Take-off run to clear 15-m (50-ft)
obstacle   950 m (3,120 ft)

Maximum weapon load
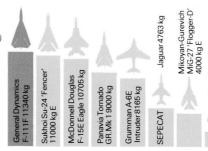

General Dynamics F-111F 11340 kg
Sukhoi Su-24 'Fencer' 11000 kg E
McDonnell Douglas F-15E Eagle 10705 kg
Panavia Tornado GR.Mk 1 9000 kg
Grumman A-6E Intruder 8165 kg
Jaguar 4763 kg
Mikoyan-Gurevich MiG-27 'Flogger-D' 4000 kg E
Nanchang Q-5 'Fantan' 2000 kg
SEPECAT

Service ceiling

General Dynamics F-111F 60,000 ft
McDonnell Douglas F-15E Eagle 60,000 ft+
Sukhoi Su-24 'Fencer' 54,100 ft E
Mikoyan-Gurevich MiG-27 'Flogger-D' 52,500 ft E
Nanchang Q-5 'Fantan' 52,500 ft
Panavia Tornado GR.Mk 1 50,000 ft+
SEPECAT Jaguar 50,000 ft+E
Grumman A-6E Intruder 42,400 ft

Maximum speed at high altitude

McDonnell Douglas F-15E Eagle Mach 2.5+
General Dynamics F-111F Mach 2.4
Panavia Tornado GR.Mk 1 Mach 2.2 'clean'
Sukhoi Su-24 'Fencer' Mach 2.18 E
Mikoyan-Gurevich MiG-27 'Flogger-D' Mach 1.7 E
SEPECAT Jaguar Mach 1.6
Nanchang Q-5 'Fantan' Mach 1.12
Grumman A-6E Intruder Mach 0.8

Maximum speed at sea level

McDonnell Douglas F-15E Eagle Mach 1.23
General Dynamics F-111F Mach 1.2
Sukhoi Su-24 'Fencer' Mach 1.2 E
Panavia Tornado GR.Mk 1 Mach 1.2
SEPECAT Jaguar Mach 1.1
Mikoyan-Gurevich MiG-27 'Flogger-D' Mach 1.1 E
Nanchang Q-5 'Fantan' Mach 0.99
Grumman A-6E Intruder Mach 0.85

Combat radius hi-lo-hi (external fuel)

Grumman A-6E Intruder 1627 km
General Dynamics F-111F 1480 km
Panavia Tornado GR.Mk 1 1390 km
McDonnell Douglas F-15E Eagle 1200 km+
Mikoyan-Gurevich MiG-27 'Flogger-D' 950 km E
Sukhoi Su-24 'Fencer' 950 km E
SEPECAT Jaguar 852 km
Nanchang Q-5 'Fantan' 690 km E

A General Dynamics FB-111

United States

Grumman A-6 Intruder

In continuous production since the late 1950s and with a new improved version likely to make its debut later in the present decade, the **Grumman A-6 Intruder** seems certain to establish a production longevity record that is unlikely to be equalled by any combat aircraft type manufactured in the West.

Development of the Intruder dates back to 1957, when 11 companies responded to a US Navy request for proposals for a new jet-powered attack aircraft capable of operating at night or in the worst conceivable weather conditions. Close study of the various contenders resulted in Grumman's model **G-128** being selected at the end of 1957 for further development as the **A2F** and eight development examples of the **A2F-1** (**A-6A** from late 1962) were duly ordered, the first making a succesful maiden flight on 19 April 1960.

Its distinctly utilitarian appearance perhaps belied the fact that it was indeed a most sophisticated machine, effectively marrying computer technology with a sturdy airframe to produce a remarkably effective warplane. Despite teething troubles with the early avionics systems, the A-6A eventually went on to compile an impressive combat record in Vietnam, often being the only aircraft able to fly and fight effectively in that theatre.

Production of the basic A-6A ceased in late 1969 after just under 500 had been built, but by then plans were well in hand for the next major attack-dedicated model, this being the

A-6E which took full advantage of progress made in the field of avionics, being fitted with Norden APQ-148 multi-mode nav/attack radar and numerous other bits and pieces of new kit.

Still in production at the time of writing, the A-6E has been progressively modernized since attaining operational status in the early 1970s, visible evidence of this process being best exemplified by the TRAM (Target Recognition Attack Multi-sensor) turret beneath the nose radome. Basically, TRAM consists of FLIR (Forward-Looking Infra-Red) and laser detection gear to provide greater accuracy in weapons delivery in all weather conditions.

Other Intruder models, most of them produced by converting existing airframes, have included the **EA-6A** ECM platform for the US Marine Corps, the **A-6B** for SAM suppression, the **A-6C** with improved night attack capability and the **KA-6D** inflight-refuelling tanker. Of these models, only the KA-6D remains active in a truly operational capacity with the US Navy.

With regard to the future, the upcoming **A-6F** will be the 'third-generation' Intruder and this model is expected to enter full production in 1990 with the new General Electric F404 unreheated turbofan. The A-6F's avionics suite will be a vast improvement over existing gear and is to include high-resolution synthetic-aperature radar and completely revised cathode ray tube-based cockpit displays.

Specification: Grumman A-6E Intruder
Origin: USA
Type: medium two-seat land/sea-based all-weather attack aircraft
Powerplant: two 4,218-kg (9,300-lb) thrust Pratt & Whitney J52-P-8A turbojet engines
Performance: maximum speed 563 kts (1043 km/h; 648 mph) at sea level; initial rate of climb 'clean' 7,620 ft (2322 m) per minute; service ceiling 'clean' 47,500 ft (14480 m); range with full weapon load 1627 km (1,011 miles)
Weights: empty 12132 kg (26,746 lb); maximum take-off (catapult launch) 26581 kg (58,600 lb); maximum take-off (field) 27397 kg (60,400 lb)
Dimensions: span 16.15 m (53 ft 0 in); length 16.69 m (54 ft 9 in); height 4.93 m (16 ft 2 in); wing area 49.13 m² (528.9 sq ft)
Armament: five external stores stations capable of accommodating maximum payload of 8165 kg (18,000 lb); options include nuclear weapons, conventional bombs, 'smart' bombs, air-to-surface missiles such as Harpoon; alternatively, auxiliary fuel tanks may be fitted to increase range at some penalty in offensive payload

A Grumman A-6E Intruder of VMA(AW)-533, a Marine attack unit based at El Toro, California.

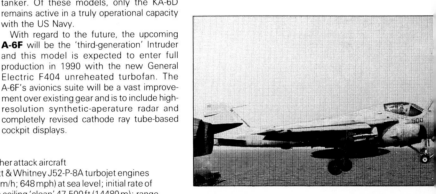

A-6E (TRAM) Intruder (lower side view: EA-6A)

An unmarked A-6E Intruder takes off from USS Coral Sea during the recent operations off Libya, which culminated in the bombing of Benghazi by US Navy A-6s.

A KA-6D of VA-55 takes off from Coral Sea, with underwing tanks and an underfuselage refuelling pod clearly visible. Attack A-6 units usually go to sea with four of these useful tankers.

Grumman EA-6B Prowler

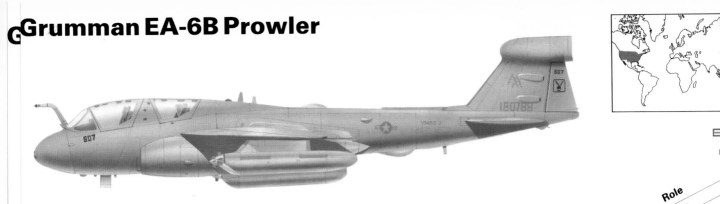

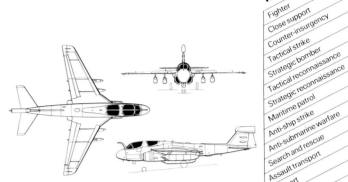

United States

A Grumman EA-6B Prowler of VMAQ-2, assigned to USS America during the Libyan operations.

Inheriting responsibility for electronic countermeasures duties from the veteran Douglas EKA-3B Skywarrior at the beginning of the 1970s, the **Grumman EA-6B Prowler** evolved from the highly successful A-6 Intruder. Although produced in relatively modest quantities, the Prowler does nevertheless form an important part of the modern carrier air wing, fulfilling functions which range from 'riding shotgun' for Navy strike aircraft intent on penetrating enemy defences through providing a protective screen around carrier task forces to acquisition of electronic intelligence.

Development of the Prowler began in the latter half of the 1960s when it was decided to purchase a new-build aircraft to perform this increasingly important role. Grumman's A-6 seemed to provide a good starting point for an ECM-dedicated type and was duly selected to provide the basis for the Prowler, which eventually appeared as a four-seater with a crew consisting of a pilot to fly the aircraft and three electronic warfare officers (EWOs) to manage the sophisticated array of ECM and electronic support measures (ESM) systems.

At the heart of the EA-6B is the ALQ-99 tactical jamming system, this being basically a package capable of detecting, sorting, classifying and dealing with electronic 'threats' across a broad spectrum of frequency bands. Operation may be accomplished automatically, semi-automatically or

manually, various antennas located around the airframe being employed to detect electronic emissions whilst up to five external pods can be carried to generate 'noise' jamming signals designed to render enemy radar ineffective.

Not surprisingly, Prowler capability has been steadily enhanced since the type first attained operational status with VAQ-132 in the summer of 1972. Early production machines were to 'Basic' standard and these have since been followed by 'ExCap' (Expanded Capability), 'ICap' (Improved Capability) and 'ICap-2' aircraft, the last being the current production model. Looking to the future, development of an 'AdvCap' (Advanced Capability) version is now in hand, and this will feature a number of improvements, including better communications jamming equipment, increased jamming power and electronically-steered antennas.

In late 1984 some 76 EA-6Bs of various subtypes were to be found in the Navy and Marine Corps inventory whilst procurement of a further 12 was in hand, and it seems likely that production will eventually surpass the 100 mark. In addition to new-build Prowlers, the Navy has also been pursuing the CILOP (conversion in lieu of procurement) policy with regard to the EA-6B, many older aircraft having been updated to late-standard configuration, and this process also looks likely to continue.

Grumman EA-6B Prowler

This US Navy Grumman EA-6B is seen in an unfamiliar environment, in front of a HAS at Zweibrücken, West Germany, during a rare off-ship deployment from USS Nimitz.

Grumman EA-6Bs, in common with most front-line US Navy aircraft, are receiving toned-down overall grey colour schemes, although many still carry white underwing ECM pods.

Specification: Grumman EA-6B Prowler with five jamming pods
Origin: USA
Type: electronic countermeasures platform
Powerplant: two 5080-kg (11,200-lb) thrust Pratt & Whitney J52-P-408 turbojet engines
Performance: maximum speed 530 kts (982 km/h; 610 mph) at sea level; cruising speed 418 kts (774 km/h; 481 mph); initial rate of climb 10,030 ft (3057 m) per minute; service ceiling 38,000 ft (11580 m); combat range with maximum external fuel 1769 km (1,099 miles)
Weights: empty 14588 kg (32,162 lb); stand-off jamming configuration take-off 24703 kg (54,461 lb); maximum take-off 29484 kg (65,000 lb)
Dimensions: span 16.15 m (53 ft 0 in); length 18.24 m (59 ft 10 in); height 4.95 m (16 ft 3 in); wing area 49.13 m (528.9 sq ft)
Armament: none

having followed during the course of 1985. In addition, two replacement training squadrons, VF-101 of the Atlantic Fleet and VF-124 of the Pacific Fleet, use the F-14A, although these units do not undertake front-line duty aboard the US Navy's large fleet of aircraft-carriers. By late 1984, 10 years after the F-14A first went to sea, Tomcat squadrons had departed from US ports for extended tours of overseas duty on no less than 42 occasions, and the type has replaced older fighters such as the McDonnell Douglas F-4 Phantom in the navy's front-line inventory.

In addition, the Tomcat has also assumed the mantle of being the navy's primary reconnaissance aircraft, although it should be emphasized that this is only a temporary measure pending the availability of the specialized RF-18 version of the McDonnell Douglas Hornet later in the present decade. In the meantime, though, the F-14A fulfils navy requirements in this area, approximately 50 aircraft having been configured to carry the TARPS beneath the rear fuselage. This package consists of a CAI KS-87B frame camera for forward-oblique or vertical photography as well as a Fairchild KA-99 panoramic camera and a Honeywell AAD-5 infra-red scanner. TARPS permits the F-14A to obtain high-quality imagery at only a modest penalty in payload capability.

Operational deployment of TARPS-compatible Tomcats began during 1982, and this variant has since been added to the complement of 11 fighter squadrons, thus permitting each F-14-capable carrier air wing to have three TARPS aircraft in one of its two F-14 squadrons. Original plans called for the acquisition of 49 TARPS-configured Tomcats and all of these were manufactured as such by the parent company. More recently, it has been decided to modify three additional examples to this standard in order that Navy Reserve squadron VF-302 can also

operate this version. Eventually, when the dedicated reconnaissance variant of the F-18 Hornet begins to enter service with the navy, the TARPS-configured Tomcats will revert to standard interceptors with full armament capability.

Iran: sole export customer

Despite the fact that it is capable of countering threats at short, medium and long ranges, the Tomcat has achieved only limited export success, most of the customers in the market for new-generation fighter aircraft opting for uncompromised air-superiority fighters such as the F-15 Eagle. Indeed, only one overseas sale has been achieved, and one rather suspects that the US government would prefer that this had not been the case, for the customer was Iran, the late Shah purchasing a total of 80 Tomcats in 1974-5. Delivered between January 1976 and July 1978, these were mainly intended for use against Mikoyan-Gurevich MiG-25s which were regularly overflying Iranian territory from the USSR, and part of the deal included the supply of 424 AIM-54A Phoenix missiles, 270 of which

The Tomcat was the first aircraft in which the wings were automatically controlled by a computer system (with manual override), which acts in response to Mach number and angle-of-attack factors. Here the wings are at minimum sweep.

were actually handed over before the ousting of the Shah in 1979. Initially equipping four squadrons at Shiraz and Khatami air bases, most (if not all) of the 75 or so surviving Iranian Tomcats are now grounded, the brunt of the aviation contribution in the long and exceedingly bloody war against Iraq having been borne by the F-4E Phantom and the Northrop F-5E Tiger II.

Glossary
BarCAP Barrier Combat Air Patrol
TARPS Tactical Air Reconnaissance Pod System
TCS Television Camera Set

Now in its second decade of operation and still supreme, the Tomcat is destined to serve for many years to come. New variants with better performance, state-of-the-art technology and improved armament will meet the high demands of Fleet defence.

US Navy F-14A Tomcat units and example aircraft

VF-1, Miramar, California
Air Wing: CVW-2
Carrier: USS Kitty Hawk (CV-63)
Aircraft: 161296/NE-107, 159855/NE-111, 158989/NE-113

VF-2*, Miramar, California
Air Wing: CVW-2
Carrier: USS Kitty Hawk (CV-63)
Aircraft: 161273/NE-201, 161299/NE-210, 158998/NE-213

VF-11, Oceana, Virginia
Air Wing: CVW-3
Carrier: USS John F. Kennedy (CV-67)
Aircraft: 159010/AC-100, 159438/AC-111, 161163/AC-112

VF-14, Oceana, Virginia
Air Wing: CVW-6
Carrier: USS Independence (CV-62)
Aircraft: 159433/AE-103, 159431/AE-106, 159595/AE-112

VF-21, Miramar, California
Air Wing: CVW-14
Carrier: USS Constellation (CV-64)
Aircraft: 161606/NK-201, 161609/NK-204, 161621/NK-211

VF-24, Miramar, California
Air Wing: CVW-9
Carrier: USS Ranger (CV-61)
Aircraft: 159592/NG-200, 160693/NG-204, 160889/NG-214

VF-31*, Oceana, Virginia
Air Wing: CVW-3
Carrier: USS John F. Kennedy (CV-67)
Aircraft: 159449/AC-204, 159421/AC-207, 159020/AC-210

VF-32*, Oceana, Virginia
Air Wing: CVW-6
Carrier: USS Independence (CV-62)
Aircraft: 159016/AE-200, 159603/AE-206, 161162/AE-214

VF-33, Oceana, Virginia
Air Wing: CVW-1
Carrier: USS America (CV-66)
Aircraft: 159426/AB-202, 159015/AB-206, 159609/AB-211

VF-41, Oceana, Virginia
Air Wing: CVW-8
Carrier: USS Nimitz (CVN-68)
Aircraft: 160395/AJ-100, 160407/AJ-112, 160399/AJ-113

VF-51, Miramar, California
Air Wing: CVW-15
Carrier: USS Carl Vinson (CVN-70)
Aircraft: 160657/NL-101, 160685/NL-110, 160694/NL-114

VF-74, Oceana, Virginia
Air Wing: CVW-17
Carrier: USS Saratoga (CV-60)
Aircraft: 160896/AA-101, 160905/AA-105, 160918/AA-112

VF-84*, Oceana, Virginia
Air Wing: CVW-8
Carrier: USS Nimitz (CVN-68)
Aircraft: 160389/AJ-202, 160405/AJ-204, 160391/AJ-210

VF-101, Oceana, Virginia
Air Wing: RAG
Aircraft: 161136/AD-103, 160902/AD-120, 159018/AD-133

VF-102*, Oceana, Virginia
Air Wing: CVW-1
Carrier: USS America (CV-66)
Aircraft: 159458/AB-101, 159006/AB-103, 161285/AB-112

VF-103*, Oceana, Virginia
Air Wing: CVW-17
Carrier: USS Saratoga (CV-60)
Aircraft: 160919/AA-200, 160898/AA-204, 161156/AA-211

VF-111*, Miramar, California
Air Wing: CVW-15
Carrier: USS Carl Vinson (CVN-70)
Aircraft: 160656/NL-200, 161270/NL-206, 160668/NL-213

VF-114, Miramar, California
Air Wing: CVW-11
Carrier: USS Enterprise (CVN-65)
Aircraft: 159825/NH-100, 159852/NH-105, 159872/NH-112

VF-124, Miramar, California
Air Wing: RAG
Aircraft: 161600/NJ-403, 159870/NJ-424, 161153/NJ-473

VF-142, Oceana, Virginia
Air Wing: CVW-7
Carrier: USS Dwight D. Eisenhower (CVN-69)
Aircraft: 160427/AG-201, 161435/AG-207, 161441/AG-213

VF-143*, Oceana, Virginia
Air Wing: CVW-7
Carrier: USS Dwight D. Eisenhower (CVN-69)
Aircraft: 160428/AG-102, 161281/AG-112, 161282/AG-114

VF-154*, Miramar, California
Air Wing: CVW-14
Carrier: USS Constellation (CV-64)
Aircraft: 161610/NK-100, 161620/NK-105, 161626/NK-110

1 × 20-mm M61A1 six-barrel cannon
6 × AIM-54C Phoenix air-to-air missiles

aximum stand-f interception

Tomcat was designed for protection of US Navy face combatant groups by stroying intruding aircraft and lise missiles at the greatest ssible distance from the ps. The AWG-9 weapon-trol system can detect ome targets at ranges of up 14 km (195 miles) according heir size, and can control up ix simultaneous agements.

Front spar
Leading edge rib construction
Slat guide rails
Port leading edge slat segments, open
Slat honeycomb construction
Port mainwheel
Torque scissor links
Main undercarriage front bracing strut
Mainwheel well door
Ventral pylon attachment
External fuel tank (capaci 265 US gal/1003 litres)
Sparrow missile launch adaptor
AIM-7F Sparrow air-to-air missile

Pilot Press Limited

Israel Pakistan United States

Grumman OV-1 Mohawk

VF-2

Air Wi
Carrie

VF-2

Air Wi
Carrie
(CVN-6

F-1

The fro
Tomca
conten
layout:
in a rel
Domin
panels
display
with th
manoe
The he
atop th
conso
of the
accele
distan
others
indica
Mach
Side p
bar, la
contro
hook,
eleva
hand s

Role

Fighter
Close support
Counter-insurgency
Tactical strike
Strategic bomber
Tactical reconnaissance
Strategic reconnaissance
Maritime patrol
Anti-ship strike
Anti-submarine warfare
Search and rescue
Assault transport
Transport
Liaison
Trainer
Inflight-refuelling tanker
Specialized

Performance

All-weather capability
Rough field capability
STOL capability
VTOL capability
Airspeed 0-250 mph
Airspeed 250 mph-Mach 1
Airspeed Mach 1 plus
Ceiling 0-20,000 ft
Ceiling 20,000-40,000 ft
Ceiling 40,000 ft plus
Range 0-1,000 miles
Range 1,000-3,000 miles
Range 3,000 miles plus

Weapons

Air-to-air missiles
Air-to-surface missiles
Cruise missiles
Cannon
Trainable guns
Naval weapons
Nuclear-capable
Rockets
'Smart' weapon kit
Weapon load 0-4,000 lb
Weapon load 4,000-15,000 lb
Weapon load 15,000 lb plus

Avionics

Electronic Counter Measures
Electronic Support Measures
Search radar
Fire control radar
Look-down/shoot-down
Terrain-following radar
Forward-looking infra-red
Laser
Television

During the operational lifetime of the **Grumman OV-1 Mohawk**, tremendous strides have been taken in the realm of army airborne reconnaissance, and what began as a traditional visual and photographic aircraft is today packed with sophisticated sensors. The **G-134**, unusual for its time in being an army aviation turboprop (two 708-kW/950-hp Lycoming T53-L-3s), was initially designated **AO-1** when the first of nine development aircraft flew on 14 April 1959, these later being redesignated **YOV-1A**. A further four were ordered to meet US Marine Corps requirements, but this proposed **OF-1** model was cancelled before the aircraft could be completed. A comprehensive array of avionics was included in the initial production **OV-1A** to enable the aircraft to meet the all-weather battlefield surveillance requirement, and two underwing stores pylons enabled up to 1225 kg (2,700 lb) of ordnance to be carried. Grumman built 64 OV-1As, equipped with KA-30 high resolution camera systems and removable pods above the wing roots for 52 upward-firing night photography flares. A small number were modified with six underwing pylons for bombs, guns and rockets to provide close support during the Vietnam War.

The **OV-1B** (90 built) introduced APS-94 side-looking airborne radar (SLAR) in a large underfuselage container, an AKT-16 VHF data link, and a further 1.83 m (6 ft 0 in) of wing span. Fuselage airbrakes were deleted, as was provision for dual controls for the two-man crew in their armour-protected, Martin-Baker J5 ejector seats. Later OV-1Bs had 858-kW (1,150-hp) T53-L-15s. Built in parallel, the **OV-1C** was an updated OV-1A with short-span wings and UAS-4 infra-red ground surveillance equipment in the underside of the rear fuselage, and late models of the 129 built also progressed to T53-L-15 engines. In the four **YOV-1D** and 37 **OV-1D** large-span aircraft which followed up to the end of production in December 1970, the SLAR could be exchanged for IR sensors within an hour, combining OV-1B/C functions in an airframe powered by further uprated engines. In addition, 72 OV-1B/C aircraft were converted to OV-1D standard by 1984, with equipment including new model APS-94F SLAR. All retain 180° visual spectrum photographic capability. The US Army will operate 110 OV-1Ds, plus 36 **RV-1D** conversions with ALQ-133 'Quicklook II', up to the end of the century. At least two OV-1Ds were supplied to Israel in mid-1976, and four OV-1s were offered to Pakistan in 1984, although delivery has not yet taken place.

Specification: Grumman OV-1D Mohawk
Origin: USA
Type: tactical reconnaissance aircraft
Powerplant: two 1044-kW (1,400-shp) Lycoming T53-L-701 turboprop engines
Performance: maximum speed 265 kts (491 km/h; 305 mph) with IR sensors, or 251 kts (465 km/h; 289 mph) with SLAR; cruising speed 210 kts (389 km/h; 242 mph) service ceiling 25,000 ft (7620 m); range 1738 km (1,080 miles) with IR, or 1653 km (1,027 miles) with SLAR
Weights: empty 5333 kg (11,757 lb); maximum take-off 8085 kg (17,826 lb) with IR, or 8164 kg (18,000 lb) with SLAR
Dimensions: span 14.63 m (48 ft 0 in); overall length 13.69 m (44 ft 11 in); fuselage length 12.50 m (41 ft 0 in); height 3.86 m (12 ft 8 in); wing area 33.45 m² (360 sq ft)

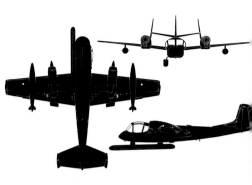

A Grumman OV-1C of the US Army.

Grumman OV-1B Mohawk

A Grumman RV-1D of the 73rd Combat Intelligence Company, US Army, based at Stuttgart in the Federal Republic of Germany. The RV-1D is equipped with ALQ-133 'Quicklook II'.

The OV-1D carries an APS-94 SLAR in its underfuselage pod, and this can be augmented by photographic and infra-red sensors. One hundred and ten will remain in service into the next century

Gru

1 Pit
2 Ra
3 Gla
4 IFF
5 Hu
   rad
6 Sc
   m
7 Ve
   jar
8 Gu
9 Ra
   eq
10 AN
   na
11 Ra
12 Inf
   (e
13 AD
14 Wi
   air
15 Te
16 Co
   bu
17 An
18 Fo
19 Ca
20 No
21 Gu
22 Ru
23 Co
   va
24 Na
25 Co
26 Ins
27 Ka
   up
28 Wi
29 Co
30 Fa
   ha
31 Eje
32 Pil
   7A
33 Sta
34 En
35 Po
36 Pit
37 Ca
   rel
38 Fo

15938
UNITED STATES ARMY

Kaman H-2 Seasprite

United States

Originating in the **HU2K-1** powered by a single General Electric T53-GE-8B turboshaft and first flown on 2 July 1959, the **Kaman Seasprite** naval rescue and utility helicopter has undergone continuous development and today represents a highly sophisticated anti-submarine weapon in the US Navy's inventory.

From the original single-turboshaft **UH-2A** and **UH-2B** of the early 1960s was developed the **UH-2C** with twin T58-GE-8B engines geared to drive a single rotor, and this in turn led to the combat search-and-rescue **HH-2C** armed with a chin Minigun turret, four-blade tail rotor and extensive armour protection around cockpit, engines and fuel tanks; this version served in the latter stages of the Vietnam War.

A major development phase was initiated with the acceptance of Kaman's Light Airborne Multi-Purpose System (LAMPS) in 1969-70. This integrated avionics package comprises the Canadian Marconi LN-66HP surveillance radar, ALR-66 passive radiation detection receivers and ASN-123 tactical navigation system operating in conjunction with ASQ-81(V)2 magnetic anomaly detector,

ARR-75 sonobuoy receiver, ASA-26B sonobuoy recorder and AKT-22(V)6 sonobuoy data link. Thus equipped, the **SH-2F** started deliveries to the US Navy in May 1973 and continued for two years, while earlier **SH-2D** helicopters were updated to include LAMPS Mk 1 in a programme that was completed in 1982. After initial production of 88 SH-2Fs and updating of 16 SH-2Ds had been completed, further orders for 36 SH-2Fs were scheduled for completion by the end of 1986. Between 1971 and 1985 400,000 flight hours had been accumulated by the LAMPS-equipped Seasprite during long-cruise assignments by warships of the US Navy.

In October 1985 an increase in the SH-2F's gross weight was authorized to 6123 kg (13,500 lb), enabling larger auxiliary fuel tanks to be carried to extend the helicopter's patrol endurance, while a single **YSH-2G** prototype was being evaluated with new fuel-efficient T700-GE-401 turboshafts and composite main rotor blades; it is currently anticipated that authority may be given to re-engine the entire SH-2F inventory with this powerplant to enable the Seasprite to remain in service into the next century.

Specification: Kaman SH-2F Seasprite
Origin: USA
Type: naval light multi-purpose helicopter
Powerplant: two 1007-kW (1,350-shp) General Electric T58-GE-8F turboshaft engines
Performance: maximum speed 130 kts (241 km/h; 150 mph) at sea level; normal cruising speed 120 kts (222 km/h; 138 mph); service ceiling 22,500 ft (6860 m); normal range 661 km 411 miles)
Weights: empty 3193 kg (7,040 lb); maximum take-off 6123 kg (13,500 lb)
Dimensions: main rotor diameter 13.41 m (44 ft 0 in); length, rotors turning 16.03 m (52 ft 7 in); height 4.72 m (15 ft 6 in); main rotor disc area 141.26 m² (1,520.53 sq ft)
Armament: up to two Mk 46 torpedoes and combinations of DIFAR and/or DICASS sonobuoys, and eight Mk 25 marine smoke markers

A Kaman SH-2F LAMPS helicopter of HSL-33, US Navy.

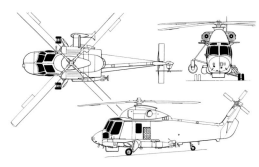

Kaman SH-2F Seasprite

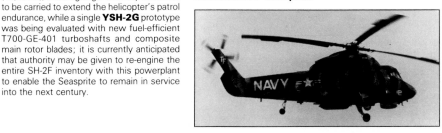

This Seasprite is a LAMPS-configured SH-2F of HSL-33 'Snakes', whose shore-base is NAS North Island, California. This aircraft was assigned to USS Bagley, a 'Knox' class frigate.

These NAS North Island-based SH-2Fs are assigned to HSL-35. US Navy Seasprites are due to receive a low-visibility grey colour scheme. Sonobuoys are ejected from the side panels.

Role
Fighter
Close support
Counter-insurgency
Tactical strike
Strategic bomber
Tactical reconnaissance
Strategic reconnaissance
Maritime patrol
Anti-ship strike
Anti-submarine warfare
Search and rescue
Assault transport
Transport
Liaison
Trainer
Inflight-refuelling tanker
Specialized

Performance
All-weather capability
Rough field capability
STOL capability
VTOL capability
Airspeed 0-250 mph
Airspeed 250 mph-Mach 1
Airspeed Mach 1 plus
Ceiling 0-20,000 ft
Ceiling 20,000-40,000 ft
Ceiling 40,000 ft plus
Range 0-1,000 miles
Range 1,000-3,000 miles
Range 3,000 miles plus

Weapons
Air-to-air missiles
Air-to-surface missiles
Cruise missiles
Cannon
Trainable guns
Naval weapons
Nuclear-capable
Rockets
'Smart' weapon kit
Weapon load 0-4,000 lb
Weapon load 4,000-15,000 lb
Weapon load 15,000 lb plus

Avionics
Electronic Counter Measures
Electronic Support Measures
Search radar
Fire control radar
Look-down/shoot-down
Terrain-following radar
Forward-looking infra-red
Laser
Television

A Kaman SH-2F Seasprite

Lockheed C-5 Galaxy

This is
...anis... designed to meet requirements formulated
...y the USAF's MATS in 1963 for a very large
Manuf... gistics transport capable of lifting a 56700-
...e C... g (125,000-lb) payload over a range of
...ompl... 2875 km (8,000 miles), the **Lockheed C-5**
...omp... **Galaxy** was selected in October 1965, the
...odel... rst **C-5A** being flown on 30 June 1968. The
...ngine... rgest landplane then built, it featured a high-
...nprov... et swept wing with leading-edge slats,
...-130... ...ide-span modified-Fowler trailing-edge
...ans... ...aps and aileron-cum-spoilers. Through-
...: the... ...ading by means of upward-hingeing nose
...rst... nd drop-down rear fuselage ramp enabled
...ered... ...rge and heavy vehicles and missiles (such
...d Re... s two M60 tanks or 10 Pershing missiles
...ace... ...with launch-tractors) to be loaded. Power
...ed t... ...was provided by four underslung, purpose-
...ines... ...eveloped General Electric TF39-GE-1 turbo-
...362... ...ans.
...xtend... By the end of 1970 30 C-5As out of an order
...rcraf... ...or 81 aircraft had flown and deliveries made
...o-to-... ...o MAC squadrons in the USA; already heavy-
...on f... ...ft services were being flown to Europe and
...om... the Far East. In the meantime the entire
...ersio... ...pecification had been extended to include a
...5 W... ...ross weight of 317515 kg (700,000 lb) and
...nd H... ...lobal deployment, calling for inflight-
...VC-1... ...efuelling compatibility with the USAF's
...uxilia... Boeing KC-135 tankers. Although the C-5's
...icrea... ...rime role was and remains heavy freighting
...Ord...

(such as global deployment of strategic missiles), its 28-wheel landing gear permitting
operation from semi-prepared runways in
potential combat areas, it is capable of lifting
345 fully-equipped troops, the entire upper
deck and cargo hold being pressurized and
air-conditioned.

In 1978 Lockheed gained authority to proceed with improved wings constructed of
7175-T73511 aluminium alloy for greater
strength and corrosion resistance, intended
to increase the service life to 30,000 hours,
and all surviving C-5As are scheduled to be
re-winged by the end of 1987. In 1982 a new
production version, the C-5B, was authorized
in which all modifications and improvements
evolved in the C-5A were to be incorporated,
including uprated TF39-GE-1C turbofans,
extended-life wing, Bendix colour weather
radar, triple Delco inertial navigators.

With C-5As now serving with the USAF's
60th, 436th, 437th and 443rd MAWs, as well
as the 105th MAG of the New York ANG,
C-5Bs are currently being delivered to the
service, with the last of 50 scheduled aircraft
being due for completion during 1987. For
more than 15 years the Galaxy remained the
world's largest military aircraft, only now
being eclipsed by the Soviet Antonov An-124
'Condor'.

*A Lockheed C-5A Galaxy of Military Airlift
Command, US Air Force.*

Lockheed C-5A Galaxy

*The prototype C-5B Galaxy is towed into position
before making its maiden flight on 10 September
1985 at the Lockheed plant at Marietta, Georgia.*

*A large number of C-5s have received this 'Euro
One' camouflage scheme, but it has caused severe
overheating problems and a lighter scheme is
likely to be adopted.*

Specification: Lockheed C-5B Galaxy
Origin: USA
Type: heavy logistics transport
Powerplant: four 19 504-kg (43,000-lb) thrust General Electric TF39-GE-1C turbofan
engines
Performance: maximum cruising speed 490 kts (908 km/h; 564 mph) at 25,000 ft
(7620 m); initial rate of climb 1,725 ft (526 m) per minute; service ceiling at 278959-kg
(615,000-lb) AUW 35,750 ft (10895 m); range with 118388-kg (261,000-lb) maximum payload
9526 km (3,434 miles)
Weights: empty equipped 169644 kg (374,000 lb); maximum take-off 379657 kg
(837,000 lb)
Dimensions: span 67.88 m (222 ft 8.5 in); length 75.54 m (247 ft 10 in) height 19.85 m
(65 ft 1.5 in); wing area 575.98 m² (6,200 sq ft)
Armament: none

United States

Role
Fighter
Close support
Counter-insurgency
Tactical strike
Strategic bomber
Tactical reconnaissance
Strategic reconnaissance
Maritime patrol
Anti-ship strike
Anti-submarine warfare
Search and rescue
Assault transport
Transport
Liaison
Trainer
Inflight-refuelling tanker
Specialized

Performance
All-weather capability
Rough field capability
STOL capability
VTOL capability
Airspeed 0-250 mph
Airspeed 250 mph-Mach 1
Airspeed Mach 1 plus
Ceiling 0-20,000 ft
Ceiling 20,000-40,000 ft
Ceiling 40,000 ft plus
Range 0-1,000 miles
Range 1,000-3,000 miles
Range 3,000 miles plus

Weapons
Air-to-air missiles
Air-to-surface missiles
Cruise missiles
Cannon
Trainable guns
Naval weapons
Nuclear-capable
Rockets
'Smart' weapon kit
Weapon load 0-4,000 lb
Weapon load 4,000-15,000 lb
Weapon load 15,000 lb plus

Avionics
Electronic Counter Measures
Electronic Support Measures
Search radar
Fire control radar
Look-down/shoot-down
Terrain-following radar
Forward-looking infra-red
Laser
Television

United States

Lockheed AC-130 Hercules

Role

- Fighter
- Close support
- Counter-insurgency
- Tactical strike
- Strategic bomber
- Tactical reconnaissance
- Strategic reconnaissance
- Maritime patrol
- Anti-ship strike
- Anti-submarine warfare
- Search and rescue
- Assault transport
- Transport
- Liaison
- Trainer
- Inflight-refuelling tanker
- Specialized

Performance

- All-weather capability
- Rough field capability
- STOL capability
- VTOL capability
- Airspeed 0-250 mph
- Airspeed 250 mph-Mach 1
- Airspeed Mach 1 plus
- Ceiling 0-20,000 ft
- Ceiling 20,000-40,000 ft
- Ceiling 40,000 ft plus
- Range 0-1,000 miles
- Range 1,000-3,000 miles
- Range 3,000 miles plus

Weapons

- Air-to-air missiles
- Air-to-surface missiles
- Cruise missiles
- Cannon
- Trainable guns
- Naval weapons
- Nuclear-capable
- Rockets
- 'Smart' weapon kit
- Weapon load 0-4,000 lb
- Weapon load 4,000-15,000 lb
- Weapon load 15,000 lb plus

Avionics

- Electronic Counter Measures
- Electronic Support Measures
- Search radar
- Fire control radar
- Look-down/shoot-down
- Terrain-following radar
- Forward-looking infra-red
- Laser
- Television

A USAF need perceived from early experience in Vietnam was quick-reaction concentrated firepower for use against small targets, especially where defenders of isolated areas were subject to nocturnal attack. The first solution was the Gunship I conversion of the Douglas C-47 as the AC-47, known informally as 'Puff the Magic Dragon' or 'Spooky'. Initially fitted with three side-firing 7.62-mm (0.3-in) general-purpose machine-guns, they were soon refitted with three 7.62-mm multi-barrelled Miniguns. Developed by the USAF Aeronautical Systems Division (ASD), the gunship applied a principle adopted by bush pilots in South America. This was the use of a weighted bucket suspended on a rope from an aircraft flying a very tight continuous turn to keep the bucket stationary at the tip of an imaginary cone for the collection of mail and the like from inaccessible sites. The gunship pilot was required to bank his aircraft at between 30° and 50° and when the target was constantly sighted fire the guns. A left-hand circuit was flown.

With the system operational, there was a need to improve firepower, sensing equipment, targeting and armour. The Fairchild C-119 was adapted as the AC-119G Shadow and AC-119K Stinger with the 17th and 18th Special Operations Squadrons (SOS) respectively, while ASD began converting the 13th production C-130A (54-1626) to Gunship II standard in 1965. This involved installation of four 20-mm Vulcan cannon, four 7.62-mm Miniguns, flare equipment and improved sighting. This aircraft was tested operationally in Vietnam in late 1967, and LTV

Electrosystems was awarded an immediate contract to modify seven JC-130A missile trackers to Lockheed AC-130A standard. Weaponry remained the same but these aircraft were fittted with a searchlight, sensors, FLIR target-acquisition and direct-view image intensifiers. Four were in service in Vietnam by the end of 1968 with the 14th Air Commando Wing operating from Ubon in Thailand. A further single C-130 was converted in the 'Surprise Package' project with two 40-mm cannon replacing two of the 20-mm variety and with computerized fire control. Nine more C-130A conversions were delivered in the 'Pave Pronto' programme.

So successful was the project that 11 C-130E models were converted to AC-130E standard in the 'Pave Spectre' programme. The aircraft were given heavier armour, better avionics and provision for more ammunition; from 1973 they were brought up to AC-130H standard with the installation of the more powerful T56-A-15 engine. The final developments for use in South East Asia were the fitting of a 105-mm howitzer and laser target designator in the 'Pave Aegis' programme. At the end of the Vietnam War remaining AC-130A/H aircraft returned to the USA to serve with the 1st Special Operations Wing at Eglin AFB. The AC-130 was used operationally again with the US occupation of Grenada in October 1983. Temporarily based at Bridgetown, Barbados, and fitted with underwing ECM pods and exhaust shrouds, AC-130H aircraft of the 16th Special Operations Squadron operated against Cuban positions.

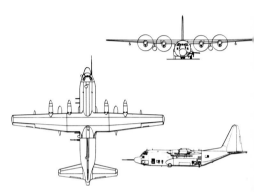

A Lockheed AC-130H 'Pave Spectre' of the 16th SOS, 1st SOW, based at Hurlburt Field, Florida.

Lockheed AC-130H Spectre

The AC-130Hs of the 16th SOS have been used over Grenada during the US invasion, flying in the gunship role, and over Central America, as unarmed night reconnaissance aircraft.

This Spectre is an AC-130A (note the three-bladed props) of the 711th SOS, 919th SOG, AFRes, based at Duke Field AFB, Florida. This unit would be assigned to TAC during time of tension or war.

Specification: Lockheed AC-130E Hercules
Origin: USA
Type: multi-sensor ground-attack gunship
Powerplant: four 3020-ekW (4,050-eshp) Allison T56-A-7 turboprop engines
Performance: maximum speed 330 kts (612 km/h; 380 mph) at 30,000 ft (9145 m); cruising speed 320 kts (592 km/h; 368 mph); initial rate of climb 1,830 ft (558 m) per minute; endurance 5 hours
Weights: empty 33063 kg (72,892 lb); maximum take-off 70307 kg (155,000 lb)
Dimensions: span 40.41 m (132 ft 7 in); length 29.79 m (97 ft 9 in); height 11.66 m (38 ft 3 in); wing area 162.11 m² (1,745 sq ft)
Armament: (AC-130H) one 105-mm (4.13-in) howitzer, two 40-mm cannon, two 20-mm cannon and four 7.62-mm (0.3-in) Miniguns

A Lockheed C-141B StarLifter

United States

Lockheed C-141 StarLifter

With an air transport fleet composed almost entirely of piston-engined aircraft in the late 1950s, the USAF's Military Air Transport Service was inadequately equipped for its growing worldwide responsibility. In May 1960 the USAF's Specific Operational Requirement 182 was drawn up, and Requests for Proposals accordingly circulated to US manufacturers. From submissions received, Lockheed was announced winner and on 13 March 1961 awarded an initial contract for five DT & E aircraft. SOR 182 specified an aircraft to airlift a payload of 27216 kg (60,000 lb) over a range of 6477 km (4,025 miles), and Lockheed's proposal probably gained favour by using proven ideas adopted from the C-130 Hercules. Thus the new design had the C-130's high-wing configuration and main landing gear units retracting into fuselage side fairings to maximize cabin volume, and a similar main loading door/ramp in the rear fuselage for straight-in cargo/vehicle loading. Conspicuous differences, apart from size, were the T-tail and podded turbofan engines pylon-mounted beneath the wings.

Given the basic designation **Lockheed C-141**, the first example (61-2775) was flown on 17 December 1963; just over 16 months later, on 23 April 1965, the type had become operational with Military Airlift Command, the successor to MATS. Operated by a flight crew of five, these aircraft were soon providing a daily service across the Pacific, outward bound with up to 138 troops or some 28440 kg (62,700 lb) of cargo, and returning with the casualties of growing conflict in Vietnam, the main cabin having room for 80 stretchers and 23 medical attendants. The last of 284 **C-141A StarLifter** aircraft was delivered to the USAF in February 1968.

Experience showed that the C-141A frequently ran out of cabin volume long before its maximum payload weight had been loaded. This problem was resolved from 1976 onward by a programme that lengthened the fuselage by 7.11 m (23 ft 4 in) and at the same time provided an inflight-refuelling capability. The prototype **YC-141B** conversion was flown on 24 March 1977, and on 29 June 1982 the last of the 270 surviving C-141As had been converted to the new **C-141B** configuration, ahead of schedule and below projected cost. This programme has, in effect, provided MAC with 90 additional transports of C-141A capacity that require no extra crew.

Specification: Lockheed C-141B StarLifter
Origin: USA
Type: strategic troop/cargo transport
Powerplant: four 9526-kg (21,000-lb) thrust Pratt & Whitney TF33-7 turbofan engines
Performance: maximum cruising speed 492 kts (912 km/h; 567 mph); long-range cruising speed 430 kts (797 km/h; 495 mph); initial rate of climb 2,920 ft (890 m) per minute; range with maximum payload 4723 km (2,935 miles); ferry range 10284 km (6,390 miles)
Weights: empty operating 67186 kg (148,120 lb); maximum take-off 155582 kg (343,000 lb)
Dimensions: span 48.74 m (159 ft 11 in); length 51.29 m (168 ft 3.5 in); height 11.96 m (39 ft 3 in); wing area 299.88 m² (3,228.0 sq ft)
Armament: none

A Lockheed C-141B StarLifter of Military Airlift Command, US Air Force.

Lockheed C-141B StarLifter

All surviving C-141s were converted to C-141B standard by stretching the fuselage. This prevent the aircraft 'bulking out' before maximum payloa weight is reached.

The C-141B has seen active service in Vietnam an in the invasion of Grenada, as well as providing logistic support for countless smaller operations of equal importance.

Lockheed P-3A and P-3B Orion

New Zealand   Norway   Portugal   Spain   United States

In August 1957 Type Specification No. 146 was issued by the US Navy, calling for a new anti-submarine aircraft to replace the Lockheed P-2 Neptune. The Lockheed proposal was based on the company's L-188 Electra passenger airliner. In May 1958 Lockheed was awarded a contract largely on the basis of the strength of the aircraft's structure and its size, which was sufficient to house an extensive array of detection systems. Lockheed modified the third Electra airframe (N1883) as the prototype with a tail-mounted magnetic anomaly detector (MAD) boom and a ventral bulge simulating a weapons bay. Following extensive adaptations (including a shortening of the fuselage) the aircraft made a successful maiden flight as the **YP3V-1** on 25 November 1959. The navy ordered an initial batch of seven aircraft in October 1960, and the first of these (BuNo 148883) flew in April of the following year. In 1962 the type was redesignated **Lockheed P-3A** and named **Orion**.

The P-3A entered service in the summer of 1962, with Patrol Squadron Eight (VP-8); other units soon followed, and by December 1963 Lockheed had delivered over 50 Orions to eight squadrons. After the production of 109 P-3As, Lockheed incorporated the DELTIC installation in an improvement programme. This doubled sonobuoy information-processing capability and also incorporated redesigned avionics. The first squadron to receive the new **P-3A DELTIC** was

VP-46 at Moffett Field, and within a short time most aircraft had been retrofitted.

In the summer of 1965, after three years experience and with 157 P-3As built, Lockheed started production of a new variant. The **P-3B** was fitted with the more powerful Allison T56-A-14 engine and was heavier than its predecessor, mainly through having provision for the AGM-12 Bullpup ASM, though it maintained basically the same electronics. The P-3B secured the first export orders and became operational with the Royal New Zealand and Norwegian air forces (five aircraft each), and with the RAAF (10 aircraft). From 1977 the USN's P-3Bs have been updated with improved navigation and acoustic-processing equipment and with provision for the AGM-84 Harpoon anti-ship missile. Production of the P-3B ceased in 1969, following the introduction of its successor, the P-3C.

P-3A/Bs remain in service with reserve units having been continuously improved. P-3As were converted to **RP-3A** standard (three aircraft) for oceanographic reconnaissance use by VXN-8, and to **WP-3A** standard (four aircraft) for weather reconnaissance by VW-4. At least five aircraft have been refitted for executive transport use as the **VP-3A**. In 1984 the Lockheed Aircraft Service Company was awarded an initial USN contract for the conversion of 30 aircraft to transport configuration as the **CP-3A**.

A Lockheed P-3B Orion of the Spanish air force.

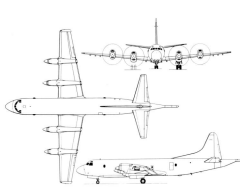

Lockheed P-3B Orion

An interesting view of a US Navy P-3B bearing down on a target submarine. Production of the P-3B ended in 1969, and most US Navy aircraft have been exported or converted.

Norwegian Orions wear an overall dark grey colour scheme, with white code letters on each side of the fuselage roundel. This aircraft is a P-3B of 333 Skvadron, based at Andoya.

Specification: Lockheed P-3A Orion
Origin: USA
Type: 10-crew anti-submarine warfare and maritime patrol aircraft
Powerplant: four 3356-kW (4,500-hp) Allison T56-A-10W turboprop engines
Performance: maximum speed 380 kts (703 km/h; 437 mph) at 15,000 ft (4570 m); patrol speed 198 kts (367 km/h; 228 mph); initial rate of climb 2,175 ft (663 m) per minute; service ceiling 28,300 ft (8625 m); maximum mission radius 4075 km (2,532 miles)
Weights: empty 27216 kg (60,000 lb); maximum take-off 57833 kg (127,500 lb)
Dimensions: span 30.38 m (99 ft 8 in); length 35.61 m (116 ft 10 in); height 10.27 m (33 ft 8.5 in); wing area 120.77 m² (1,300.0 sq ft)
Armament: a combination of mines, depth bombs, torpedoes, sonobuoys and rockets can be carried to maximum weights of 3289 kg (7,250 lb) in the lower-fuselage weapons bay and of 7257 kg (16,000 lb) on the 10 underwing stations

Role
Fighter
Close support
Counter-insurgency
Tactical strike
Strategic bomber
Tactical reconnaissance
Strategic reconnaissance
Maritime patrol
Anti-ship strike
Anti-submarine warfare
Search and rescue
Assault transport
Transport
Liaison
Trainer
Inflight-refuelling tanker
Specialized

Performance
All-weather capability
Rough field capability
STOL capability
VTOL capability
Airspeed 0-250 mph
Airspeed 250 mph-Mach 1
Airspeed Mach 1 plus
Ceiling 0-20,000 ft
Ceiling 20,000-40,000 ft
Ceiling 40,000 ft plus
Range 0-1,000 miles
Range 1,000-3,000 miles
Range 3,000 miles plus

Weapons
Air-to-air missiles
Air-to-surface missiles
Cruise missiles
Cannon
Trainable guns
Naval weapons
Nuclear-capable
Rockets
'Smart' weapon kit
Weapon load 0-4,000 lb
Weapon load 4,000-15,000 lb
Weapon load 15,000 lb plus

Avionics
Electronic Counter Measures
Electronic Support Measures
Search radar
Fire control radar
Look-down/shoot-down
Terrain-following radar
Forward-looking infra-red
Laser
Television

Lockheed P-3C Orion

United States

Australia Iran Japan Netherlands

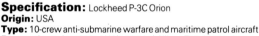

Although the P-3B offered superior power in comparison with the P-3A, there was a need for a more electronically advanced version of the Orion to counter advances in the technology of nuclear submarines. The result was the **Lockheed P-3C Orion**, first flown in September 1968. This much-improved type entered service with VP-56 in 1969. The primary advance was the adoption of the A-NEW system of sensors and control equipment, the heart of which was the UNIVAC ASQ-114 digital computer. This produced more easily interpretable data, allowing the crew more time to perform the task of hunting submarines. Other areas of modification with the P-3C included improved navigation and communications systems.

Since entering service, the P-3C has also been subjected to several important technological updates. The first produced the **P-3C Update I** in 1974 and involved expansion of the computer's memory and some modifications to the navigation system. The **P-3C Update II** programme, undertaken in 1977, involved the introduction of the ARS-3 sonobuoy system enabling the aircraft to locate buoys without having to overfly them and of an infra-red detection system (IRDS) allowing the aircraft to track automatically a detected target by day or night. Against this background of further electronic development,

Update II also conferred on the P-3C the ability to operate with the McDonnell Douglas AGM-84 Harpoon anti-ship missile. The third and most extensive modification, incorporated from 1984 in the **P-3C Update III** programme, involved the installation of the IBM Proteus signal processor which works more efficiently than the previous system. Also included were a new sonobuoy receiver and an improved auxiliary power unit. Now in development is the **P-3C Update IV** programme.

Export successes have been notable for such a complex and expensive aircraft. In 1975 the Imperial Iranian air force acquired six aircraft designated **P-3F** for long-range surface surveillance and anti-submarine warfare duties; these were basic P-3C models equipped for inflight-refuelling (the only P-3s with such a facility). Other operators include Australia, the Netherlands and Japan, making the Orion one of the most widely used aircraft in its field. In addition two P-3Cs were procured as weather reconnaissance **WP-3D** aircraft (N42RF and N43RF) for the National Oceanographic and Atmospheric Administration (NOAA). The 51st P-3C was modified with additional fuel capacity for atmospheric research and magnetic survey, and as the sole **RP-3D** this aircraft is operated by VXN-8 in 'Project Magnet'.

Specification: Lockheed P-3C Orion
Origin: USA
Type: 10-crew anti-submarine warfare and maritime patrol aircraft
Powerplant: four 3661-kW (4,910-hp) Allison T56-A-14 turboprop engines
Performance: maximum speed 411 kts (761 km/h; 473 mph) at 15,000 ft (4570 m); patrol speed 206 kts (381 km/h; 237 mph); initial rate of climb 1,950 ft (594 m) per minute; service ceiling 28,300 ft (8625 m); maximum mission radius 3835 km (2,383 miles)
Weights: empty 27892 kg (61,491 lb); maximum take-off 61235 kg (135,000 lb)
Dimensions: span 30.38 m (99 ft 8 in); length 35.61 m (116 ft 10 in); height 10.27 m (33 ft 8.5 in); wing area 120.77 m² (1,300.0 sq ft)
Armament: one 907-kg (2,000 lb) or three 454-kg (1,000-lb) mines, or eight depth bombs, or torpedoes, or combinations of these weapons in the lower-fuselage weapons bay, plus up to 7257 kg (16,000 lb) of mines, torpedoes, rockets or AGM-84A Harpoon anti-ship missiles on the 10 underwing stations, and 87 sonobuoys launched from tubes in the lower fuselage

A Lockheed P-3C Orion of 51 Kokutai, JMSDF, based at Shimofusa.

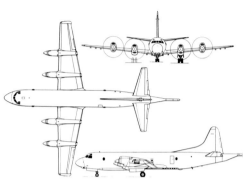

Lockheed P-3C Orion

This is one of two civil-registered WP-3D aircraft operated by the US Department of Commerce, on behalf of the National Oceanographic and Atmospheric Administration for long-range weather reconnaissance.

This Royal Australian Air Force P-3C belongs to No. 10 Squadron, based at Edinburgh. Australia's neighbour, New Zealand, operates the earlier P-3

Lockheed EP-3 Orion

United States

For weapons to be applied most effectively, knowledge of the potential opposition is essential. Nowhere is this more true than in the area of electronics. Modern navies (especially) depend upon a wide range of communications and identification systems in order to function. It therefore follows that detailed information about the characteristics of radars and radios is necessary if they are to be avoided or (better still) neutralized. For this reason, the major navies have long employed a range of electronic intelligence (Elint) vehicles, including aircraft. The US Navy had used the Lockheed EC-121 version of the Constellation airliner, but by the mid-1960s these aircraft were becoming outdated.

Initially the US Navy converted one P-3A (BuNo 149673) to **Lockheed EP-3A Orion** configuration for use by the Naval Air Test Center (NATC), the Naval Weapons Laboratory (NWL) and latterly Air Test & Evaluation Squadron One (VX-1) at NAS Patuxent River. The aircraft was fitted with additional radomes and used to test a range of electronic surveillance equipment. The magnetic anomaly detector (MAD) boom on the tail was deleted. In 1969 two P-3Bs (BuNos 149669 and 149678) were converted into **EP-3B** aircraft for use with VQ-1; both were subsequently updated to **EP-3E** standard, but were maintained by the same squadron. Between 1971 and 1975, 10 more powerful EP-3Es entered service with the two operational fleet air reconnaissance countermeasures

squadrons, VQ-1 and VQ-2, which are assigned the task of giving 'signal warfare support' to various units, particularly to the large aircraft carriers. VQ-1 operates out of NAS Agana on Guam and VQ-2 covers the Mediterranean and Eastern Atlantic from its base at NAS Rota in Spain.

The EP-3E is a modification of the basic patrol P-3A with the anti-submarine warfare equipment replaced by electronic equipment for analysing radar signals. The new electronics installed within the EP-3E include the ALQ-110 signals-gathering system from United Technology Laboratory, the ALD-8 radio direction finder from E-Systems, the ALR-52 automatic frequency-measuring receiver from ARGO-Systems, and the ALR-60 from GTE-Sylvania for the multiple recording of radio communications. Externally, the main features which distinguish the EP-3E from the conventional P-3 is a flat, circular radome under the forward fuselage, and two oblong black antennae domes on top of and underneath the fuselage. The work of these aircraft involves collecting, storing, and analysing signals emitted by radar or radio: major surface vessels employ dozens of separate systems and if the signals are successfully analysed, it is possible to identify the installations, their purpose and range. To make the task of the squadrons as difficult as possible, the Soviet navy frequently alters the radiation patterns of its ships.

A Lockheed EP-3E of VQ-1, based at NAS Agana, Guam.

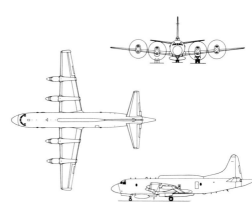

Lockheed EP-3E Orion

This EP-3A is one of those used by the Pacific Missile Test Center, based at Point Mugu, California, for miscellaneous missile tracking and calibration duties.

Squatting down on its nosewheel, this EP-3E of VQ-2 winds up to full power before taking off from RAF Wyton, an occasional port of call for this Rota-based Elint unit.

Specification: Lockheed EP-3 Orion
Origin: USA
Type: Elint platform
Powerplant: four 3661-kW (4,910-hp) Allison T56-A-15 turboprop engines
Performance: maximum speed 380 kts (703 km/h; 437 mph) at 15,000 ft (4570 m); patrol speed 180 kts (333 km/h; 207 mph); initial rate of climb 2,175 ft (663 m) per minute; service ceiling 28,000 ft (8535 m); maximum mission radius 4075 km (2,532 miles)
Weight: maximum take-off 64410 kg (142,000 lb)
Dimensions: span 30.38 m (99 ft 8 in); length 35.61 m (116 ft 10 in); height 10.27 m (33 ft 8.5 in); wing area 120.77 m² (1,300.0 sq ft)
Armament: none

Role
- Fighter
- Close support
- Counter-insurgency
- Tactical strike
- Strategic bomber
- Tactical reconnaissance
- Strategic reconnaissance
- Maritime patrol
- Anti-ship strike
- Anti-submarine warfare
- Search and rescue
- Assault transport
- Transport
- Liaison
- Trainer
- Inflight-refuelling tanker
- Specialized

Performance
- All-weather capability
- Rough field capability
- STOL capability
- VTOL capability
- Airspeed 0-250 mph
- Airspeed 250 mph-Mach 1
- Airspeed Mach 1 plus
- Ceiling 0-20,000 ft
- Ceiling 20,000-40,000 ft
- Ceiling 40,000 ft plus
- Range 0-1,000 miles
- Range 1,000-3,000 miles
- Range 3,000 miles plus

Weapons
- Air-to-air missiles
- Air-to-surface missiles
- Cruise missiles
- Cannon
- Trainable guns
- Naval weapons
- Nuclear-capable
- Rockets
- 'Smart' weapon kit
- Weapon load 0-4,000 lb
- Weapon load 4,000-15,000 lb
- Weapon load 15,000 lb plus

Avionics
- Electronic Counter Measures
- Electronic Support Measures
- Search radar
- Fire control radar
- Look-down/shoot-down
- Terrain-following radar
- Forward-looking infra-red
- Laser
- Television

Lockheed S-3 Viking

The growing capability of the submarines in service with the Soviet navy in the 1960s, plus certain domestic factors, highlighted to the US Navy a need for an advanced carrier-borne ASW aircraft. In late 1966 procurement for this VSX requirement began, with Lockheed gaining in August 1969 an initial contract for development of such an aircraft under the designation **Lockheed S-3A**, later named **Viking**.

Lockheed made great efforts to ensure that its design submission, and ultimately the production aircraft, would give the US Navy the aircraft it needed, the company teaming with LTV (Ling-Temco-Vought) to benefit from the latter's experience in ship-based aircraft, and with Univac Federal Systems, specialists in ASW systems. LTV designed and built the engine pods, landing gear, tail unit and wing; Univac produced the complete ASW system; and Lockheed built the fuselage, integrated the systems and carried out final assembly and test. The first of eight pre-production **YS-3A** aircraft (BuNo 157992) made the type's maiden flight on 21 January 1972 and the first batch of production S-3As was authorized in April 1972. Just under two years later, on 20 February 1974, the S-3A entered service with training squadron VS-41 at NAS North Island, San Diego. VS-21, also based at NAS North Island, was the first operational unit and in July 1975 took the S-3A for its first carrier deployment aboard the USS *John F. Kennedy*. When production ended in mid-1978, a total of 187 S-3As had been built.

In early 1980 demonstration examples of a Carrier Onboard Delivery (COD) **US-3A** and a tanker **KS-3A** were evaluated by the Navy but failed to gain orders, although three of the YS-3As and one-off KS-3A were later converted to US-3A configuration. Also in 1980, Lockheed was awarded a WSIP (Weapon System Improvement Program) contract to give the S-3As expanded ASW capability. This introduced a new generation of avionics and provisions to carry the Harpoon anti-ship missile. The first two WSIP conversions, designated **S-3B**, began service trials in 1985 and two more S-3As are currently undergoing modification; a decision whether to modify the remaining 160 S-3As to S-3B configuration will depend upon the test and evaluation programme now in progress.

A Lockheed S-3 Viking wearing toned-down insignia and the markings of VS-38 the 'Red Griffins'.

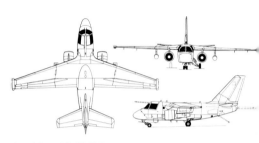

Lockheed S-3 Viking

Seen on the flight deck of USS America is this S-3A Viking of VS-32 'Norsemen', home-based at NAS Cecil Field, Florida, but here forming a component of CVW-1 (Carrier Air Wing One).

This VS-29 S-3A is landing on USS Kitty Hawk. VS-29, the 'Vikings', are a Pacific Fleet anti-submarine warfare unit and are home based at NAS North Island, California.

Specification: Lockheed S-3A Viking
Origin: USA
Type: carrier-based ASW aircraft
Powerplant: two 4207-kg (9,275-lb) thrust General Electric TF34-2 turbofan engines
Performance: maximum speed 450 kts (834 km/h; 518mph) at 25,000 ft (7620m); loiter speed 160 kts (296 km/h; 184mph); initial rate of climb 4,200 ft (1280m) per minute; service ceiling 35,000 ft (10670m); combat range more than 3701 km (2,300 miles)
Weights: empty 12088 kg (26,650 lb); maximum take-off 23831 kg (52,539 lb)
Dimensions: span, open 20.93 m (68 ft 8 in); and folded 8.99 m (29 ft 6 in); length 16.26 m (53 ft 4 in) and with tail folded 15.06 m (49 ft 5 in); height 6.93 m (22 ft 9 in) and with tail folded 4.65 m (15 ft 3 in); wing area 55.55 m² (598.0 sq ft)
Armament: internal weapons bay for bombs, depth bombs, destructors, mines or torpedoes, plus two underwing pylons suitable for auxiliary fuel tanks, cluster bombs, flare launchers or rocket pods

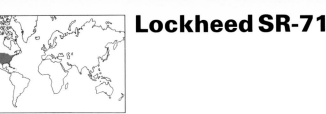

Lockheed SR-71

United States

Development of the **Lockheed SR-71** was shrouded in secrecy, and much 'information' about this remarkable type is based on assumption and analysis rather than on direct fact. The SR-71 came into service as a result of a decision by the Central Intelligence Agency to acquire an aircraft with both a higher service ceiling and a greater maximum speed than the Lockheed U-2. The new aircraft was to carry out clandestine reconnaissance over the USSR and other sensitive territory, and a contract was awarded to Lockheed in August 1959.

Because of the specific nature of the aircraft's requirements, including a maximum speed of Mach 3 and a ceiling of 85,000 ft (25910 m), unprecedented problems were encountered during design and construction. These problems emanated from the need to employ refined aerodynamics and construction materials to withstand the inevitable high temperatures. The airframe had to be constructed from titanium, and engineering problems arose with the propulsion and hydraulic systems, which were also constructed on the basis of new materials and techniques. As long range was also required at the high cruise speed, the aircraft has a highly swept delta wing with a camber on the leading edge to induce low drag.

It is believed that approximately 15 aircraft based on the design and designated **A-12** were delivered to the CIA from 1962; they were single-seaters, although one was modi-

fied as a trainer and two had an additional seat for a launch officer for the D-21 drone programme. A further three research prototypes (designated **YF-12A**) were built as two-seat interceptors in 1963, with Hughes ASG-18 radar. The A-12s, currently in store at Palmdale, were employed by the USAF for the CIA until the SR-71 (originally designated **RS-71**) came into service from 1964. The SR-71 has a more efficient airframe, greater fuel capacity and a more complex reconnaissance system, but is not fitted with a missile bay.

The first SR-71s were delivered in 1966 to the 4200th SRW, a new unit based at Beale AFB in California, where the special Boeing KC-135Q tankers of the 100th ARW (required for inflight-refuelling with the special JP-7 fuel) were also based. Of the initial batch of 29, two were designated **SR-71B** and fitted with dual pilot controls for use as trainer aircraft; another trainer was produced by converting one YF-12A into an **SR-71C**, and one SR-71A was redesignated YF-12C for NASA research purposes. In June 1966 the 4200th was renumbered the 9th SRW and the SR-71s assigned to the 1st SRS; detachments fly regularly from RAF Mildenhall in the UK and Kadena AB in Okinawa. The 'Blackbird' has established several world speed records (including the fastest flight time from London to New York), and in favourable conditions is capable of reaching a speed of around Mach 3.3.

Specification: Lockheed SR-71A
Origin: USA
Type: strategic reconnaissance aircraft
Powerplant: two 10433-kg (23,000-lb) dry and 14742-kg (32,500-lb) afterburning thrust Pratt & Whitney JT11D-20B (J58) bleed turbojet engines
Performance: maximum speed at 80,000 ft (24385 m) more than Mach 3 or 1,737 kts (3219 km/h; 2,000 mph); ceiling more than 80,000 ft (24385 m); unrefuelled range at maximum speed 4800 km (2,983 miles)
Weights: empty 27216 kg (60,000 lb); maximum take-off 77111 kg (170,000 lb)
Dimensions: span 16.94 m (55 ft 7 in); length 32.74 m (107 ft 5 in); height 5.64 m (18 ft 6 in); wing area 167.22 m² (1,800.0 sq ft)
Armament: none

A Lockheed SR-71 of the 9th SRW based at Beale AFB, California.

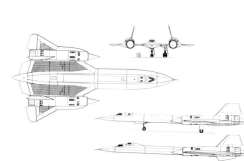

Lockheed SR-71A (lower side view: SR-71B)

There have been three twin-stick SR-71s. Two were purpose-built SR-71Bs, and one SR-71C, 'The Bastard', was converted from a YF-12A when one of the original trainers was written off.

SR-71 'Blackbirds' fly from two permanent forward-operating bases, with Detachment One, 9th SRW at Kadena AFB, Okinawa, and Detachment Four at RAF Mildenhall, Suffolk. KC-135Q tankers are co-deployed.

Role
Fighter
Close support
Counter-insurgency
Tactical strike
Strategic bomber
Tactical reconnaissance
Strategic reconnaissance
Maritime patrol
Anti-ship strike
Anti-submarine warfare
Search and rescue
Assault transport
Transport
Liaison
Trainer
Inflight-refuelling tanker
Specialized

Performance
All-weather capability
Rough field capability
STOL capability
VTOL capability
Airspeed 0-250 mph
Airspeed 250 mph-Mach 1
Airspeed Mach 1 plus
Ceiling 0-20,000 ft
Ceiling 20,000-40,000 ft
Ceiling 40,000ft plus
Range 0-1,000 miles
Range 1,000-3,000 miles
Range 3,000 miles plus

Weapons
Air-to-air missiles
Air-to-surface missiles
Cruise missiles
Cannon
Trainable guns
Naval weapons
Nuclear-capable
Rockets
'Smart' weapon kit
Weapon load 0-4,000 lb
Weapon load 4,000-15,000 lb
Weapon load 15,000 lb plus

Avionics
Electronic Counter Measures
Electronic Support Measures
Search radar
Fire control radar
Look-down/shoot-down
Terrain-following radar
Forward-looking infra-red
Laser
Television

Lockheed TR-1

Role

Fighter
Close support
Counter-insurgency
Tactical strike
Strategic bomber
Tactical reconnaissance
Strategic reconnaissance
Maritime patrol
Anti-ship strike
Anti-submarine warfare
Search and rescue
Assault transport
Transport
Liaison
Inflight-refuelling tanker
Trainer
Specialized

Performance

All-weather capability
Rough field capability
STOL capability
VTOL capability
Airspeed 0-250 mph
Airspeed 250 mph-Mach 1
Airspeed Mach 1 plus
Ceiling 0-20,000 ft
Ceiling 20,000-40,000 ft
Ceiling 40,000 ft plus
Range 0-1,000 miles
Range 1,000-3,000 miles
Range 3,000 miles plus

Weapons

Air-to-air missiles
Air-to-surface missiles
Cruise missiles
Cannon
Trainable guns
Naval weapons
Nuclear-capable
Rockets
'Smart' weapon kit
Weapon load 0-4,000 lb
Weapon load 4,000-15,000 lb
Weapon load 15,000 lb plus

Avionics

Electronic Counter Measures
Electronic Support Measures
Search radar
Fire control radar
Look-down/shoot-down
Terrain-following radar
Forward-looking infra-red
Laser
Television

In 1978 the USAF announced a new programme for a tactical reconnaissance aircraft, and in 1979 the U-2R line, which had been dormant for a decade, reopened for production of the **TR-1A**. On 11 May 1981, the first aircraft took to the air. It was the **ER-2**, a demilitarised version for NASA Ames, and was used for earth resources and other high altitude research. Following on 1 August 1981 was the first TR-1A for the USAF.

The TR-1A differs only in secondary systems from the original U-2R, and in primary role. Battlefield surveillance is undertaken with high-resolution radars such as the Hughes ASARS (Advanced Synthetic Aperture Radar System), which allows the TR-1A to patrol for many hours behind friendly lines, the radar searching for enemy tank concentrations and other installations at long oblique ranges. TR-1As retain the strategic reconnaissance capability of the U-2R, and are sometimes seen with large 'farms' of Comint and Elint gathering antennas or windows for optical sensors. The Precision Location Strike System had been developed for use with the TR-1A for locating hostile radar emissions,

but the programme has been cancelled for technical and budgetary problems. It may be replaced by a cheaper and less sophsiticated system.

TR-1As currently serve with two units, the 9th SRW and 17th RW. With the former they serve with the 99th SRS alongside the remaining U-2Rs, and may have replaced lost U-2 airframes. Shortly before the TR-1s first flight, the British government announced that a squadron would be based at RAF Alconbury, and the first aircraft for the 95th RS, 17th RW, arrived in February 1983 for European operations. An original total of 18 was envisaged, but has since been cut to 14 on budgetary grounds.

Training on the type is handled by the 4029th SRTS, 9th SRW 'Dragon Tamers', which operates a pair of **TR-1B**s. This trainer version is not combat-capable, and features a second, raised cockpit replacing the Q-bay. The U-2R/TR-1A has also been apparently evaluated for the AEW role, one U-2R having been seen with a large dorsal radome.

A Lockheed TR-1A of the Alconbury-based 95th RS, 17th RW.

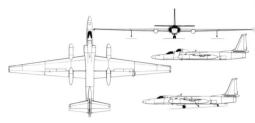

Lockheed TR-1A (upper side view: TR-1B)

This underside view of a TR-1A shows to advantage its long, slender wings and huge 'superpods' containing mission equipment, as well as the sinister matt-black colour scheme.

This 17th RW aircraft has clearly been operating at high altitude, since ice is still visible under its wings as it comes in to land at RAF Alconbury. TR-1s have flown from this base since February 1983.

Specification: Lockheed TR-1A
Origin: USA
Type: single-seat high-altitude reconnaissance aircraft
Powerplant: one 7711-kg (17,000-lb) thrust Pratt & Whitney J75-P-13B turbojet engine
Performance: maximum cruising speed at more than 70,000 ft (21336 m) 373 kts (692 km/h; 430 mph); service ceiling 80,000 ft (24385 m); maximum range 10050 km (6,250 miles)
Weights: empty 7030 kg (15,500 lb); maximum take-off 18733 kg (41,300 lb)
Dimensions: span 31.39 m (103 ft 0 in); length 19.13 m (62 ft 9 in); height 4.88 m (16 ft 0 in); wing area 92.9 m^2 (1,000 sq ft)
Armament: none

Lockheed U-2R

Following the explosion of the first Soviet hydrogen bomb in August 1953 and the emergence of the Myasishchyev M-4 'Bison' jet bomber, the USA had an urgent need for a more technically advanced form of espionage. With developments in photographic technology the need could be met by high-level reconnaissance. The **Lockheed U-2** was conceived in the spring of 1954, in response to a call from the USAF and the Central Intelligence Agency (CIA) for an aircraft capable of cruising at extremely high altitudes. Introduced in 1956 the U-2 is essentially a jet-powered glider and fulfilled its role adequately for several years. But by the mid-1960s many had been lost, primarily as the result of flying an aircraft renowned for its poor handling characteristics. Consequently, in August 1966 the CIA and USAF signed a contract with Lockheed for the design and construction of a considerably more advanced variant of the U-2, designated the U-2R. The new aircraft was to offer increased range and improved controlability, and to carry a greater payload.

The U-2R was a complete redesign, correcting the original poor engine/airframe match and allowing for greater sensor payload. Handling at low altitude was particularly improved. The incompatibility between the engine and the airframe in the U-2C existed because the airframe was too weak to handle the maximum thrust produced by the engine.

In the U-2R the J75-P-13B and the wing aerofoil section were the only features shared with the earlier design. Apart from a family likeness the U-2R was a new aircraft: wing span was increased by 20 per cent and wing area by 75 per cent, whilst the maximum take-off weight went up by some 77 per cent. Provision was made for two extra-large wing sensor pods, and these distinguish the type in service.

After the first flight on 28 August 1967, six aircraft went to the CIA, the balance going to the 349th SRS, 100th SRW by late 1968. U-2Rs were used widely in South East Asia, flying from U-Tapao RTNAF in Thailand until 1976. The aircraft were also involved in Project 'Senior Book' requiring semi-remotely directed flights around China.

In 1972 the US Navy was loaned two U-2Rs for trials to test the electronics patrol-experiment (EP-X) concept using a new range of sensors for monitoring ship movements. The CIA had earlier, in November 1969, flown a U-2R from the carrier USS *America*. Agency aircraft were detached to the Middle East from 1970 and from 1976 there were permanent detachments of the 99th SRS, 9th SRW at Akrotiri and RAF Mildenhall for signals intelligence gathering (Sigint). Lockheed proposed an unmanned version of the U-2R in response to the ill-fated USAF 'Compass Cope' remotely piloted vehicle (RPV) programme.

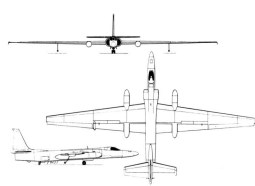

A Lockheed U-2R used for testing an advanced synthetic aperture radar.

Lockheed U-2R

This U-2R is seen in service with the 9th SRW, based at Beale AFB, California. The U-2R differs from the TR-1 only in its internal equipment fit, and in its primary role of strategic reconnaissance.

This U-2R, while remaining on the strength of the 9th SRW, was used by Lockheed to test ASARS (Advanced Synthetic Aperture Radar System). The U-2R saw war service in Vietnam, and has been used over Central America.

Specification: Lockheed U-2R

Origin: USA
Type: single-seat high-altitude reconnaissance aircraft
Powerplant: one 7711-kg (17,000-lb) thrust Pratt & Whitney J75-P-13B turbojet engine
Performance: maximum speed 373 kts (692 km/h; 430 mph); service ceiling 80,000 ft (24385 m); maximum range about 10060 km (6,250 miles)
Weights: empty 6849 kg (15,100 lb); maximum take-off 18597 kg (41,000 lb)
Dimensions: span 31.39 m (103 ft 0 in); length 19.17 m (62 ft 11 in); height 4.88 m (16 ft 0 in); wing area 92.9 m² (1,000 sq ft)
Armament: none

Role
- Fighter
- Close support
- Counter-insurgency
- Tactical strike
- Strategic bomber
- *Tactical reconnaissance*
- *Strategic reconnaissance*
- Maritime patrol
- Anti-ship strike
- Anti-submarine warfare
- Search and rescue
- Assault transport
- Transport
- Liaison
- Trainer
- Inflight-refuelling tanker
- Specialized

Performance
- All-weather capability
- Rough field capability
- STOL capability
- VTOL capability
- Airspeed 0-250 mph
- Airspeed 250 mph-Mach 1
- Airspeed Mach 1 plus
- Ceiling 0-20,000 ft
- Ceiling 20,000-40,000 ft
- *Ceiling 40,000ft plus*
- Range 0-1,000 miles
- Range 1,000-3,000 miles
- *Range 3,000 miles plus*

Weapons
- Air-to-air missiles
- Air-to-surface missiles
- Cruise missiles
- Cannon
- Trainable guns
- Naval weapons
- Nuclear-capable
- Rockets
- 'Smart' weapon kit
- Weapon load 0-4,000 lb
- Weapon load 4,000-15,000 lb
- Weapon load 15,000 lb plus

Avionics
- Electronic Counter Measures
- Electronic Support Measures
- Search radar
- Fire control radar
- Look-down/shoot-down
- Terrain-following radar
- Forward-looking infra-red
- Laser
- Television

McDonnell Douglas A-4 Skyhawk

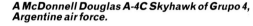

A classic aeroplane by any criterion, the relatively small, compact and lightweight **Douglas A-4 Skyhawk** single-seat naval attack bomber has remained in front line service ever since it first joined the US Navy in 1956. What may be termed the first generation of Skyhawks included those versions based on variants up to and including the A-4F. Of low-set delta wing planform, the Skyhawk first flew in prototype form (XA4D-1) on 22 June 1954 with a Wright J65 turbojet (in effect an Armstrong Siddeley Sapphire produced under licence) and featured prominent lateral air inlets on the sides of the fuselage above the wing root leading edges. Considerable wing strength derived from the use of single-piece tip-to-tip spars machined from solid planks; an exceptionally low thickness/chord ratio gave a speed performance well in excess of many contemporary fighters yet, with automatic wing slats, variable-incidence tailplane and long-travel nosewheel landing gear, the Skyhawk remained entirely tractable as a shipborne high-performance aircraft.

After 165 **A4D-1** aircraft had been built, the **A4D-2** (later redesignated the **A-4B**) introduced provision for Martin Bullpup air-to-surface missiles, navigation and bombing computer, powered rudder with unique central 'skin' with external stiffeners, and inflight-refuelling (both as buddy tanker and receiver); 542 were produced for the US Navy and Marines. Of these, 66 were rebuilt

in the late 1960s as the **A-4P** and **A-4Q** for the Argentine air force and navy respectively, being much in evidence during the Falkland Islands campaign of 1982; 40 others were rebuilt as the **A-4S** for the Singapore Air Defence Command with 30-mm guns in place of the US Navy's 20-mm type.

Some 638 A-4C limited all-weather/night attack aircraft started delivery in 1959, introducing improved autopilot, LABS and terrain-avoidance radar, and gave outstanding service during the Vietnam War; few remain in service, although about 77 rebuilt **A-4L** aircraft with J65 engines and dorsal avionic 'humps' are currently in storage. Some 499 **A-4E** aircraft were produced in the early and mid-1960s with a zero/90-kt (167-km/h, 104-mph) ejector seat, five store pylons and J52 turbojet, many of these becoming the first of some 300 Skyhawks of various versions delivered to Israel over the next 10 years, the great majority of which remain in service today. The **A-4F** (of which 147 examples were built) introduced the dorsal avionics hump into the production line, as well as lift dumpers and spoilers, steerable nosewheel, zero/zero seat and extra cockpit armour. A high proportion of these remain in USN and USMC service, while export derivatives included 14 **A-4G** aircraft for the Royal Australian Navy and 10 **A-4K** aircraft for the Royal New Zealand Air Force (the latter with braking parachute).

Specification: McDonnell Douglas A-4F Skyhawk
Origin: USA
Type: single-seat carrierborne attack fighter-bomber
Powerplant: one 4218-kg (9,300-lb) thrust Pratt & Whitney J52-P-8A turbojet engine
Performance: maximum speed with 1814-kg (4,000-lb) bombload 515 kts (954 km/h; 593 mph) at 34,000 ft (10365 m); initial rate of climb 5,620 ft (1713 m) per minute; maximum unrefuelled range 3307 km (2,055 miles)
Weights: empty equipped 4739 kg (10,448 lb); maximum take-off 12437 kg (27,420 lb)
Dimensions: span 8.38 m (27 ft 6 in); length without refuelling probe 12.27 m (40 ft 3.25 in); height 4.57 m (15 ft 0 in); wing area 24.15 m² (260 sq ft)
Armament: two 20-mm Mk 12 cannon in wing roots; underfuselage mounting for single or multiple store carriers (stressed to 1588 kg; 3,500 lb); and four underwing hardpoints, inboard pair stressed to 1021 kg (2,250 lb) and plumbed for external fuel tanks, outboard pair (dry) stressed to 454 kg (1,000 lb)

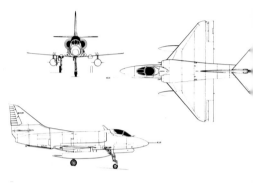

A McDonnell Douglas A-4C Skyhawk of Grupo 4, Argentine air force.

McDonnell Douglas A-4 Skyhawk

The A-4K Skyhawk replaced the Canberra B(I).Mk 12 in RNZAF service and serves with No. 75 Squadron at Ohakea. This aircraft carries a full load of bombs and fuel tanks, and a pair of AIM-9Ds.

The Indonesian air force operates ex-Israeli A-4Es complete with extended IR-suppressing tailpipe and dorsal avionics hump. This aircraft belongs to Skwadron Udara II of No. 300 Wing at Maidun.

McDonnell Douglas A-4 Skyhawk II

introduction to the Skyhawk of the Pratt & Whitney J52-P-408A turbojet, with its 20 per cent power increase, heralded the beginning of a new generation of the remarkable little attack aircraft, now generally known as the **McDonnell Douglas A-4 Skyhawk II**. Retaining the now-characteristic dorsal avionics hump, the **A-4M** (162 produced for the US Marine Corps during the 1970s, plus four for Kuwait), also introduced doubled ammunition provision, angle-rate bombing system (ARBS), enlarged windscreen, ram-air turbogenerator, cranked inflight-refuelling probe and braking parachute. These Skyhawks entered service with marine attack squadrons and only now are being phased out with the arrival in service of the McDonnell Douglas AV-8B Harrier II; they will then continue to serve alongside the TAV-8B with attack training squadrons. Similar to the A-4M, and built simultaneously, were 117 **A-4N** aircraft for the Israeli air force, which however adopted 30-mm wing-root cannon and included more advanced avionics, decoy flare dispensers and provision for the carriage of Israeli weapons.

There is no doubt that, other than in an advanced-technology combat environment, the Skyhawk II is still a remarkably potent weapon, capable of delivering a worthwhile payload accurately, and still able to operate

from a carrier deck or 1220-m (4,000-ft) runway. Post-delivery modifications have included the addition of radar warning and ECM equipment in the rear fuselage and in a fairing at the top of the fin.

Final new-build Skyhawks in 1979 included a small number of **A-4Y** aircraft for the US Marine Corps which included head-up display and an improved ARBS, and some A-4Ms were scheduled for modification to this standard. In the Far East eight ex-Australian A-4Gs transferred to the RNZAF in 1984-5 were expected, together with New Zealand's own A-4Ks, to undergo an update programme which, depending on costs of an avionic refit, would bring the Skyhawks much closer to the Skyhawk II standard. In the Singapore air force a proof-of-concept proposal has been made to re-engine its A-4S Skyhawks with non-reheated General Electric F404 turbofans, followed by a possible avionics update which will place these aircraft firmly in the 'second generation' of A-4s. The Royal Malaysian air force took delivery of 34 single-seat **A-4PTM** aircraft during 1985 to equip two squadrons, and in the same year the last of about 30 ex-Israeli A-4Es joined the Indonesian Armed Forces – Air Force (TNI-AU) amid reports that these too would be re-engined in due course to A-4M standard.

Specification: McDonnell Douglas A-4M Skyhawk II
Origin: USA
Type: single-seat attack fighter-bomber
Powerplant: one 5080-kg (11,200-lb) thrust Pratt & Whitney J52-P-408A turbojet engine
Performance: maximum speed with 1814-kg (4,000-lb) bombload 560 kts (1038 km/h; 645 mph) at 34,000 ft (10365 m); initial rate of climb 8,440 ft (2573 m) per minute; maximum unrefuelled range 3307 km (2,055 miles)
Weights: empty equipped 4747 kg (10,465 lb); maximum take-off 12438 kg (27,420 lb)
Dimensions: span 8.38 m (27 ft 6 in); length without refuelling probe 12.29 m (40 ft 3.75 in); eight 4.57 m (15 ft 0 in); wing area 24.15 m² (260 sq ft)
Armament: two 20-mm Mk 12 cannon in wing roots (30-mm DEFA cannon optional in exported versions); underfuselage mounting for single or multiple store carriers (stressed to 1588 kg; 3,500 lb); and four underwing hardpoints, inboard pair stressed to 1021 kg (2,250 lb) and plumbed for external fuel tanks, outboard pair (dry) stressed to 454 kg (1,000 lb)

A McDonnell Douglas A-4N Skyhawk of the Israel Defence Force/Air Force, with extended anti-SAM tailpipe.

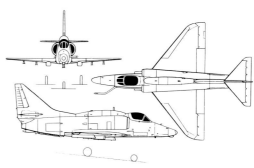

McDonnell Douglas A-4M Skyhawk II

These A-4M Skyhawks belong to the El Toro-based VMA-214, 'Black Sheep'. The rear aircraft wears the old-style high-visibility markings.

Malaysia's A-4 Skyhawks are designated A-4 PTM (Peculiar To Malaysia) and are basically surplus A-Cs, Ds and Ls modified to approximately A-4M standard, some with provision for the AGM-65 Maverick missile.

Role
- Fighter
- Close support
- Counter-insurgency
- Tactical strike
- Tactical bomber
- Strategic bomber
- Tactical reconnaissance
- Strategic reconnaissance
- Maritime patrol
- Anti-ship strike
- Anti-submarine warfare
- Search and rescue
- Assault transport
- Transport
- Liaison
- Trainer
- Inflight-refuelling tanker
- Specialized

Performance
- All-weather capability
- Rough field capability
- STOL capability
- VTOL capability
- Airspeed 0-250 mph
- Airspeed 250 mph-Mach 1
- Airspeed Mach 1 plus
- Ceiling 0-20,000 ft
- Ceiling 20,000-40,000 ft
- Ceiling 40,000 ft plus
- Range 0-1,000 miles
- Range 1,000-3,000 miles
- Range 3,000 miles plus

Weapons
- Air-to-air missiles
- Air-to-surface missiles
- Cruise missiles
- Cannon
- Trainable guns
- Naval weapons
- Nuclear-capable
- Rockets
- 'Smart' weapon kit
- Weapon load 0-4,000 lb
- Weapon load 4,000-15,000 lb
- Weapon load 15,000 lb plus

Avionics
- Electronic Counter Measures
- Electronic Support Measures
- Search radar
- Fire control radar
- Look-down/shoot-down
- Terrain-following radar
- Forward-looking infra-red
- Laser
- Television

McDonnell Douglas OA-4M Skyhawk

United States

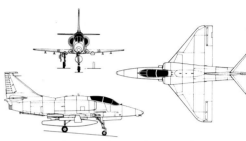

A McDonnell Douglas OA-4M of H&MS 32, based at MCAS Cherry Point, North Carolina.

In 1979 the US Marine Corps took delivery of the first examples of what was then thought likely to be the final variant of a quite outstanding military aeroplane. This was the two-seat **McDonnell Douglas OA-4M Skyhawk**, an extensively modified version of the TA-4F/J developed for forward air control duties. Featuring the same fin profile as the A-4M Skyhawk II with tip-mounted ECM fairing, the rebuilt OA-4M represents a much tidied-up aircraft with the dorsal avionics 'hump' faired neatly into the lines of the rear cockpit, which occupies the fuselage bay normally accommodating the main 908-litre (240-US gal) fuel tank. Deletion of this fuel tank results in the OA-4M almost always carrying a ventral tank of 568-litre (150-US gal) capacity. Indeed store-carrying emphasis is usually confined to fuel tanks, dependence for self-defence being placed on the pair of wing root-mounted 20-mm cannon which have been retained. Avionics remain much the same as in the former two-seaters for contingency use of AAMs and/or ASMs, but

the nature of the OA-4M's tactical role has dictated an upgrading of data link and secure communications systems. Among the items of equipment now omitted are the inflight-refuelling probe and braking parachute.

A total of 22 OA-4Ms was delivered between 1979 and 1981 to the US Marine Corps (after a single aircraft which was technically an **OA-4F** and served as a feasibility demonstrator). These aircraft were delivered to the USMC's headquarters and maintenance squadrons, H&MS-12 at MCAS Iwakuni, H&MS-13 at MCAS El Toro, California, and H&MS-14 and -32 at MCAS Cherry Point, North Carolina. The aircraft for conversion were confined to the TA-4Fs and TA-4Js originally purchased in the mid-1960s, but with 263 A-4s of various versions still listed in the US Navy's 1984 inventory and at least 144 with the US Marine Corps (other than the OA-4Ms) it is still possible that further updated versions of the classic Skyhawk will be pursued, particularly for some of the world's smaller air forces.

McDonnell Douglas OA-4M Skyhawk II

Specification: McDonnell Douglas OA-4M Skyhawk
Origin: USA
Type: two-seat land- or carrier-based aircraft for forward air control duties
Powerplant: one 5080-kg (11,200-lb) thrust Pratt & Whitney J52-P-408 turbojet engine
Performance: maximum speed 582 kts (1078 km/h; 670 mph) at low altitude; low-level combat radius with 568-litre (150-US gal) ventral tank 370 km (230 miles)
Weights: empty equipped 4872 kg (10,740 lb); maximum take-off 11113 kg (24,500 lb)
Dimensions: span 8.38 m (27 ft 6 in); length 12.99 m (42 ft 7.25 in); height 4.71 m (15 ft 5.5 in); wing area 24.15 m² (260.0 sq ft)
Armament: two wing root-mounted 20-mm cannon and four wing pylons normally capable of carrying up to 2948 kg (6,500 lb) of fuel tanks, bombs or missiles

Headquarters and Maintenance Squadron 32, based at MCAS Cherry Point, operates the OA-4M for fast-FAC duties. The OA-4M is an armed version of the TA-4F, and is used only by the USMC.

Seen on approach at MCAS Iwakjuni, Japan, is this OA-4M of H&MS 12, which acts as the fast-FAC unit for the Pacific Fleet.

McDonnell Douglas KC-10A Extender

United States

An outcome of a US Air Force requirement, recognized during the mid-1970s, for an advanced tanker/cargo aircraft (ATCA), the McDonnell Douglas DC-10-30 three-turbofan airliner was selected in December 1977 for development to perform this role, designated **McDonnell Douglas KC-10** and later named **Extender**. Following initial research, development and tooling contracts, orders for a total of 16 production **KC-10A** aircraft had been placed by January 1982, with future planning announced to increase the fleet of these tankers to 60 by the end of 1987, subject to annual congressional approval.

Modification of the basic commercial DC-10-30CF to the military configuration was extensive, comprising in the main of the inclusion of seven bladder fuel cells in the lower fuselage compartments (containing a total of 53446 kg/117,829 lb of fuel), provision of an air flight-refuelling boom under the rear fuselage, a boom operator's station, and inclusion of various alternative seating layouts in the forward section of the main cabin. An advanced boom operating system, employing digital fly-by-wire control procedure, was provided by Sperry Flight Systems, and an alternative hose/reel probe-and-drogue installation was also incorporated for use by US Navy and Marine Corps aircraft. A refuelling receptacle enables the KC-10A itself to be refuelled in flight, but even without this facility the total fuel load capable of being carried, including the tanker's own fuel system, amounts to 108062 kg (238,236 lb), any of which can be used either to extend the tanker's range or replenish other aircraft in flight. In practice this enables the KC-10A to pass 90718 kg (200,000 lb) of fuel to other aircraft 3540 km (2,200 miles) from its home base and then return to that base. Thus it would require just 17 KC-10As to support an entire fighter squadron on a nonstop flight from the USA to the Middle East, at the same time transporting all ground personnel and equipment simultaneously. The task would otherwise require the deployment of 40 Boeing KC-135s. Avionics now provided include a beacon transponder and a radar beacon mode, enabling the KC-10A to act as a pathfinder for such a long-range deployment of fighter aircraft.

First flight by a KC-10A was made on 12 July 1980, and by the end of 1985 Extenders were in service with the 22nd ARW at March AFB, California, the 2nd BW at Barksdale AFB, Louisiana, and the 68th ARG at Seymour Johnson AFB, North Carolina, with Air Force Reserve (Associate) Squadron crews sharing the aircraft of the active duty squadrons.

McDonnell Douglas KC-10A, Strategic Air Command, US Air Force.

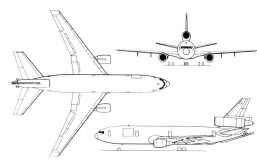

McDonnell Douglas KC-10A Extender

As well as boom capability, the KC-10A has a hose and drogue for probe-equipped receivers. Here an AV-8B prepares to take on fuel.

Definitive colour scheme for the KC-10A is this charcoal grey with light grey undersides. Note the central main wheel inherited from the DC-10 Series 30.

Specification: McDonnell Douglas KC-10A Extender
Origin: USA
Type: advanced tanker/cargo aircraft
Powerplant: three 23814-kg (52,500-lb) thrust General Electric CF6-50C2 turbofan engines
Performance: maximum speed at 25,000 ft (7620 m) 530 kts (982 km/h; 610 mph); maximum cruising speed 490 kts (908 km/h; 564 mph) at 30,000 ft (9145 m); maximum rate of climb at sea level 2,680 ft (817 m) per minute; unrefuelled range with maximum cargo 7033 km (4,370 miles)
Weights: empty equipped, as tanker 109328 kg (241,027 lb); maximum take-off 267620 kg (590,000 lb)
Dimensions: span 50.40 m (165 ft 4.4 in); length 55.35 m (181 ft 7 in); height 17.70 m (58 ft 1 in); wing area 367.7 m² (3,958 sq ft)
Armament: none

Role
Fighter
Close support
Counter-insurgency
Tactical strike
Strategic bomber
Tactical reconnaissance
Strategic reconnaissance
Maritime patrol
Anti-ship strike
Anti-submarine warfare
Search and rescue
Assault transport
Transport
Liaison
Trainer
Inflight-refuelling tanker
Specialized

Performance
All-weather capability
Rough field capability
STOL capability
VTOL capability
Airspeed 0-250 mph
Airspeed 250 mph-Mach 1
Airspeed Mach 1 plus
Airspeed Mach 1 plus
Ceiling 0-20,000 ft
Ceiling 20,000-40,000 ft
Ceiling 40,000 ft plus
Range 0-1,000 miles
Range 1,000-3,000 miles
Range 3,000 miles plus

Weapons
Air-to-air missiles
Air-to-surface missiles
Cruise missiles
Cannon
Trainable guns
Naval weapons
Nuclear-capable
Rockets
'Smart' weapon kit
Weapon load 0-4,000 lb
Weapon load 4,000-15,000 lb
Weapon load 15,000 lb plus

Avionics
Electronic Counter Measures
Electronic Support Measures
Search radar
Fire control radar
Look-down/shoot-down
Terrain-following radar
Forward-looking infra-red
Laser
Television

Phantom II: The St Louis Slugger

Aircraft may come and go, but the truly great designs live forever. So it is with the mighty F-4 Phantom II, a design which continues to meet a wide range of operational requirements around the world. In the vanguard of users are the US armed forces, for whom this big, bold beast has helped win many a battle in a variety of operational scenarios over nearly three decades.

For any enemy ground forces unlucky enough to see the broad profile of the F-4 hurtling down towards them, admiration for its versatility and sheer power would attest to the aircraft's excellent fighting qualities. Here an F-4G rolls in to attack a radar.

The slat-wing F-4S Phantoms aboard USS *Midway* (CV-41) in the Western Pacific are soon to be replaced by McDonnell Douglas F/A-18A Hornets, leaving no Phantoms on carrier decks anywhere in the world. By 1988, the US Navy's Phantom inventory will have been whittled down to a mere two reserve squadrons. But the Phantom was exclusively Navy property when the story began in the early 1950s (at the McDonnell Aircraft Company's St Louis facility) with Herman Barkey's design team conceiving a brute-sized, twin-engine fighter originally meant for the strike role and designated AH-1. When it first flew on 27 May 1958 with test pilot Robert C. Little at the controls, the F4H-1 Phantom had been through extensive design changes and was now a fleet interceptor, designed to protect US Navy carrier battle groups using APQ-50 radar and missiles such as the radar-guided AAM-N-6 (later AIM-7) Sparrow and IR-homing AAM-N-7 (later AIM-9) Sidewinder. Much of the effectiveness of the Phantom was credited to its powerplant, two 7326-kg (16,150-lb) thrust General Electric J79-GE-2A afterburning turbojets in the first aircraft with improved variants in later Phantoms. In its era the J79 was a breakthrough, solving the need for a high-ratio compressor by using a single high-pressure rotor with upstream rows of intermediate stator blades able to be pivoted to exactly the right angular setting for the airflow. The

engines gave the aircraft enormous power and double insurance against battle damage. They also were renowned for leaving black smoke trails to entice enemy AAA gunners and, while the US Navy's F-4B variant is today 'smokeless', most still do.

Forty-seven F-4A developmental airframes were followed by the US Navy/ Marine Corps F-4B Phantom, which scored the first and last MiG kills of the South East Asia war. In service with the fleet by 1962, the Navy aircraft quickly lost their purely interceptor status and became dogfighters and mud movers. A family of reconnaissance Phantoms and another of Phantoms for foreign users, outside the scope of this narrative, followed. The F-4B had J79-GE-8A/B engines, APQ-72 radar with an 81-cm (32-in) dish, and the Lear AJB-3 bombing system; 651 came off the production line. Some 228 were rebuilt to F-4N standard under a SLEP which introduced updated items such as the helmet-sight VTAS, SEAM and improved avionics.

The F-4J, first flown 27 May 1966, was equipped with 8119-kg (17,900-lb) thrust J79-GE-19 engines and added to the Phantom's capability an improved TACAN, the upgraded AJB-7 bombing system, a slatted tailplane, and drooped ailerons intended to reduce carrier approach speed from 137 to 125 kts (254 to 232 km/h; 158 to 144 mph). On 10 May 1972 in an F-4J Phantom (BuNo 155800)

of VF-96 'Fighting Falcons', Lieutenant Randall Cunningham became the Vietnam war's first pilot ace by scoring his third, fourth and fifth MiG kills. Of 522 F-4Js delivered to the Navy, 248 were retrofitted with various improvements, including leading-edge manoueuvre slats, to receive the designation F-4S. In other conversion programmes, 44 QF-4B and 40 QF-4N target drones were used as fodder for missile and ordnance tests.

Marine machine

When Brigadier General Michael P. Sullivan recently became the first man to attain 5,000 flight hours in the Phantom, he illustrated the longevity and importance of the F-4 type for the US Marine Corps. In 1962 the Marines were just a step behind the Navy in acquiring the F-4B model. In April 1965 they introduced the F-4B to South Vietnam when VMFA-531

Only two squadrons of Phantoms remain in front-line US Navy service, although there are several reserve units. A number of aircraft are used for armament and equipment test purposes, such as this VX-4 F-4J, seen in the company of Lockheed's test SR-71A.

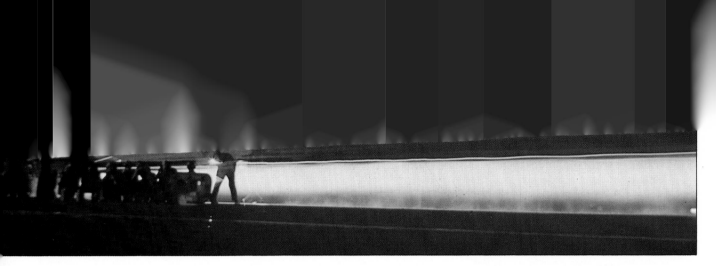

'Gray Ghosts' arrived at Da Nang. The Marines also operated the F-4J and F-4N before transitioning to today's F-4s. They are expected on occasion to fill in for their Navy brethren on carrier decks. On 11 September 1972, Major Thomas 'Bear' Lasseter and Captain John D. Cummings flying an F-4J Phantom (BuNo 155526) of VMFA-333 'Shamrocks' went into North Vietnam from USS *America* (CV-66) and shot down a MiG-21, the only Marine air-to-air kill of the South East Asia conflict.

The Marines regard their air arm as an adjunct to their elite ground fighting force and are more interested in the Phantom as a warplane that can loiter for extended periods in a target area than as a fighter possessing long range. Close air support being so essential to the Marines, it must be said that the Phantom is a generation behind present-day strike aircraft for precision delivery of ordnance.

The Phantom remains the most numerous fighter in the Marine Corps, and three squadrons at MCAS Beaufort, South Carolina will not convert to the F/A-18A Hornet until 1988. Three more Marine F-4S squadrons which bask in the sun at MCAS Kaneohe Bay, Hawaii will not see the Hornet until 1993, and no plans have been made to replace the F-4S in reserve units.

In a typical real-world situation, the 3rd Marine Division at Camp Pendleton, California might be rushed to the Persian Gulf to block a Soviet invasion. F-4S

Phantoms might deploy with the aid of inflight-refuelling to a friendly country granting 'user rights', like Oman or Somalia. While newer fighters clear the air of enemy opposition, the big, powerful F-4S Phantom would support the Marines on the ground, carrying the diversity of ordnance loads for which the Phantom is famous. Against a hard target, the load might be six 750-lb (340-kg) iron bombs, while fluid troop concentrations might be attacked with CBU-58 Rockeye II cluster bombs.

Air Force fighter

In January 1962, Colonels Gordon Graham and George Laven delivered to the US Air Force two examples of the F-110A Phantom, redesignated F-4C later in that year, which was almost a carbon copy of the machine designed to fly from carrier decks. The Air Force fighter needed a self-contained cartridge main engine starter not found on the Navy variant, but the F-4C remained essentially a land-based version of a nautical craft. Production amounted to 583 aircraft, many of them participating in heavy fighting in South East Asia. As noted, a few remain on duty with ANG squadrons today, but the F-4C was in certain respects a transition for the Air Force: having eaten humble pie to acquire a Navy aircraft, the Air Force wanted better ordnance delivery. It also wanted something the Navy never had, namely a gun.

A sight soon to disappear into the annals of history – the launch of US Navy F-4s from an aircraft-carrier somewhere on the world's oceans. For many years the backbone of US Navy Fleet defence and strike forces, the Phantom II will soon end its days at sea.

The F-4D Phantom, first flown 9 December 1965, was the first step towards translating carrier-based potency into Air Force needs. The D model introduced the partly solid-state APQ-109 fire-control radar (highly advanced in its day, but a handicap now), a lead-computing gunsight, and an ASQ-91 weapon release computer making it able to deliver 'smart' bombs or PGMs. The F-4D was also supposed to introduce the IR-homing AIM-4D Falcon missile, but these were received so poorly in South East Asia that Robin Olds ordered the Falcons trashed and rewired his F-4Ds to continue using Sidewinders. The senior US airman in the UK today, Major General Thomas McInerney, helped introduce the F-4D to combat in 1967 and was impressed that its new systems permitted bomb release from higher altitude, while other strike aircraft had to get closer to targets like the

Once a significant part of USAFE, the Phantom numbers are rapidly dwindling; these 86th TFW aircraft are being replaced by F-16C/Ds. When current replacement plans are complete, only the 26th TRW RF-4Cs and the 52nd TFW F-4G 'Wild Weasels' will remain in Europe.

Thanh Hoa Bridge, so creating greater exposure to ground fire. McInerney and his companions still wanted a gun, and the centreline SUU-16/A pod carrying a 20-mm cannon was not sufficient. The SUU-23/A pod introduced in the late 1960s is an improvement, but is still weighty and creates drag.

At last – a gun

The gun, an internally mounted M61A1 Vulcan 20-mm 'Gatling' style cannon with 640 rounds, finally appeared aboard the F-4E Phantom, first flown on 30 June 1967. The cannon-armed Phantom had been demanded by pilots, including Olds who missed his fifth air-to-air kill and ace status when (in an F-4D) he was too close to a MiG to use a missile and possessed no gun.

In the end, it was ACM training rather than an internal gun which enabled US airmen to prevail over the North Vietnamese MiG, but the F-4E became the most numerous of Phantoms and the principal export model, no fewer than 949 being built. As pointed out by Colonel Edward Hillding, whose 469th TFS introduced the E model to combat at Korat in November 1968 (with McInerney again in attendance), 'The F-4E was a wholly different Phantom – longer, heavier, different fuel [capacity], different radar.' The F-4E had 8119-kg thrust J79-GE-17 engines, smaller APQ-120 nose radar, and an extra (seventh) fuel cell in the rear fuselage to counterbalance the weight of the gun. Until 1969, all Air Force Phantoms were flown by two pilots, and the F-4E was first to introduce the present-day crew of pilot and navigator, the latter officially termed a WSO. From 1972, F-4Es still in production were built with a slatted leading edge permitting much tighter accelerative manoeuvres to be made.

After testing other types including the F-4D variant and the Grumman EA-6B Prowler, the Air Force adopted the F-4G as its standard 'Advanced Wild Weasel' platform, replacing the Republic F-105F and F-105G (and a small handful of special F-4Cs) which pioneered 'Wild Weasel' missions in Vietnam. The term

embraces EW and SAM suppression missions by dedicated electronic warplanes hunting down hostile SAM installations (using radar for lock-on, tracking or missile guidance) and destroying them before or during an attack by other friendly aircraft on nearby targets.

'Weasel' weaponry

Some 116 F-4E airframes were converted to F-4G standard, having the 20-mm gun deleted and being equipped with the APR-38 system which provides comprehensive radar homing and warning and employs no fewer than 52 special aerials, including those in the former gun pod and others in a new fairing at the top of the vertical tail. Ordnance carried by the 'Wild Weasel' includes electro-optical AGM-65 Maverick missiles on each inboard pylon, two AGM-88A HARMs outboard, and AIM-9L Sidewinder all-aspect missiles for air-to-air engagements.

While the 'pure fighter' F-4E begins its ANG service by joining the 131st TFW, Missouri ANG at Lambert-St Louis Airport (where three airframes are evaluating a new, single-piece, bird-resistant windscreen likely to be retrofitted to all Phantoms) reports persist that a further number of F-4E airframes, perhaps a large number, will be converted to F-4G 'Wild Weasels'. It has taken three decades to get from Phantom to 'Wild Weasel', but the F-4G is only beginning its contribution to the solid record of achievement.

Though showing its age somewhat against the modern service aircraft, the F-4S still plays a significant role within US Marine Corps aviation operations. Its ruggedness and heavy payload capabilities make it an excellent close air support/strike aircraft.

Glossary

AAA Anti-Aircraft Artillery
AMRAAM Advanced Medium-Range Air-to-Air Missile
AB Air Base
ACM Air Combat Manoeuvring
AFB Air Force Base
ASFRes Air Force Reserve
ANG Air National Guard
EW Electronic Warfare
HARM High-speed Anti-Radiation Missile
IR Infra-Red
MCAS Marine Corps Air Station
PGM Precision-Guided Munition
RIO Radar Intercept Officer
SAM Surface-to-Air Missile
SEAM Sidewinder Expanded-Acquisition Mode
SLEP Service Life Extension Program
TAC Tactical Air Command
TACAN TACtical Air Navigation
TFS Tactical Fighter Squadron
TFW Tactical Fighter Wing
VTAS Visual Target-Acquisition System
WSO Weapons System Officer

The latest and most capable of the F-4 models operated by the US Air Force is the F-4G 'Wild Weasel V', the widely-dispersed force enabling anti-radiation operations to be conducted in support of other F-4 attack operations, e.g. eliminating enemy SAM radar sites.

F-4 in service:

United States Air Force, Tactical Air Command

Tasked with organizing, training, equipping and maintaining combat forces which can deploy rapidly, and to ensure that the USAF strategic air defence forces can meet both peacetime and wartime air defence requirements, Tactical Air Command employs the F-4 at the forefront of its operations. As with other Commands the F-4 is gradually giving way to the F-15 and F-16, but it still plays an important role as a tactical fighter and electronic combat suppression aircraft. What was Air Defense Tactical Air Command (ADTAC) is now the 1st Air Force, this being responsible for the command and control of the interceptor forces, while the tactical F-4 elements come under the command of the 9th and 12th Air Forces. In times of war these forces would be considerably bolstered by tactical and interceptor squadrons from the Air National Guard and Air Force Reserve.

This McDonnell Douglas F-4E, with the prominent undernose cannon fairing, is in the markings of the 69th TFS/347th TFW.

9th Air Force
4th Tactical Fighter Wing
Base: Seymour-Johnson AFB, North Carolina
Tailcode letters: 'SJ'
Squadrons: 334th, 335th, 336th & 337th TFS

Aircraft model: F-4E
Example aircraft: (334th TFS) 20162, 31176, 31182, 41627; (335th TFS) 21478, 70379, 31183; (336th TFS) 20161, 31171, 40665, 41639; (337th TFS) 60379, 70272, 60361

31st Tactical Fighter Wing
Base: Homestead AFB, Florida
Tailcode letters: 'ZF'
Squadrons: 307th, 308th & 309th TFS
Aircraft models: F-4D/E
Example aircraft: (307th TFS) 67698; (308th TFS) 50729, 67635; (309th TFS) 67463

347th Tactical Fighter Wing
Base: Moody AFB, Georgia
Tailcode letters: 'MY'
Squadrons: 68th, 69th & 70th TFS
Aircraft model: F-4E
Example aircraft: (68th TFS) 70360, 80320, 80357, 80495; (69th TFS) 70396, 80389, 80427, 80494; (70th TFS) 80318, 80366, 80423, 80449

12th Air Force

35th Tactical Training Wing
Base: George AFB, California
Tailcode letters: 'GA'
Squadrons: 20th & 21st TFTS
Aircraft model: F-4E
Example aircraft: (20th TFTS) 70235, 70288, 70311; (21st TFTS) 60338, 70241, 80351

37th Tactical Fighter Wing
Base: George AFB, California
Tailcode letters: 'WW'

Squadrons: 561st, 562nd & 563rd TFS
Aircraft models: F-4E/G
Example aircraft: 561st TFS (F-4G) 97209, 97303, 97561, 97574; 562nd TFS (F-4E) 70233, 90270, (F-4G) 97288, 90284; 563rd TFS (F-4G) 90279, 97204, 97550

Tactical Air Warfare Center
Base: Eglin AFB, Florida
Tailcode letters: 'OT'
Example aircraft: (F-4E) 20168, 60306, 97589

United States Pacific Air Forces

As the air component of the unified Pacific Command, PACAF's mission is to plan and execute offensive and defensive air operations assigned to it, defending US interests stretching over a vast area which covers more than half the Earth's surface, including more than 35 countries. Active airfields are dotted round the region, principally in Japan, South Korea, the Philippines and Hawaii. The 5th and 13th Air Force administer PACAF operations, the F-4 units (still the most numerically important in the region) coming under their control.

5th Air Force
51st Tactical Fighter Wing
Bases: Osan AB, South Korea (36th TFS); Taegu AB, South Korea (497th TFS)
Tailcode letters: 'OS' (36th TFS); 'GU' (497th TFS)

Aircraft model: F-4E
Example aircraft: (36th TFS) 70351, 80407, 80329, 80376; (497th TFS) 80305, 80323, 80453, 97294

13th Air Force
3rd Tactical Fighter Wing
Base: Clark AFB, Philippines
Tailcode letters: 'PN'
Squadrons: 3rd TFS & 90th TFS
Aircraft models: F-4E/G

Example aircraft: 3rd TFS (F-4E) 80355, 10237, 11073, 31198; 90th TFS (F-4E) 80310, 90290, 11391; (F-4G) 90267, 97208, 97583

The sand and two-tone green 'Vietnam' tactical camouflage is worn less and less by today's USAF F-4s, most having adopted the 'European One' colours. This 3rd TFW F-4E illustrates the older scheme, along with flamboyant shark's-mouth on the lower nose.

United States Air Forces in Europe

For so long a major element within the USAFE aircraft force, the F-4 is now rapidly disappearing, giving way to the General Dynamics F-16 Fighting Falcon. The 86th TFW is well advanced with its re-equipment plans, its F-4Es being returned to the USA and distributed amongst Air National Guard units in the main. The mix of F-4Es and F-4Gs which equip the three squadrons of the 52nd TFW will start to replace their E models with F-16Cs during 1987 on a one-for-one basis, a programme that is intended to be finished by the end of 1987. Preceding this, a dozen F-4Es will return to the USA in mid-1986, their place in West Germany being taken by a dozen F-4Gs. These units come under the control of the 17th Air Force, the units making a valuable contribution to NATO and the defence of Western Europe.

17th Air Force
52nd Tactical Fighter Wing
Base: Spangdahlem AB, West Germany
Tailcode letters: 'SP'
Squadrons: 23rd TFS, 81st TFS & 480th TFS
Aircraft models: F-4E/G
Example aircraft: 23rd TFS (F-4E) 21482, 40666, 41059; (F-4G) 90255, 97228, 97566; 81st TFS (F-4E) 40657, 41038, 41645; (F-4G) 90286, 97293,

97587; 480th TFS (F-4E) 20167, 21485, 40653; (F-4G) 90269, 97270, 97579

86th Tactical Fighter Wing
Base: Ramstein AB, West Germany
Tailcode letters: 'RS'
Squadron: 526th TFS
Aircraft model: F-4E
Example aircraft: 80381, 80408, 90244

This F-4E Phantom II's yellow and black fin-stripe and 'SP' tailcode letters identify it as an 81st TFS/52nd TFW machine, based at Spangdahlem AB in West Germany.

United States Air Force, Air National Guard

By far the largest user of the F-4 in the US armed forces, the Air National Guard force is based around the F-4C/D/E with the Cs being progressively replaced by the later models, the F-4E becoming more prevalent as it is retired from USAFE and home-based units in favour of types such as the F-15 Eagle and F-16 Fighting Falcon. The Phantom II is the ANGs primary tactical fighter, its importance underlined by the fact that there are current programmes which will modify F-4D and -E airframes to allow carriage of the AIM-9L and -M models of the Sidewinder AAM, and the fitting of low-smoke engines.

Current duties for the ANG Phantom II force include interception, close air support, air superiority and battlefield interdiction. In times of war the majority of ANG F-4 units would be 'gained' by Tactical Air Command, most of the units being assigned to the 1st Air Force for fighter interception duties (the seven FISs and the 114th TFTS). Out on its own is the 199th TFS which would join PACAF. In peacetime flying, the importance of the ANG F-4 units can be appreciated by the fact that it provides 26 per cent of the Air Force's tactical fighters and some 73 per cent of the interceptor force – the F-4 playing its part to the full.

Amongst the most colourful ANG F-4s are the aircraft of the 171st FIS/191st FIG, Michigan ANG. Illustrated is an F-4C.

110th TFS/131st TFW Missouri ANG
Base: St. Louis IAP, Missouri
Tailcode letters: 'SL'
Aircraft model: F-4E
Example aircraft: 80338, 80410, 90305, 90307

111th FIS/147th FIG Texas ANG
Base: Ellington AFB, Texas
Aircraft model: F-4C
Example aircraft: 40712, 40828, 40908

113th TFS/181st TFG Indiana ANG
Base: Hullman Regional AP, Indiana

Tailcode letters: 'HF'
Aircraft model: F-4C
Example aircraft: 37657, 40675, 40724

114th TFTS/142nd FIG Oregon ANG
Base: Kingsley Field, Oregon
Aircraft model: F-4C
Example aircraft: 37549, 40673, 40888

121st TFS/113th TFW District of Columbia ANG
Base: Andrews AFB, Maryland
Tailcode letters: 'DC'

123rd FIS/142nd FIG Oregon ANG
Base: Portland IAP, Oregon
Aircraft model: F-4C
Example aircraft: 37670, 40707, 40893

127th TFTS/184th TFG Kansas ANG
Base: McConnell AFB, Kansas
Aircraft model: F-4D
Example aircraft: 50705, 60274, 68693

128th TFS/116th TFW Georgia ANG
Base: Dobbins AFB, Georgia
Aircraft model: F-4D
Example aircraft: 67614, 67735, 68689

134th TFS/158th TFG Vermont ANG
Base: Burlington IAP, Vermont

Tailcode letters: 'VT'
Aircraft model: F-4D
Example aircraft: 50790, 60243, 60266

136th FIS/107th FIG New York ANG
Base: Niagara Falls IAP, New York
Aircraft model: F-4C
Example aircraft: 37581, 40660, 40822

141st TFS/108th TFW New Jersey ANG
Base: McGuire AFB, New Jersey
Tailcode letters: 'NJ'
Aircraft model: F-4E
Example aircraft: 80375, 80526, 80534

160th TFS/187th TFG Alabama ANG
Base: Dannelly Field, Alabama
Tailcode letters: 'AL'
Aircraft model: F-4D
Example aircraft: 67644, 67708, 67754

163rd TFS/122nd TFW Indiana ANG
Base: Fort Wayne MAP, Indiana
Tailcode letters: 'FW'
Aircraft model: F-4E
Example aircraft: 80512

171st FIS/191st FIG Michigan ANG
Base: Selfridge ANGB, Michigan
Aircraft models: F-4C/D
Example aircraft: (F-4C) 37514, 37626; (F-4D) 50737

177th TFTS/184th TFG Kansas ANG
Base: McConnell AFB, Kansas
Aircraft model: F-4D
Example aircraft: 67520, 67633, 67759

178th FIS/119th FIG North Dakota ANG
Base: Hector Field, North Dakota
Aircraft model: F-4D
Example aircraft: 40977, 50647, 67498

184th TFS/188th TFG Arkansas ANG
Base: Fort Smith MAP, Arkansas
Aircraft model: F-4C
Example aircraft: 37411, 37646, 40912

194th FIS/144th FIW California ANG
Base: Fresno Air Terminal, California
Aircraft model: F-4D
Example aircraft: 50740, 60279, 67741

196th TFS/163rd TFG California ANG
Base: March AFB, California
Aircraft models: F-4C/D
Example aircraft: (F-4C) 37686, 37693, 40665, 40923

199th TFS/154th CG Hawaii ANG
Base: Hickam AFB, Hawaii
Aircraft model: F-4C
Example aircraft: 37647, 40851, 40913

United States Air Force Reserve

Given the mainly transport-orientated nature of AFRes operations and aircraft-equipped units, it is not surprising that the Phantom II is serving with only a handful of Tactical Fighter Squadrons (TFSs). This small but effective force is now exclusively equipped with the F-4D, though no doubt the F-4E will start filtering down from front-line units in due course. The squadrons are organized along the standard Squadron/Wing structure, with squadrons based away from the Wing HQ receiving support from the Group HQ. Squadrons based at Wing HQ report directly to that Wing HQ. All the squadrons will be 'gained' by Tactical Air Command in times of war, part of a total of 12 AFRes squadrons which would report to this Command within the front-line Air Force.

6th Air Force

89th TFS/906th TFG
Base: Wright-Patterson AFB, Ohio
Tailcode letters: 'DO'
Aircraft model: F-4D
Example aircraft: 67699, 67706, 67749, 67755

93rd TFS/482nd TFW
Base: Homestead AFB, Florida
Tailcode letters: 'FM'
Aircraft model: F-4D
Example aircraft: 67552, 67563, 68715, 68824

457th TFS/301st TFW
Base: Carswell AFB, Texas

Tailcode letters: 'TH'
Aircraft model: F-4D
Example aircraft: 68737, 68786, 68794, 68825

465th TFS/507th TFG
Base: Tinker AFB, Oklahoma
Tailcode letters: 'SH'
Aircraft model: F-4D
Example aircraft: 67618, 67750, 68701, 68709

704th TFS/924th TFG
Base: Bergstrom AFB, Texas
Tailcode letters: 'TX'
Aircraft model: F-4D
Example aircraft: 68739, 68788, 68802, 68819

United States Air Force Test and Evaluation units

The F-4 continues to serve with various agencies for a wide range of purposes, much of this revolving around weapons and their operational use, this also being covered by test and evaluation units within Tactical Air Command. Air Force Systems Command is concerned with advances in aerospace technology and their applications in an operational environment. This is particularly applied to the design, construction and testing of various projects, the 3246th Test Wing (ADTC) using its F-4s for work relating to all non-nuclear weapons for tactical forces. The 6512th Test Squadron (AFFTC) evaluates aircraft following their delivery by the manufacturers, usually retaining some examples for further research work, close co-operation being maintained by both the units with their counterparts in TAC.

The Ogden Air Logistics Center is responsible for the major overhauls and modification/upgrading programmes associated with the USAF F-4 forces, in addition to the standard planned inspections and service life overhauls, the unit retaining a small number of aircraft for its own use. This unit is controlled by Air Force Logistics Command.

Air Force Systems Command

Air Force Flight Test Center
Base: Edwards AFB, California
Tailcode letters: 'ED'
Squadron: 6512th TS
Example aircraft: (F-4C) 37408; (F-4D) 67483; (F-4E) 60289, 60294

Armament Development & Test Center
Base: Edwards AFB, California
Tailcode letters: 'AD'
Wing: 3246th TW
Example aircraft: (F-4C) 40869; (F-4D) 68699; (F-4E) 11072, 20126

Air Force Logistics Command Ogden Air Logistics Center
Base: Hill AFB, Utah
Example aircraft: (F-4D) 67455, 67688; (F-4E) 60301, 80450

United States Navy

After a long and highly distinguished service career as the US Navy's primary front-line fighter, the venerable F-4 Phantom II had all but given way to the Grumman F-14A Tomcat and McDonnell Douglas F/A-18A Hornet. Today, only two squadrons remain active, both flying as part of the Pacific Fleet aircraft carrier forces, but their days with the F-4S are numbered. Shortly they will begin transitioning to the Hornet.

VF-151 'Vigilantes'
Carrier: USS *Midway* (CV-41)
Air Wing: CVW-5
Tailcode letters: 'NF'
Aircraft model: F-4S
Example aircraft: 153868-203, 153910-206, 155565-212

VF-161 'Chargers'
Carrier: USS *Midway* (CV-41)
Air Wing: CVW-5
Tailcode letters: 'NF'
Aircraft model: F-4S
Example aircraft: 157261-100, 155746-105, 155897-113

A VF-161 F-4S wears one of several low-visibility tactical colour schemes.

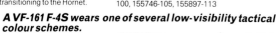

United States Naval Air Reserve

As with the front-line US Navy forces the Reserve forces are in the process of retiring their remaining active Phantom IIs in favour of more modern types. The two remaining squadrons currently fly the F-4S, newer models having been handed down over the years from the front-line units as they re-equipped. From August 1986 the F-4S will start to be retired from the two units as the first Grumman F-14A Tomcats arrive at NAS Dallas for ground instruction and maintenance training.

VF-201 'Red Raiders'
Air Wing: CVWR-20
Home base: NAS Dallas, Texas
Tailcode letters: 'AF'
Aircraft model: F-4S
Example aircraft: 153828-102, 153887-103, 155572-110

VF-202
Air Wing: CVWR-20
Home base: NAS Dallas, Texas

Tailcode letters: 'AF'
Aircraft model: F-4S
Example aircraft: 155893-207, 153904-211, 153824-213

The Texas home-base of VF-201 is represented on the fin of this F-4S by a state map.

Youngest of the AFRes F-4D units is the 89th TFS/906th TFG based at Wright-Patterson AFB, Ohio. Note the stylized black trim around the cockpits and on the canopy framing.

McDonnell Douglas F-4E Phantom II cutaway drawing key

1 Starboard tailplane
2 Static discharger
3 Honeycomb trailing edge panels
4 Tailplane mass balance weight
5 Tailplane spar construction
6 Drag chute housing
7 Tailcone/drag chute hinged door
8 Fuselage fuel tanks vent pipe
9 Honeycomb rudder construction
10 Rudder balance
11 Tail warning radar fairing
12 Tail navigation light
13 Fin tip antenna fairing
14 Communications antenna
15 Fin rear spar
16 Variable intensity formation lighting strip

17 Rudder control jack
18 Tailplane pivot mounting
19 Tailplane pivot seal
20 Fixed leading edge slat
21 Tailplane hydraulic jack
22 Fin front spar
23 Stabilator feel system pressure probe
24 Anti-collision light
25 Stabilator feel system balance mechanism
26 Tailcone cooling air duct
27 Heat resistant tailcone skinning
28 Arrester hook housing
29 Arrester hook, lowered
30 Starboard fully variable exhaust nozzle

31 Rudder artificial feel system bellows
32 Fin leading edge
33 Ram air intake
34 Fuselage No 7 fuel cell, capacity 318 litres (84 US gal)
35 Engine bay cooling air outlet louvres
36 Arrester hook actuator and damper
37 Fuel vent piping
38 Fuselage No 6 fuel cell, capacity 806 litres (213 US gal)
39 Jet pipe shroud construction

40 Engine bay hinged access doors
41 Rear AIM-7E-2 Sparrow to-air missile
42 Semi-recessed missile housing
43 Jet pipe nozzle actuator
44 Afterburner jet pipe
45 Fuselage No 5 fuel cell, capacity 681 litres (18 gal)
46 Fuel tank access panel
47 Fuel system piping
48 Tailplane control cable
49 Fuselage No 4 fuel cell, capacity 761 litres (20 gal)

United States Navy Test and Evaluation units

F-4 in its navalized forms continues to serve with several the US Navy's test and evaluation units, most of these ating under the control of Naval Air Systems Command, Navy agency responsible for the development, urement and service support of aircraft and their ciated systems. A mixture of Navy F-4 models are in use, gh in general their numbers are decreasing. Duties de support of Strike Aircraft Test Directorate evaluation rierborne aircraft and their equipment, use by the Naval pons Center in support of weapons development and forms of delivery within the context of modern air are – the testing of new missiles on behalf of the Pacific sile Test Center.

VX-4 'Evaluators'
Base: NAS Point Mugu, California
Tailcode letters: 'XF'
Example aircraft: (F-4S) 155539/XF-1, 158360/XF-7

Lakehurst Naval Air Test Center
Base: NAS Lakehurst, New Jersey
Example aircraft: (F-4N) 150485/MG-10

Naval Weapons Center
Base: NAF China Lake, California
Example aircraft: (QF-4N) 150993/407, 152303/408

Pacific Missile Test Center
Base: NAS Point Mugu, California
Example aircraft: (F-4J) 155563/92, 151504/94

Strike Aircraft Test Directorate/Naval Air Test Center
Base: NAS Patuxent River, Maryland
Tailcode letters: '7T'
Example aircraft: (F-4J) 153077/101, 157286/120

1 Starboard engine bay construction
2 TACAN antenna
3 Fuselage No 3 fuel cell, capacity 556 litres (147 US gal)
4 Engine oil tank
5 General Electric J79-GE-17A turbojet engine
6 Engine accessories
7 Wing rear spar attachment
8 Mainwheel door
9 Main undercarriage wheel well
10 Lateral control servo actuator
11 Hydraulic accumulator
12 Lower surface airbrake jack
13 Flap hydraulic jack
14 Starboard flap
15 Honeycomb control surface construction
16 Starboard aileron
17 Aileron power control unit
18 Flutter damper

68 Spoiler housing
69 Wing tank fuel vent
70 Dihedral outer wing panel
71 Rear identification light
72 Wing tip formation lighting
73 Starboard navigation light
74 Radar warning antenna
75 Outer wing panel construction
76 Outboard leading edge slat
77 Slat control linkage
78 Slat hydraulic jack
79 Outer wing panel attachment
80 Starboard wing fence
81 Fuel vent system shut-off valves
82 Top of main undercarriage leg

83 Outboard pylon attachment housing
84 Inboard slat hydraulic jack
85 Starboard outer pylon
86 Mainwheel leg door
87 Mainwheel brake discs
88 Starboard mainwheel
89 Starboard external fuel tank, capacity 1400 litres (370 US gal)
90 Inboard leading edge slat, open
91 Slat hinge linkages
92 Main undercarriage retraction jack
93 Undercarriage uplock
94 Starboard wing fuel tank, capacity 1192 litres (315 US gal)
95 Integral fuel tank construction

96 Inboard pylon fixing
97 Leading edge ranging antenna
98 Starboard inboard pylon
99 Twin missile launcher
100 AIM-9 Sidewinder
101 Hinged leading edge access panel
102 Wing front spar
103 Hydraulic reservoir
104 Centre fuselage formation lighting
105 Fuselage main frame
106 Engine intake compressor face
107 Intake duct construction
108 Fuselage No 2 fuel cell, capacity 700 litres (185 US gal)
109 Air-to-air refuelling receptacle, open
110 Port main undercarriage leg
111 Aileron power control unit
112 Port aileron
113 Aileron flutter damper
114 Port spoiler
115 Spoiler hydraulic jack
116 Wing fuel tank vent pipe
117 Port outer wing panel
118 Rearward identification light
119 Wing tip formation lighting
120 Port navigation light
121 Radar warning antenna
122 Port outboard leading edge slat
123 Slat hydraulic jack
124 Wing fence
125 Leading edge dog tooth
126 Inboard leading edge slat, open
127 Port external fuel tank, capacity 1400 litres (370 US gal)

128 Inboard slat hydraulic jack
129 Port wing fuel tank, capacity 1192 litres (315 US gal)
130 Upper fuselage light
131 IFF antenna
132 Avionics equipment bay
133 Gyro platform
134 Fuselage No 1 fuel cell, capacity 814 litres (215 US gal)
135 Intake duct
136 Hydraulic connections
137 Starter cartridge container
138 Pneumatic system air bottle
139 Engine bleed air supply pipe
140 Forward AIM-7 missile housing
141 Ventral fuel tank, capacity 2271 litres (600 US gal)
142 Bleed air louvre assembly, lower
143 Avionics equipment bay
144 Variable intake ramp jack
145 Bleed air louvre assembly, upper
146 Radar operator's Martin-Baker ejection seat
147 Safety harness
148 Face blind seat firing handle
149 Rear cockpit canopy cover
150 Front canopy hinges
151 Inter-canopy bridge section glazing
152 Radar operator's instrument console
153 Canopy jack
154 Port intake
155 Pilot's Martin-Baker ejection seat
156 Intake front ramp
157 Starboard intake
158 Bleed air holes
159 Boundary layer splitter plate
160 ALQ-119 electronic countermeasures pod (replaces forward Sparrow missile)

161 HOBOS 907-kg (2000-lb) guided bomb
162 Nosewheel door
163 AIM-7E-2 Sparrow missile semi-recessed housing
164 Forward formation lighting
165 Air conditioning plant
166 Battery
167 Pilot's starboard side console
168 Ejection seat safety harness
169 Engine throttles
170 Port intake front ramp
171 Forward cockpit canopy cover
172 Port inboard wing pylon
173 Pylon attachments
174 Triple ejector release unit
175 Mk 82 low profile 227-kg (500-lb) bombs
176 Extended bomb fuses
177 Windscreen panels
178 Pilot's lead computing sight
179 Instrument panel shroud
180 Control column
181 Rudder pedals
182 Cockpit front pressure bulkhead
183 Refrigeration plant
184 Communications antenna
185 Nosewheel jack
186 Nose undercarriage leg strut
187 Twin nosewheels
188 Nosewheel torque links
189 Landing and taxiing lamps
190 Air conditioning ram air intake
191 Angle of attack probe
192 Ammunition drum 640 rounds
193 Rain dispersal duct nozzle
194 ADF antenna
195 Gun bay frame construction
196 M61A-1 20-mm rotary barrel cannon
197 Cannon fairing
198 AN/APQ-120 fire control radar
199 Radar antenna mounting
200 Gun muzzle fairing
201 Radar scanner
202 Radome
203 Pitot tube

© Pilot Press Ltd

United States Marine Corps

The Phantom II remains a sizeable force within USMC front-line service though it is slowly giving way to the F/A-18A Hornet for its future fighter-attack duties. The F-4s are tasked with attaining air-superiority and providing close air support, assisting other elements by gaining the advantage over beach-heads. The original re-equipment plans called for the replacement of the F-4 by the F-14A Tomcat, but this was changed in favour of the Hornet, the Marine Corps accepting the consequent time delay. Four Marine Air Wings exist for the purpose of controlling the numerous front-line and training units, these being further sub-divided into Marine Aircraft Groups, the number of MAGs varying within each MAW. The Wings and Groups are divided between the Fleet Marine Force Pacific (FMFPac) and Fleet Marine Brigade, which has a single MAG.

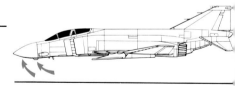

Despite the loss of their highly colourful markings in recent years, VMFA-333 has maintained its prominent shamrocks on the tailfin, albeit in a darker shade of grey.

2nd Marine Aircraft Wing/Marine Aircraft Group 31

VMFA-122 'Crusaders'
Base: MCAS Beaufort, South Carolina
Tailcode letters: 'DC'
Aircraft model: F-4S
Example aircraft:
157260/DC-9, 155783/DC-11

VMFA 134
Base: MCAS El Toro, California
Tailcode letters: 'MF'
Aircraft model: F-4N
Example aircraft: 152244/MF-106

VMFA-251 'Thunderbolts'
Base: MCAS Beaufort, South Carolina
Tailcode letters: 'DW'

Aircraft model: F-4S
Example aircraft:
158321/DW-07, 155805/DW-10, 155550/DW-15

VMFA-333 'Shamrocks'
Base: MCAS Beaufort, South Carolina
Tailcode letters: 'DN'
Aircraft model: F-4S
Example aircraft:
155792/DN-06, 158348/DN-11, 158352/DN-12

VMFA-451 'Warlords'
Base: MCAS Beaufort, South Carolina
Tailcode letters: 'VM'
Aircraft model: F-4S
Example aircraft:
155517/VM-02, 157309/VM-11

1st Marine Aircraft Wing/Marine Aircraft Group 15

VMFA-232 'Red Devils'
Base: MCAS Kaneohe Bay, Hawaii (but relocated to NAS Barbers Point, Hawaii until late 1986)
Tailcode letters: 'WT'
Aircraft model: F-4S
Example aircraft:
153889/WT-02, 157283/WT-07

1st Marine Brigade/Marine Aircraft Group 24

VMFA-212 'Lancers'
Base: MCAS Kaneohe Bay, Hawaii (but relocated to NAS Barbers Point, Hawaii until late 1986)
Tailcode letters: 'WD'
Aircraft model: F-4S
Example aircraft:
153791/WD-01, 153902/WD-06, 157281/WD-11

VMFA-235 'Death Angels'
Base: MCAS Kaneohe Bay, Hawaii (but relocated to NAS Barbers Point, Hawaii until late 1986)

3rd Marine Aircraft Wing/Marine Combat Crew Readiness Training Group 10

VMFAT-101
Base: MCAS Yuma, Arizona
Tailcode letters: 'SH'
Aircraft model: F-4S
Example aircraft:
158351/SH-31, 157291/SH-35

Tailcode letters: 'DB'
Aircraft model: F-4S
Example aircraft:
155547/DB-01, 158353/DB-12, 158362/DB-14

United States Marine Corps Air Reserve Force

Two squadrons within the Air Force Reserve are currently flying the F-4S as part of the 4th Marine Aircraft Wing, organized along the lines of the front line Wing/Group structure. Attempts to introduce more modern equipment and sub-variants have included the F-4S, which serves with the two Phantom II units.

4th Marine Aircraft Wing

VMFA-112
Base: NAS Dallas, Texas
Tailcode letters: 'MA'
Aircraft model: F-4S
Example aircraft:
153856/MA-00, 155527/MA-03, 155531/MA-04

VMFA-321 'Black Barons'
Base: NAF Washington, DC
Tailcode letters: 'MG'
Aircraft model: F-4S
Example aircraft:
153809/MG-01, 153860/MG-10, 153832/MG-14

F-4 Phantom II US fighter variants

XF4H-1: two prototypes built to meet the US Navy's fleet defence requirement of the mid-1950s; these had the original short, pointed nose and shallow canopies, plus 12° dihedral on the outer wing panels and 23° anhedral on the stabilators

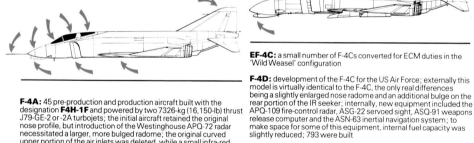

F-4A: 45 pre-production and production aircraft built with the designation **F4H-1F** and powered by two 7326-kg (16,150-lb) thrust J79-GE-2 or -2A turbojets; the initial aircraft retained the original nose profile, but introduction of the Westinghouse APQ-72 radar necessitated a larger, more bulged radome; the original curved upper portion of the air inlets was deleted, while a small infra-red sensor housing was added beneath the nose

TF-4A: a small number of F-4As converted for training duties; the arrester hook and combat equipment were deleted

F-4B: the first major production variant with a total of 649 built (originally under the designation **F4H-1**) for the US Navy and Marine Corps; powered by two J79-GE-8A or J79-GE-8B turbojets each rated at 7711-kg (17,000-lb) static thrust, this model featured the larger nose radome and IR sensor as standard fits; the original rear canopy was replaced by a deeper, more bubble-shaped canopy; inflight-refuelling was possible with a probe on the starboard forward fuselage, while underwing pylons could carry Sparrow or Sidewinder air-to-air missiles

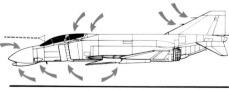

DF-4B: rebuilt F-4Bs used as drone mother ships for the remote control of QF-4Bs

EF-4B: one F-4B converted for ECM training

NF-4B: one F-4B used for development testing

QF-4B: 44 F-4Bs converted for use as pilotless target drones

F-4C: variant of the F-4B for the US Air Force, originally designated **F-110A** and powered by J79-GE-15s of 7711-kg thrust; external differences include wider low-pressure main tyres and an inflight-refuelling receptacle in the fuselage spine aft of the cockpits; internally, the avionics were completely revised to include the ASN-48 inertial navigation system, APQ-100 radar and AJB-7 bombing system; dual flight controls were fitted as standard; 583 were built, production ending in 1966

EF-4C: a small number of F-4Cs converted for ECM duties in the 'Wild Weasel' configuration

F-4D: development of the F-4C for the US Air Force; externally this model is virtually identical to the F-4C, the only real differences being a slightly enlarged nose radome and an additional bulge on the rear portion of the IR seeker; internally, new equipment included the APQ-109 fire-control radar, ASG-22 servoed sight, ASQ-91 weapons release computer and the ASN-63 inertial navigation system; to make space for some of this equipment, internal fuel capacity was slightly reduced; 793 were built

EF-4D: a number of F-4Ds converted for ECM duties in the 'Wild Weasel' configuration

YF-4E: one YRF-4C converted for tests as the F-4E prototype

F-4E: multi-role variant for the US Air Force; among the significant additions were wing leading-edge slats which replaced the original blown leading-edge flaps, slotted stabilators, and an internally-mounted M61A1 20-mm multi-barrel cannon with a prominent undernose firing point; in the mid-1970s a cylindrical housing was added to the inner leading edge of the port wing, this carrying the Northrop Target Identification System Electro-Optical (TISEO) to aid positive identification of targets; a new powerplant, in the form of two 8119-kg (17,900-lb) thrust J79-GE-17s, was also fitted, along with an APQ-120C fire-control radar and a seventh fuselage fuel cell

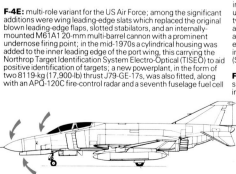

F-4G: originally 12 F-4Bs fitted with ASW-21 digital data-link system and used by the US Navy over Vietnam; the aircraft were later reconverted to F-4B configuration

F-4G 'Advanced Wild Weasel': 116 F-4Es converted for use in the electronic warfare role to suppress enemy radar emitters; externally, the F-4G is easily distinguished by the prominent fairing atop the vertical tail, this housing antennas for the APR-38 radar homing and warning system, further APR-38 subsystems being housed in a chin pod replacing the fire point for the cannon, which has been removed; much new equipment is fitted to enable the F-4G to carry out its mission, this being reflected in the rear cockpit especially, where the front instrument panel extends up to the top of the canopy; a large variety of armaments can be carried to eliminate electromagnetic emitters

YF-4J: three F-4Bs converted for testing as prototypes for the F-4J

F-4J: development of the F-4B for Navy/Marine Corps use primarily as an interceptor, but with a ground attack capability; slotted stabilators and 16.5° drooping ailerons fitted to reduce carrier approach speeds; the thicker tyres, main wheels and main wings adopted from USAF models; a later fit saw ECM fairings added to the air inlets, along with main wing leading-edge slats; the IR seeker pod was deleted from its undernose position, and the afterburner nozzles extended in length; internally, the Westinghouse AWG-10 pulse-Doppler fire-control system and the Lear Siegler AJB-7 bombing system were added as standard fits

F-4N: a conversion programme to update some 228 F-4Bs involving the remanufacturing of the airframe structure and the updating of the avionics; the F-4N retains the thinner wheels and tyres and J79-GE-8 engines, while incorporating ECM fairings on the air inlets (longer fairings than on the F-4J), and in some cases having an additional antenna fairing at the top of the vertical tail leading edge; the undernose IR seeker is retained; avionics updates include the addition of a Sidewinder Expanded Acquisition Mode (SEAM), dogfight computer and Identification Friend or Foe (IFF)

F-4S: a conversion of the F-4J including outer-wing manoeuvring slats, smokeless or low-smoke J79-GE-10B turbojets and an improved AWG-10A weapons-control system

F-4 Phantom II warload

Enhanced air-to-air interception

1 × SUU-23/A Vulcan six-barrel 20-mm cannon pod with 1,200 rounds mounted on the underfuselage centreline station
4 × AIM-9L Sidewinder IR-homing AAMs, one pair shoulder-mounted on each inner pylon triple ejector rack
4 × AIM-7D Sparrow semi-active radar-homing AAMs, each semi-recessed in one of the four underfuselage stations
2 × 370-US gal (1401-litre) drop tanks, one on each outer underwing station

One feature lacking from the early models of the F-4 was an internally-mounted cannon, such a weapon being omitted in the belief that guided missiles would be all-conquering. Reality proved this to be wrong and the Vulcan cannon pod has become a regular sight on the F-4C and F-4D as well as the Navy/Marine Corps models.

Ground attack

12 × Mk 82 Snakeye high-drag 500-lb (227-kg) bombs, three on each inner underwing pylon triple ejector rack and six mounted in two triple clusters on the underfuselage centreline multiple ejector rack
1 × ALQ-119 dual-mode ECM jammer pod, mounted in the forward port semi-recessed station
2 × 370-US gal (1401-litre) drop tanks, one on each outer underwing pylon

A wide variety of bombs can be carried depending on specific mission requirements, this configuration representing the usual quantities of bombs carried per pylon. Taking off with maximum thrust, the aircraft climbs to its optimum cruise altitude, later dropping down to sea level and searching out the target(s). A search time of 5 minutes is available at military thrust, plus a reserve of 20 minutes loiter at sea level.

Standard air-to-air interception

4 × AIM-9L Sidewinder IR-homing AAMs one pair shoulder-mounted on each inner pylon triple ejector rack
4 × AIM-7D Sparrow semi-active radar-homing AAMs, each semi-recessed in one of the four underfuselage stations
2 × 370-US gal (1401-litre) drop tanks, one on each outer underwing station

Common on US Navy F-4s for many years, this configuration is still used by Air National Guard and Air Force Reserve units tasked with intercepting enemy intruders over the USA. The patrol often involves flying at maximum endurance altitudes, full use being made of the powerful engines to give high closing speeds on the target. The AIM-9s provide a short-range attack capability, while the AIM-7s allow for a degree of stand-off target destruction.

F-4E precision attack/close-air support

1 × M61A1 Vulcan 20-mm cannon with 640 rounds mounted internally in the forward fuselage
6 × AGM-65 Maverick air-to-surface missiles, mounted in groups of three on the inner underwing pylon triple ejector racks
1 × ALQ-131 advanced ECM jamming pod, mounted in the forward port semi-recessed station
2 × 370-US gal (1401-litre) drop tanks, one on each outer underwing station

This is one of the modern weapons configurations available to the large F-4E force, both in Europe and North America, various models of the Maverick being compatible with the F-4E fire-control system. If there is a stabilized ground laser designator or other aircraft flying with laser designating equipment, the AGM-65C/E can be used, while the AGM-65D IR Maverick can be launched day or night in adverse weather conditions.

F-4G anti-radar attack

1 × AGM-45A Shrike anti-radiation air-to-surface missile mounted on the port inner underwing pylon
1 × AGM-65 Maverick air-to-surface missile mounted on the starboard inner underwing pylon
1 × ALQ-119 dual-mode ECM jammer pod mounted in the forward port underfuselage semi-recessed station
2 × 370-US gal (1401-litre) drop tanks, one on each outer underwing pylon
1 × 600-US gal (2271-litre) drop tank mounted on the underfuselage centreline station

Designed specifically to go in, root out and destroy enemy air-defence systems, the F-4G 'Advanced Wild Weasel' offers formidable detection and attack capabilities through a wide range of weapons and its highly effective APR-38 system. If there is a stabilized ground laser designator providing threat information and data for automatic weapons release and a blind-bombing capability. In this configuration the emphasis is on attack.

F-4G advanced anti-radar attack

2 × AIM-9M Sidewinder IR-homing AAMs, one on each inner underwing pylon
2 × AGM-88A HARM anti-radiation air-to-surface missiles, one on each outer underwing pylon
2 × AIM-7F Sparrow semi-active radar-homing AAMs, one semi-recessed in each of the two rear underfuselage stations
1 × ALQ-131 advanced ECM jamming pod mounted in the forward port underfuselage semi-recessed station
1 × 600-US gal (2271-litre) drop tank mounted on the underfuselage centreline station

This is the latest radar-suppression configuration now being used by F-4G 'Advanced Wild Weasel' units with the HARM (High-speed Anti-Radiation Missile) replacing the Shrike as the primary attack weapon and allowing for a greater range of potential targets to be attacked other than those associated with surface-to-air systems.

Specification: F-4E Phantom II

Wings

Span	11.71 m	(38 ft 5 in)
Width wings folded	8.39 m	(27 ft 6.5 in)
Area	29.24 m²	(530.0 sq ft)

Fuselage and tail unit

Accommodation	pilot and radar intercept officer on ejector seats	
Length overall	19.20 m	(63 ft 0 in)
Height overall	5.03 m	(16 ft 6 in)
Tailplane span	5.47 m	(17 ft 11.5 in)

Landing gear

Retractable tricycle landing gear with single-wheel main and twin wheel nose units

Wheelbase	7.12 m	(23 ft 4.5 in)
Wheel track	5.45 m	(17 ft 10.5 in)

Weights

Empty	13757 kg	(30,328 lb)
Combat take-off	18818 kg	(41,487 lb)
Maximum take-off	28030 kg	(61,795 lb)
Maximum external load	7257 kg	(16,000 lb)
Internal fuel load	5575 kg	(12,290 lb)
Maximum external fuel	4005 kg	(8,830 lb)

F-4E Phantom II recognition features

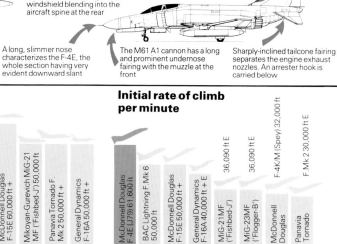

The fuselage sides are bulged but with smooth contours to house the side-by-side engine arrangement

Pronounced anhedral on the one-piece, all-moving stabilator

Very wide-track, single-wheel main landing gear

Outer main wing sections have 12° dihedral

Very noticeable downward angle of the fuselage when viewed head-on

Very deep but relatively narrow engine air intakes, the boundary-layer splitter plate extending well forward

Very broad, swept vertical tail surfaces

Long, narrow and smoothly-contoured main canopies and windshield blending into the aircraft spine at the rear

The fuselage tapers very sharply aft of the engine exhaust nozzles

A long, slimmer nose characterizes the F-4E, the whole section having very evident downward slant

The M61 A1 cannon has a long and prominent undernose fairing with the muzzle at the front

Sharply-inclined tailcone fairing separates the engine exhaust nozzles. An arrester hook is carried below

---

Performance:

Maximum speed, at 40,000 ft (12190 m) Mach 2.25 or 1290 kts (2390 km/h; 1,485 mph)

Maximum speed at sea level	Mach 1.18 or 780 kts	(1445 km/h; 898 mph)
Cruising speed at optimum altitude	508 kts	(941 km/h; 585 mph)
Initial rate of climb	61,400 ft	(18715 m) per minute
Combat ceiling	57,200 ft	(17435 m)
Service ceiling	62,250 ft	(18975 m)
Combat radius Hi-Lo-Hi with two 1400 litre (370 US gal) tanks	680 km	(423 miles)
Ferry range	3034 km	(1,885 miles)
Take-off distance to clear 50 ft (15 m) obstacle	1792 m	(5,880 ft)

Service ceiling

- McDonnell Douglas F-4E (J79) 62,250 ft
- Mikoyan-Gurevich MiG-23MF ('Flogger-B') 61,000 ft E
- BAC Lightning F.Mk 6 60,000 ft +
- McDonnell Douglas F-4K/M (Spey) 60,000 ft
- McDonnell Douglas F-15E 60,000 ft +
- Mikoyan-Gurevich MiG-21 MF ('Fishbed-J') 50,000 ft
- Panavia Tornado F.Mk 2 50,000 ft
- General Dynamics F-16A 50,000 ft +

Initial rate of climb per minute

- McDonnell Douglas F-4E (J79) 61,600 ft
- BAC Lightning F.Mk 6 50,000 ft
- McDonnell Douglas F-15E 50,000 ft +
- General Dynamics F-16A 40,000 ft + E
- MiG-21MF ('Fishbed-J') 36,090 ft E
- MiG-23MF ('Flogger-B') 36,090 ft E
- McDonnell Douglas F-4K/M (Spey) 32,000 ft
- Panavia Tornado F.Mk 2 30,000 ft E

Maximum speed at high altitude

McDonnell Douglas F-15E Mach 2.5 +	
Mikoyan-Gurevich MiG-23MF ('Flogger-B')	Mach 2.35 E
BAC Lightning F.Mk 6 Mach 2.27	
McDonnell Douglas F-4E (J79) Mach 2.25	
Panavia Tornado F.Mk 2 Mach 2.16	
McDonnell Douglas F-4K/M (Spey)	Mach 2.1
Mikoyan-Gurevich MiG-21MF ('Fishbed-J')	Mach 2.1
General Dynamics F-16A Mach 2.0 +	

Maximum speed at sea level

McDonnell Douglas F-15E Mach 1.23	
McDonnell Douglas F-4K/M (Spey) Mach 1.2	
Mikoyan-Gurevich MiG-23MF ('Flogger-B')	Mach 1.2 E
McDonnell Douglas F-4E (J79) Mach 1.18	
Panavia Tornado F.Mk 2 Mach 1.1	
Mikoyan-Gurevich MiG-21MF ('Fishbed-J')	Mach 1.06
BAC Lightning F.Mk 6 Mach 1.06	
General Dynamics F-16A Mach 1.0	

Combat radius Hi-Lo-Hi

McDonnell Douglas F-15E 1200 km +	
Mikoyan-Gurevich MiG-23MF ('Flogger-B')	1000 km E
General Dynamics F-16A 925 km +	
McDonnell Douglas F-4K/M (Spey)	805 km
Mikoyan-Gurevich MiG-21MF	('Fishbed-J') 740 km
Panavia Tornado F.Mk 2	725 km E
McDonnell Douglas F-4E	(J79) 680 km
BAC Lightning F.Mk 6	600 km

ley during the closing months of 1976, and the first of these was classed mission-ready in mid-January 1977, by which time the delivery of Eagles earmarked for service with the 36th TFW had begun, these also finding their way to Langley. Eventually, with training complete, 20 F-15As and three TF-15As set course across the Atlantic on 27 April 1977, these all reaching Bitburg safely during the same afternoon. The 36th TFW's other two squadrons made use of the same training scheme, the 53rd TFS deploying to Bitburg in July while the 22nd TFS followed in October.

Ongoing production

Continuing procurement of the F-15A variant enabled two more TAC wings and one more USAFE squadron to be equipped during the 1977-9 timeframe, production thereafter switching to the F-15C and the basically similar two-seat F-15D.

Flown for the first time on 27 February 1979, the F-15C has been the major production model for the past few years and, while there are no noticeable external differences between the F-15A and the F-15C, the later derivative does feature an improved version of the Hughes APG-63 radar and additional fuel capacity. In addition, it is also compatible with the company-developed FAST (Fuel and Sensor Tactical) packs, whereby conformal fuel tanks and/or sensor packages can be attached to the outside of each air inlet, these permitting close to 2268 kg (5,000 lb) of extra fuel or a variety of sensors (such as reconnaissance cameras, infra-red equipment, radar warning receivers, laser designators and low-light-level television cameras) to be carried. Thus, overall capability of the Eagle has been significantly enhanced.

Operational deployment of the F-15C and F-15D began in 1979. The 18th TFW at Kadena, Okinawa was the first unit to receive this version, re-equipment of this wing's three squadrons being effected between September 1979 and April 1980. Subsequent deliveries were made to existing Eagle units, most of which were

In the United States, Japan, Germany and the Netherlands, USAF Eagles are alert, waiting for the call to action. The Eagle is widely regarded as the best fighter in the world, able to dominate contested airspace with its wide envelope of capabilities.

progressively re-equipped during the early 1980s.

Re-equipment for CONUS

The availability of older F-15As made more or less redundant by the advent of the F-15C has enabled a number of other units to re-equip with the Eagle, and one particularly advantageous manifestation of this process has been the progressive updating of those elements dedicated to the air defence of the continental USA. Mainly equipped with the Convair F-106A Delta Dart, a fine interceptor in its own right but one now rather long in the tooth, these units have been long overdue for an infusion of more modern equipment. This process finally got under way in August 1981 when Air Defense Tactical Air Command's 48th Fighter Interceptor Squadron at Langley received its first F-15A; the squadron attained operational status during 1982. The McChord-based 318th FIS followed in 1983, and plans are in hand for at least three more ADTAC interceptor squadrons to convert to the Eagle during the next few years. The command's Air Defense Weapons Center at Tyndall AFB, Florida was re-equipped in 1984, this essentially fulfilling a training function. In addition to their primary role of countering the threat posed by bomber aircraft, some ADTAC squadrons are to be employed in the ASAT anti-satellite mission, current planning calling for 36 Eagles to be configured to carry this Vought-developed weapon.

As well as the versions already discussed, the USAF is to receive 392

A view of the F-15's underside shows the relatively large wing and stabilators, and their smooth contours blending into the fuselage. The wingtips are clipped at a diagonal angle to solve wing loading and buffet problems, while the stabilators' leading-edge saw-tooth eradicates flutter.

examples of a dedicated all-weather interdictor/strike variant designated F-15E but known by the parent company as the 'Strike Eagle'. Flown for the first time on 8 July 1980, this began life as a company-funded private venture incorporating improvements to the radar and avionics systems. It very quickly caught the eye of the USAF, which called for a comparative evaluation between the Strike Eagle and the General Dynamics F-16E model of the Fighting Falcon. Conducted at Edwards AFB during the course of 1983, this evaluation resulted in a decision for the F-15E, and deliveries are presently expected to begin in 1988, initially to supplement and eventually to replace the General Dynamics F-111. Equipment to be installed in the F-15E includes the LANTIRN night nav/attack pod system, FLIR sensors, threat-warning displays, digital map displays, APG-70 radar, a wide-angle HUD, an improved mission computer and provision for AIM-120 AMRAAM missiles in place of the AIM-7F Sparrow which, in conjunction with the AIM-9L Sidewinder heat-seeking missile and the integral M61 Vulcan cannon, presently constitutes the Eagle's talons.

Although most Eagles built to date have been earmarked for service with the USAF, the type has also achieved a measure of success on the export market, overseas customers comprising Israel, Japan and Saudi Arabia.

Glossary

ASAT Anti-SATellite
EW Electronic Warfare
FAST Fuel And Sensor Tactical
FLIR Forward-Looking Infra-Red
HUD Head-Up Display
LANTIRN Low-Altitude Navigation and Targeting IR for Night
MiGCAP MiG Combat Air Patrol

US Air Force F-15 Eagle in service units and example aircraft

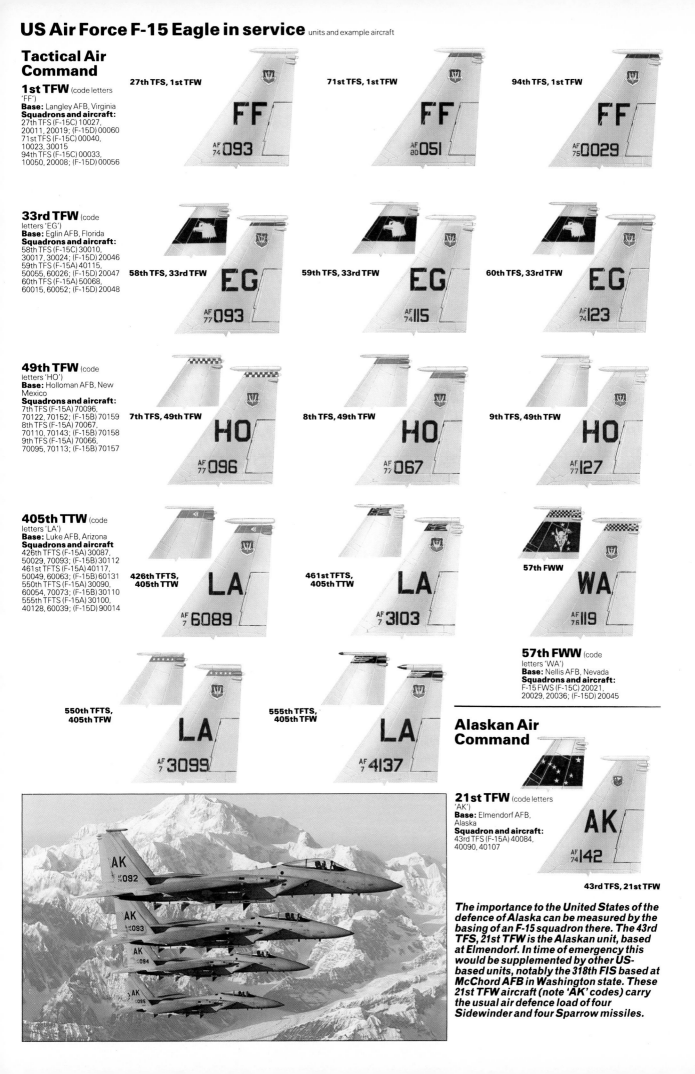

Tactical Air Command

1st TFW (code letters 'FF')
Base: Langley AFB, Virginia
Squadrons and aircraft:
27th TFS (F-15C) 10027, 20011, 20019; (F-15D) 00060
71st TFS (F-15C) 00040, 10023, 30015
94th TFS (F-15C) 00033, 10050, 20008; (F-15D) 00056

27th TFS, 1st TFW

71st TFS, 1st TFW

94th TFS, 1st TFW

AF 74 093

AF 80 051

AF 75 0029

33rd TFW (code letters 'EG')
Base: Eglin AFB, Florida
Squadrons and aircraft:
58th TFS (F-15C) 30010, 30017, 30024; (F-15D) 20046
59th TFS (F-15A) 40115, 50055, 60026; (F-15D) 20047
60th TFS (F-15A) 50068, 60015, 60052; (F-15D) 20048

58th TFS, 33rd TFW

59th TFS, 33rd TFW

60th TFS, 33rd TFW

EG AF 77 093

EG AF 74 115

EG AF 74 123

49th TFW (code letters 'HO')
Base: Holloman AFB, New Mexico
Squadrons and aircraft:
7th TFS (F-15A) 70096, 70122, 70152; (F-15B) 70159
8th TFS (F-15A) 70067, 70110, 70143; (F-15B) 70158
9th TFS (F-15A) 70066, 70095, 70113; (F-15B) 70157

7th TFS, 49th TFW

8th TFS, 49th TFW

9th TFS, 49th TFW

HO AF 77 096

HO AF 77 067

HO AF 77 127

405th TTW (code letters 'LA')
Base: Luke AFB, Arizona
Squadrons and aircraft
426th TFTS (F-15A) 30087, 50029, 70093; (F-15B) 30112
461st TFTS (F-15A) 40117, 50049, 60063; (F-15B) 60131
550th TFTS (F-15A) 30090, 60054, 70073; (F-15B) 30110
555th TFTS (F-15A) 30100, 40128, 60039; (F-15D) 90014

426th TFTS, 405th TTW

461st TFTS, 405th TTW

57th FWW

LA AF 7 6089

LA AF 7 3103

WA AF 76 119

550th TFTS, 405th TFW

555th TFTS, 405th TFW

LA AF 7 3099

LA AF 7 4137

57th FWW (code letters 'WA')
Base: Nellis AFB, Nevada
Squadrons and aircraft:
F-15 FWS (F-15C) 20021, 20029, 20036; (F-15D) 20045

Alaskan Air Command

21st TFW (code letters 'AK')
Base: Elmendorf AFB, Alaska
Squadron and aircraft:
43rd TFS (F-15A) 40084, 40090, 40107

AK AF 74 142

43rd TFS, 21st TFW

The importance to the United States of the defence of Alaska can be measured by the basing of an F-15 squadron there. The 43rd TFS, 21st TFW is the Alaskan unit, based at Elmendorf. In time of emergency this would be supplemented by other US-based units, notably the 318th FIS based at McChord AFB in Washington state. These 21st TFW aircraft (note 'AK' codes) carry the usual air defence load of four Sidewinder and four Sparrow missiles.

Air Defense Tactical Air Command

325th TTW (code letters 'TY')
Base: Tyndall AFB, Florida
Squadrons and aircraft:
1st TFTS (F-15A) 40101, 40132, 50027; (F-15B) 40140
2nd TFTS (F-15A) 40112, 50022, 50080; (F-15B) 50086

1st TFTS, 325th TTW

2nd TFTS, 325th TTW

48th FIS
Base: Langley AFB, Virginia
Aircraft: (F-15A) 60084, 60097, 60117

48th FIS

United States Air Forces in Europe

36th TFW (code letters 'BT')
Base: Bitburg AB, West Germany
Squadrons and aircraft:
22nd TFS (F-15C) 90057, 00010, 00026; (F-15D) 90011
53rd TFS (F-15C) 90067, 00011, 00028; (F-15D) 90010
525th TFS (F-15C) 90041, 90061, 00018; (F-15D) 90007

22nd TFS, 36th TFW

53rd TFS, 36th TFW

525th TFS, 36th TFW

Pacific Air Forces

18th TFW (code letters 'ZZ')
Base: Kadena AB, Okinawa
Squadrons and aircraft:
12th TFS, 44th TFS, 67th TFS (F-15C) 80477, 80479, 80481, 80497, 80512, 80537, 80543; (F-15D) 80562

all squadrons, 18th TFW

Non-operational units

4485th TS (code letters 'OT')
Base: Eglin AFB, Florida
Aircraft: (F-15A) 70064; (F-15C) 80542

6512nd TS/ AFFTC (code letters 'ED')
Base: Edwards AFB, California
Aircraft: (F-15A) 60084, 70139; (F-15B) 70166; (F-15C) 80468

3246th TW/ AFAD (code letters 'AD')
Base: Eglin AFB, Florida
Aircraft: (F-15A) 50035; (F-15B) 70160

4485th TS

Warner Robin ALC (code letters 'R...
Base: Robins AFB, Ge...
Aircraft: (F-15A) 700...

McDonnell Douglas F-15C Eagle cutaway drawing key

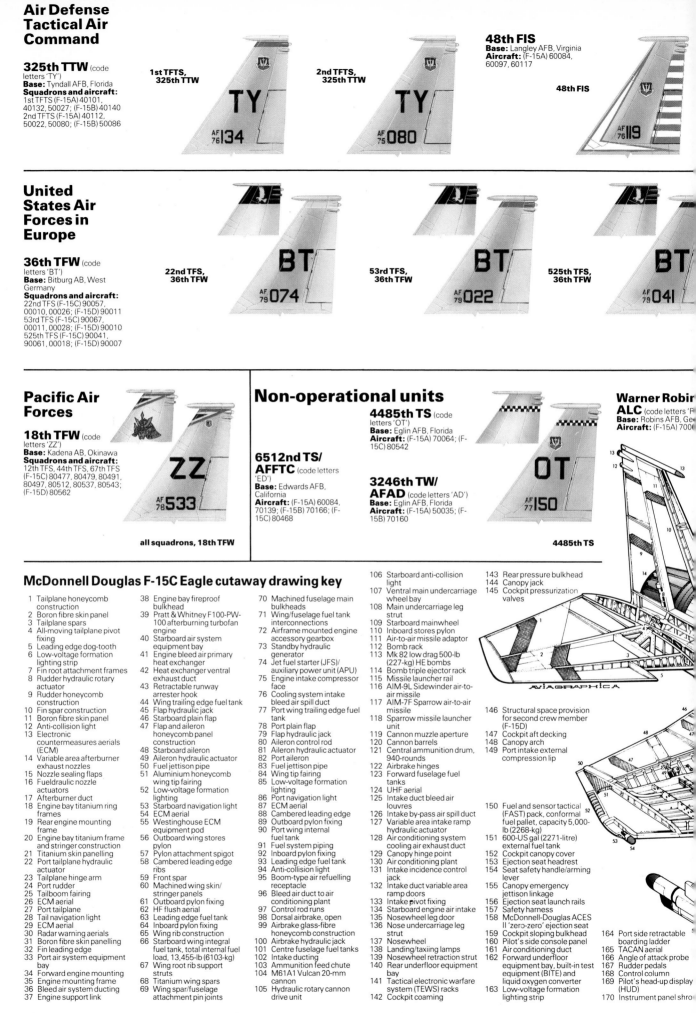

1 Tailplane honeycomb construction
2 Boron fibre skin panel
3 Tailplane spars
4 All-moving tailplane pivot fixing
5 Leading edge dog-tooth
6 Low-voltage formation lighting strip
7 Fin root attachment frames
8 Rudder hydraulic rotary actuator
9 Rudder honeycomb construction
10 Fin spar construction
11 Boron fibre skin panel
12 Anti-collision light
13 Electronic countermeasures aerials (ECM)
14 Variable area afterburner exhaust nozzles
15 Nozzle sealing flaps
16 Fuel hydraulic nozzle actuators
17 Afterburner duct
18 Engine bay titanium ring frames
19 Rear engine mounting frame
20 Engine bay titanium frame and stringer construction
21 Titanium skin panelling
22 Port tailplane hydraulic actuator
23 Tailplane hinge arm
24 Port rudder
25 Tailboom fairing
26 ECM aerial
27 Port tailplane
28 Tail navigation light
29 ECM aerial
30 Radar warning aerials
31 Boron fibre skin panelling
32 Fin leading edge
33 Port air system equipment bay
34 Forward engine mounting
35 Engine mounting frame
36 Bleed air system ducting
37 Engine support link

38 Engine bay fireproof bulkhead
39 Pratt & Whitney F100-PW-100 afterburning turbofan engine
40 Starboard air system equipment bay
41 Engine bleed air primary heat exchanger
42 Heat exchanger ventral exhaust duct
43 Retractable runway arrester hook
44 Wing trailing edge fuel tank
45 Flap hydraulic jack
46 Starboard plain flap
47 Flap and aileron honeycomb panel construction
48 Starboard aileron
49 Aileron hydraulic actuator
50 Fuel jettison pipe
51 Aluminium honeycomb wing tip fairing
52 Low-voltage formation lighting
53 Starboard navigation light
54 ECM aerial
55 Westinghouse ECM equipment pod
56 Outboard wing stores pylon
57 Pylon attachment spigot
58 Cambered leading edge ribs
59 Front spar
60 Machined wing skin/ stringer panels
61 Outboard pylon fixing
62 HF flush aerial
63 Leading edge fuel tank
64 Inboard pylon fixing
65 Wing rib construction
66 Starboard wing integral fuel tank, total internal fuel load, 13,455-lb (6103-kg)
67 Wing root rib support struts
68 Titanium wing spars
69 Wing spar/fuselage attachment pin joints

70 Machined fuselage main bulkheads
71 Wing/fuselage fuel tank interconnections
72 Airframe mounted engine accessory gearbox
73 Standby hydraulic generator
74 Jet fuel starter (JFS)/ auxiliary power unit (APU)
75 Engine intake compressor face
76 Cooling system intake bleed air spill duct
77 Port wing trailing edge fuel tank
78 Port plain flap
79 Flap hydraulic jack
80 Aileron control rod
81 Aileron hydraulic actuator
82 Port aileron
83 Fuel jettison pipe
84 Wing tip fairing
85 Low-voltage formation lighting
86 Port navigation light
87 ECM aerial
88 Cambered leading edge
89 Outboard pylon fixing
90 Port wing internal fuel tank
91 Fuel system piping
92 Inboard pylon fixing
93 Leading edge fuel tank
94 Anti-collision light
95 Boom-type air refuelling receptacle
96 Bleed air duct to air conditioning plant
97 Control rod runs
98 Dorsal airbrake, open
99 Airbrake glass-fibre honeycomb construction
100 Airbrake hydraulic jack
101 Centre fuselage fuel tanks
102 Intake ducting
103 Ammunition feed chute
104 M61A1 Vulcan 20-mm cannon
105 Hydraulic rotary cannon drive unit

106 Starboard anti-collision light
107 Ventral main undercarriage wheel bay
108 Main undercarriage leg strut
109 Starboard mainwheel
110 Inboard stores pylon
111 Air-to-air missile adaptor
112 Bomb rack
113 Mk 82 low drag 500-lb (227-kg) HE bombs
114 Bomb triple ejector rack
115 Missile launcher rail
116 AIM-9L Sidewinder air-to-air missile
117 AIM-7F Sparrow air-to-air missile
118 Sparrow missile launcher unit
119 Cannon muzzle aperture
120 Cannon barrels
121 Central ammunition drum, 940-rounds
122 Airbrake hinges
123 Forward fuselage fuel tanks
124 UHF aerial
125 Intake duct bleed air louvres
126 Intake by-pass air spill duct
127 Variable area intake ramp hydraulic actuator
128 Air conditioning system cooling air exhaust duct
129 Cannon hinge point
130 Air conditioning plant
131 Intake incidence control jack
132 Intake duct variable area ramp doors
133 Intake pivot fixing
134 Starboard engine air intake
135 Nosewheel leg door
136 Nose undercarriage leg strut
137 Nosewheel
138 Landing/taxiing lamps
139 Nosewheel retraction strut
140 Rear underfloor equipment bay
141 Tactical electronic warfare system (TEWS) racks
142 Cockpit coaming

143 Rear pressure bulkhead
144 Canopy jack
145 Cockpit pressurization valves

146 Structural space provision for second crew member (F-15D)
147 Cockpit aft decking
148 Canopy arch
149 Port intake external compression lip

150 Fuel and sensor tactical (FAST) pack, conformal fuel pallet, capacity 5,000-lb (2268-kg)
151 600-US gal (2271-litre) external fuel tank
152 Cockpit canopy cover
153 Ejection seat headrest
154 Seat safety handle/arming lever
155 Canopy emergency jettison linkage
156 Ejection seat launch rails
157 Safety harness
158 McDonnell-Douglas ACES II 'zero-zero' ejection seat
159 Cockpit sloping bulkhead
160 Pilot's side console panel
161 Air conditioning duct
162 Forward underfloor equipment bay, built-in test equipment (BITE) and liquid oxygen converter
163 Low-voltage formation lighting strip

164 Port side retractable boarding ladder
165 TACAN aerial
166 Angle of attack probe
167 Rudder pedals
168 Control column
169 Pilot's head-up display (HUD)
170 Instrument panel shro...

F-15 Eagle recognition points

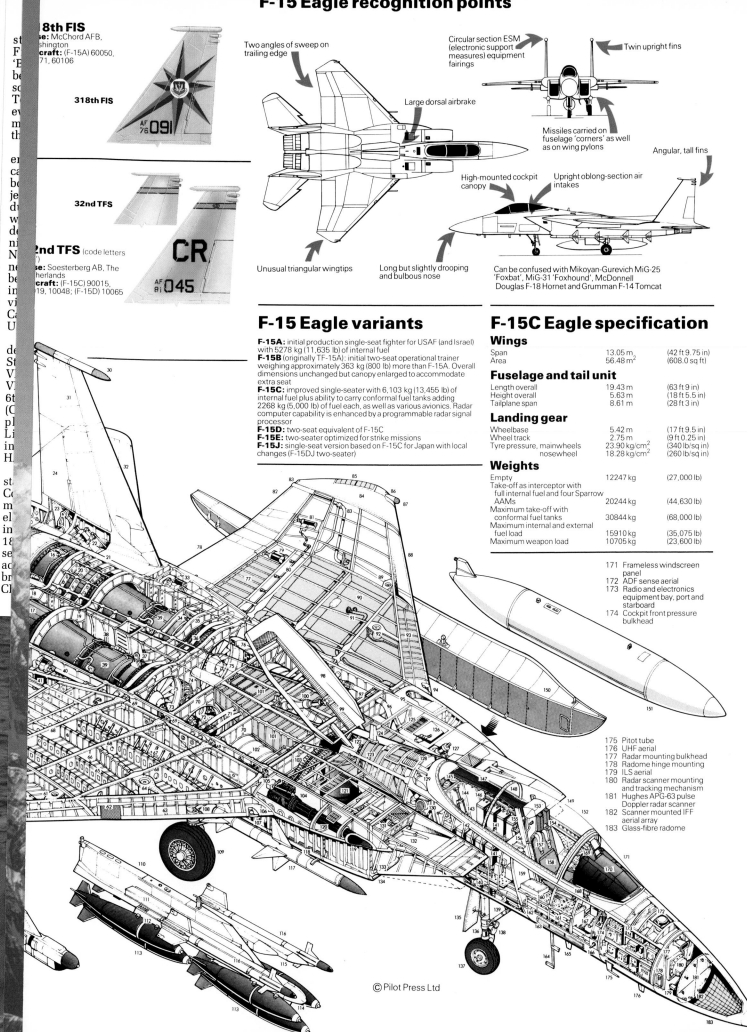

318th FIS

18th FIS
Base: McChord AFB, Washington
Aircraft: (F-15A) 60050, ...71, 60106

32nd TFS

32nd TFS (code letters ...)
Base: Soesterberg AB, The Netherlands
Aircraft: (F-15C) 90015, ...19, 10048; (F-15D) 10065

Two angles of sweep on trailing edge

Large dorsal airbrake

Unusual triangular wingtips

Long but slightly drooping and bulbous nose

Circular section ESM (electronic support measures) equipment fairings

Twin upright fins

Missiles carried on fuselage 'corners' as well as on wing pylons

Angular, tall fins

High-mounted cockpit canopy

Upright oblong-section air intakes

Can be confused with Mikoyan-Gurevich MiG-25 'Foxbat', MiG-31 'Foxhound', McDonnell Douglas F-18 Hornet and Grumman F-14 Tomcat

F-15 Eagle variants

F-15A: initial production single-seat fighter for USAF (and Israel) with 5278 kg (11,635 lb) of internal fuel
F-15B (originally TF-15A): initial two-seat operational trainer weighing approximately 363 kg (800 lb) more than F-15A. Overall dimensions unchanged but canopy enlarged to accommodate extra seat
F-15C: improved single-seater with 6,103 kg (13,455 lb) of internal fuel plus ability to carry conformal fuel tanks adding 2268 kg (5,000 lb) of fuel each, as well as various avionics. Radar computer capability is enhanced by a programmable radar signal processor
F-15D: two-seat equivalent of F-15C
F-15E: two-seater optimized for strike missions
F-15J: single-seat version based on F-15C for Japan with local changes (F-15DJ two-seater)

F-15C Eagle specification

Wings

Span	13.05 m	(42 ft 9.75 in)
Area	56.48 m²	(608.0 sq ft)

Fuselage and tail unit

Length overall	19.43 m	(63 ft 9 in)
Height overall	5.63 m	(18 ft 5.5 in)
Tailplane span	8.61 m	(28 ft 3 in)

Landing gear

Wheelbase	5.42 m	(17 ft 9.5 in)
Wheel track	2.75 m	(9 ft 0.25 in)
Tyre pressure, mainwheels	23.90 kg/cm²	(340 lb/sq in)
nosewheel	18.28 kg/cm²	(260 lb/sq in)

Weights

Empty	12247 kg	(27,000 lb)
Take-off as interceptor with full internal fuel and four Sparrow AAMs	20244 kg	(44,630 lb)
Maximum take-off with conformal fuel tanks	30844 kg	(68,000 lb)
Maximum internal and external fuel load	15910 kg	(35,075 lb)
Maximum weapon load	10705 kg	(23,600 lb)

171 Frameless windscreen panel
172 ADF sense aerial
173 Radio and electronics equipment bay, port and starboard
174 Cockpit front pressure bulkhead

175 Pitot tube
176 UHF aerial
177 Radar mounting bulkhead
178 Radome hinge mounting
179 ILS aerial
180 Radar scanner mounting and tracking mechanism
181 Hughes APG-63 pulse Doppler radar scanner
182 Scanner mounted IFF aerial array
183 Glass-fibre radome

Warload

1×M61 A1 20-mm six-barrel cannon with 570 rounds of ammunition mounted in the nose
2×AIM-9M Sidewinder heat-seeking air-to-air missiles, one on each wingtip missile rail
2×AIM-7M Sparrow radar-guided air-to-air missiles, one per underfuselage pylon

Standard air-to-air interception
F/A-18As acting in the Fleet defence mode often carry this combination of armament as a basic weapons fit. The AIM-9Ms provide a close-range kill capability, while the radar-guided AIM-7Ms are used for medium-range/stand-off interceptions. A fixed cannon is now back in vogue on modern military fighters, the Hornets' M61A1 having a maximum fire rate of 6,000 rounds per minute.

1×M61 A1 20-mm six-barrel cannon with 570 rounds of ammunition mounted in the nose
6×AIM-9M Sidewinder heat-seeking air-to-air missiles, one on each wingtip missile rail, and two on each outer wing pylon
2×AIM-7M Sparrow radar-guided air-to-air missiles, one per underfuselage pylon
1×1249-litre (330 US gal) fuel tank on the centreline station

Enhanced air-to-air interception
This configuration allows the Hornet to attack more targets or deal effectively with one particularly stubborn victim. The additional AIM-9Ms can be replaced by two extra AIM-7Ms if so desired, one per outer pylon. The fuel tank is optional, the increase in endurance it offers being offset to a degree by the increased drag produced by the missiles on the wing pylons.

1×M61 A1 20-mm six-barrel cannon with 570 rounds of ammunition mounted in the nose
2×AIM-9M Sidewinder heat-seeking air-to-air missiles, one on each wingtip missile rail
2×AGM-88A HARM air-to-ground missiles, one per outer wing pylon
2×1249-litre (330 US gal) fuel tanks, one per inner wing pylon

Anti-radiation target attack
One of the weapons configurations carried by F/A-18A Hornets in action against Libya with the HARM (High-Speed Anti-Radiation Missile) taking out coastal radar sites. The two fuel tanks allow extended loiter time between missile firings, while the almost obligatory AIM-9Ms provide a degree of self-defence. Approximate range of firing for HARM is 20 km (12 miles), with firing profile being selected from self-protection, target of opportunity and pre-briefed modes of operation.

1×M61 A1 20-mm six-barrel cannon with 570 rounds of ammunition mounted in the nose
2×AIM-9M Sidewinder heat-seeking air-to-air missiles, one on each wingtip missile rail
2×AGM-84A Harpoon air-to-surface missiles, one per outer wing pylon
2×1249-litre (330 US gal) fuel tanks, one per inner wing pylon

Anti-shipping attack
Royal Australian Air Force (RAAF) Hornets are projected users of the Harpoon ASM for operation over the seas surrounding this nation. In theory, up to four AGM-84As could be carried, but the additional weight and drag make two missiles and additional fuel reserves a more likely configuration. Plans are in hand to extend use of this missile to US Navy F/A-18As in the future.

1×M61 A1 20-mm six-barrel cannon with 570 rounds of ammunition mounted in the nose
2×AIM-9M Sidewinder heat-seeking air-to-air missiles, one on each wingtip missile rail
4×GBU-10E/B Mk 84 907-kg (2,000-lb) Paveway II laser-guided bombs, one on each of the four underwing pylons
1×Martin Marietta AN/ASQ-173 laser spot tracker/strike camera (LST/SCAM) on the starboard underfuselage pylon
1×Ford AN/AAS-38 forward-looking infra-red (FLIR) pod on the port underfuselage pylon
1×1249-litre (330 US gal) fuel tank on the centreline station

All-weather precision attack
An impressive array of ordnance and associated equipment is carried for stand-off precision attacks against a wide range of targets. The AN/AAS-38 FLIR gives the pilot a clear picture of terrain both ahead and aft, even in bad weather, the image being displayed on the Master Monitor Display. The LST/SCAM contains a detector which can acquire laser-designated targets, and also a strike camera for photo-coverage of targets both before and after attack. Both sensor pods normally operate in conjunction with the head-up display for the pilot's weapons-aiming needs, the Paveway IIs being delivered in the same manner as conventional bombs.

2×AIM-9M Sidewinder heat-seeking air-to-air missiles, one on each wing-tip missile rail
1×Fairchild-Weston F-924 panoramic camera
1×Fairchild-Weston KA-99 low/medium-altitude framing camera
1×Honeywell AAD-5 infra-red linescan

Multi-sensor Reconnaissance
Among possible derivatives of the basic F/A-18 Hornet is the F/A-18(R), a reconnaissance model which is set to enter service with the US Navy and Marine Corps. The nose-mounted gun package is removed and replaced by the twin-sensor package. The equipment noted above is not necessarily the final configuration, but the presence of the dependable AIM-9P is almost certain as a degree of self-protection given the lack of M61 A1 firepower.

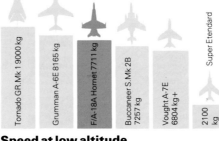

An illustration of a Canadian Armed Forces CF-18B configured for the standard air-to-air intercept mission, two AIM-9M Sidewinders and two AIM-7M Sparrows augmenting the internally mounted cannon. The wingtip carriage of the Sidewinder is noteable for the downward deflection of the missile. Just visible ahead and below the very front of the leading edge extension is the port for the highly powerful searchlight fitted to Canadian machines for night illumination of potential enemy aircraft.

Performance:

Maximum speed at altitude exceeds	Mach 1.8; 1032 kts	1913 km/h (1,189 mph) (15240 m)
Service ceiling about	50,000 ft	
Combat radius on a fighter mission	740 km	(460 miles)
Initial rate of climb	45,000 ft	(13716 m) per minute
Take-off distance less than	427 m (1,400 ft)	

Weapons load

Tornado GR.Mk 1 9000 kg
Grumman A-6E 8165 kg
F/A-18A Hornet 7711 kg
Buccaneer S.Mk 2B 7257 kg
Vought A-7E 6804 kg+
2100 kg
Super Etendard

Service ceiling
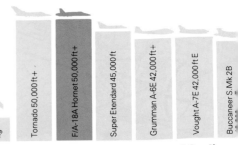

Tornado 50,000 ft+
F/A-18A Hornet 50,000 ft+
Super Etendard 45,000 ft
Grumman A-6E 42,000 ft+
Vought A-7E 42,000 ft E
Buccaneer S.Mk 2B

Speed at high altitude
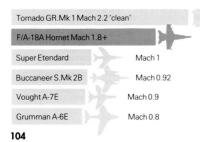

Tornado GR.Mk 1 Mach 2.2 'clean'
F/A-18A Hornet Mach 1.8+
Super Etendard Mach 1
Buccaneer S.Mk 2B Mach 0.92
Vought A-7E Mach 0.9
Grumman A-6E Mach 0.8

Speed at low altitude

Tornado GR.Mk 1 Mach 1.2
F/A-18A Hornet Mach 1
Super Etendard Mach 0.95
Vought A-7E Mach 0.9
Buccaneer S.Mk 2B Mach 0.85
Grumman A-6E Mach 0.85

Operational range (internal fuel)

Buccaneer S.Mk 2B 3700 km
Vought A-7E 2300 km
F/A-18A Hornet 2130 km
Grumman A-6E 1627 km
Super Etendard 1500 km
Tornado GR.Mk 1 1390 km

McDonnell Douglas Helicopter (Hughes) OH-6A

Denmark   Dominican Rep   Japan   Nicaragua

United States   El Salvador

A McDonnell Douglas Helicopter (Hughes) OH-6A Cayuse of the US Army.

Requiring a new light observation helicopter (LOH) to replace the Bell and Hiller aircraft then in service for the observation role, the US Army drew up its specification for the aircraft in 1960. The Army was looking for high performance, turboshaft power, easy maintenance, and low initial cost, and one might have expected this to limit the number of contenders for the LOH competition. However, it was a period when the nation's helicopter industry was looking for work and all the major companies put in one or more proposals. In the following year three manufacturers each received a contract for five prototypes of their submission, the competitors being Bell (YHO-4A), Hiller (YHO-5A) and Hughes (**YHO-6A**). Flown initially on 27 February 1963 (and by then redesignated **YOH-6A**) the Hughes prototypes took part in a seven-month evaluation at Fort Rucker, Alabama, being selected the winner on 26 May 1965 and ordered into production as the **OH-6A** with the name **Cayuse**.

Although Hughes then had little experience in helicopter design (the Model 269 was at that time in the early production stage) the LOH submission, company designation **Hughes Model 369**, introduced an innovative four-blade rotor offering good control and manoeuvre characteristics. The use of four blades (instead of two) meant that individual blade loading was lower and that a power-boosted (and thus complex) control system was not needed.

Initial production delivery of OH-6As to the US Army began in September 1966 and the new type's performance and reliability in combat in Vietnam left little doubt that the anticipated procurement of some 4,000 would follow. However, the war in Vietnam created enormous demands for aircraft, resulting in material shortages and rising costs, and when Hughes began to push up prices and fall behind on deliveries the Army decided to re-open the LOH competition in late 1967 (won by Bell Helicopters) after contracting for 1,434 OH-6As, all of them delivered by the end of 1970. Some 350 remain in service in 1986 with the US Army National Guard.

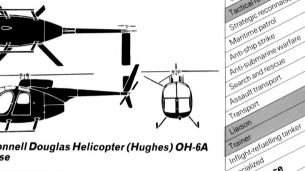

McDonnell Douglas Helicopter (Hughes) OH-6A Cayuse

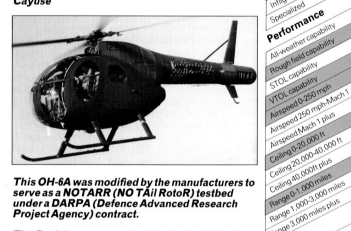

This OH-6A was modified by the manufacturers to serve as a NOTARR (NO TAil RotoR) testbed under a DARPA (Defence Advanced Research Project Agency) contract.

The Danish army operates about a dozen Hughes Model 369s from Vandel in central Jutland. These aircraft are mainly used for observation and reconnaissance duties.

Specification: McDonnell Douglas (Hughes) OH-6A Cayuse
Origin: USA
Type: light observation helicopter
Powerplant: one 236-kW (317-shp) Allison T63-A-5A turboshaft engine derated to 188 kW (252 shp) for take-off
Performance: maximum speed 130 kts (241 km/h; 150 mph) at sea level; cruising speed 116 kts (216 km/h; 134 mph); initial climb rate 1,840 ft (561 m) per minute; service ceiling 15,800 ft (4815 m); range with standard fuel 612 km (380 miles)
Weights: empty equipped 557 kg (1,229 lb); maximum take-off 1225 kg (2,700 lb)
Dimensions: main rotor diameter 8.03 m (26 ft 4 in); length, rotors turning 9.24 m (30 ft 3.75 in); height 2.48 m (8 ft 1.5 in); main rotor disc area 50.60 m² (544.63 sq ft)
Armament: provision for short pylon on the port side of the fuselage to mount an XM27 7.62-mm (0.3-in) six-barrel Minigun or an XM75 grenade-launcher

Role
- Fighter
- Close support
- Counter-insurgency
- Tactical strike
- Strategic bomber
- Tactical reconnaissance
- Strategic reconnaissance
- Maritime patrol
- Anti-ship strike
- Anti-submarine warfare
- Search and rescue
- Assault transport
- Transport
- Liaison
- Trainer
- Inflight-refuelling tanker
- Specialized

Performance
- All-weather capability
- Rough field capability
- STOL capability
- VTOL capability
- Airspeed 0-250 mph
- Airspeed 250 mph-Mach 1
- Airspeed Mach 1 plus
- Ceiling 0-20,000 ft
- Ceiling 20,000-40,000 ft
- Ceiling 40,000 ft plus
- Range 0-1,000 miles
- Range 1,000-3,000 miles
- Range 3,000 miles plus

Weapons
- Air-to-air missiles
- Air-to-surface missiles
- Cruise missiles
- Cannon
- Trainable guns
- Naval weapons
- Nuclear-capable
- Rockets
- 'Smart' weapon kit
- Weapon load 0-4,000 lb
- Weapon load 4,000-15,000 lb
- Weapon load 15,000 lb plus

Avionics
- Electronic Counter Measures
- Electronic Support Measures
- Search radar
- Fire control radar
- Look-down/shoot-down
- Terrain-following radar
- Forward-looking infra-red
- Laser
- Television

Specification: AH-64A Apache

Rotors

Main rotor diameter	14.63 m	(48 ft 0 in)
Main rotor disc area	168.11 m²	(1,809.5 sq ft)
Tail rotor diameter	2.79 m	(9 ft 2 in)
Tail rotor disc area	6.13 m²	(66.0 sq ft)

Fuselage and tail unit

Accommodation	two flight crew in tandem seating	
Length overall, both rotors turning	17.76 m	(58 ft 3.2 in)
Height over tail rotor	4.30 m	(14 ft 1.25 in)
Height to top of air data sensor	4.66 m	(15 ft 3.5 in)

Wings and tailplane

Wing span	5.23 m	(17 ft 2 in)
Tailplane span	3.40 m	(11 ft 2 in)

Landing gear

Two non-retractable rearward-folding mainwheels and a lockable tailwheel

Wheel track	2.03 m	(6 ft 8 in)
Wheelbase	10.59 m	(34 ft 9 in)

Powerplant

Two General Electric T700-GE-701 turboshafts

Rating, each	1265 kW	(1,696 shp)
One engine out rating	1285 kW	(1,723 shp)

AH-64A Apache recognition features

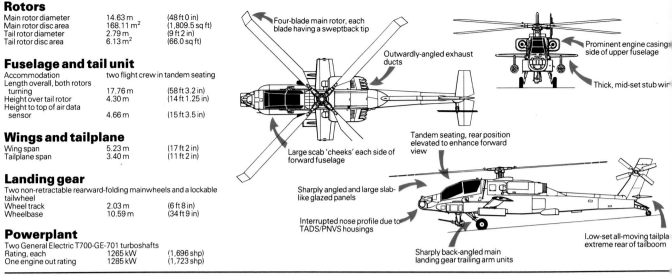

Four-blade main rotor, each blade having a sweptback tip

Outwardly-angled exhaust ducts

Prominent engine casing side of upper fuselage

Thick, mid-set stub win[g]

Tandem seating, rear position elevated to enhance forward view

Large scab 'cheeks' each side of forward fuselage

Sharply angled and large slab-like glazed panels

Interrupted nose profile due to TADS/PNVS housings

Sharply back-angled main landing gear trailing arm units

Low-set all-moving tailpla[ne] extreme rear of tailboom

AH-64A Apache variants

YAH-64: development of Hughes Model 77 in response to US Army's Advanced Attack Helicopter competition; six prototypes, including one ground test vehicle; five flying prototypes known as Air Vehicles 02 to 06 (AV02 to AV06); first flight by AV02 on 30 September 1975, powered by two General Electric T700-GE-700 turboshafts; the prototypes originally had a T-tail configuration and pointed nose, but the former was eventually repositioned much lower down; as the Phase I and II programmes progressed, several major modifications were introduced to the various prototypes, these being incorporated in the final production model

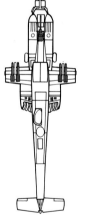

AH-64A Apache: production standard model, first flew on 9 January 1984: the first two were assigned to non-operational tasks as dedicated test vehicles; powered by T700-GE-701 turboshafts derated to provide reserve power for combat emergencies; the tailplane has been relocated to the base of the fin, single-curvature glazing has replaced the flat panels originally fitted, longer forward fuselage fairings cover expanded avionics bays, the tail rotor has been moved up some 7.6 cm (30 in) and the rotor diameter increased, the nose profile has been significantly altered by the addition of the TADS/PNVS turrets; a total of 593 are currently on order for the US Army

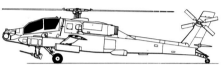
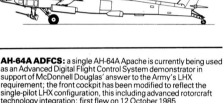

AH-64A ADFCS: a single AH-64A Apache is currently being used as an Advanced Digital Flight Control System demonstrator in support of McDonnell Douglas' answer to the Army's LHX requirement; the front cockpit has been modified to reflect the single-pilot LHX configuration, this including advanced rotorcraft technology integration; first flew on 12 October 1985

Sea Apache: a company-initiated programme to tailor the AH-64A Apache to US Navy and Marine Corps requirements; the USMC version would retain the TADS/PNVS equipment, but the Chain Gun would be deleted; would be capable of firing TOW missiles, Zuni unguided rockets and wingtip-mounted AIM-9L Sidewinders; the Navy model would also retain the TADS/PNVS equipment, but also get surface-search radar housed in a mast mount or ventral radome in place of the Chain Gun; would be capable of carrying up to four Harpoon or Penguin missiles, and six AIM-9L Sidewinders; the tail section would be folding and the tailwheel moved forward. Common features would include upgraded brakes, Doppler INS, additional tie-down points and a new rotor hub to permit a 45° movement of the rotor blades to facilitate deck storage; no orders to date.

AH-64B/G Apache: company proposal for co-developmen[t] co-production with West Germany of an advanced variant to r[meet] the German's PAH-2 requirement; features would include advanced crew station avionics and flight controls to reduce c[rew] workload, improvements in gun and ammunition performanc[e,] better air-to-air missile aiming; a small TV camera would be fi[tted] the extreme rear of the tailfin to enhance crew rearward visio[n]; state-of-the-art data transfer system and pre-programmed m[ission] cassettes would be used to reduce pre-flight tasks time; com[puter] capacity would be tripled to a 192,000 word memory; overall, [per] cent commonality with the AH-64A Apache; no orders to date[

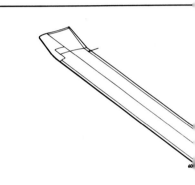

© Pilot Press Ltd

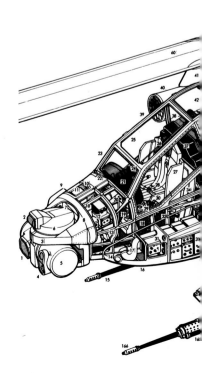

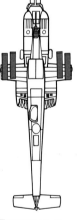

■ 1×M230 Chain Gun 30-mm automatic cannon with 320 rounds of ammunition
8×AGM-114A Hellfire anti-armour missiles

Basic anti-armour (primary mission)

In action the Apache would be extremely unlikely to carry its maximum permissable external weapon load of 16 Hellfire missiles as this would considerably degrade overall performance. Each Hellfire missile can be independently targeted and has a maximum effective range of 8 km (5 miles)

■ 1×M230 Chain Gun 30-mm automatic cannon with 320 rounds of ammunition
16×AGM-114A Hellfire anti-armour missiles

Anti-armour (Middle East operations)

Operating in hot-and-high conditions of 4,000 ft (1220 m) and 35°C (95°F), the Apache could just manage a full load of missiles. Maximum speed would be cut to 147 kts (272 km/h; 169 mph) with a mission endurance time of just under 2 hours. The vertical rate of climb is 450 ft (137 m) per minute.

■ 1×M230 Chain Gun 30-mm automatic cannon with 1,200 rounds of ammunition
38×2.75-in (69.85-mm) FFARs in two 19-round pods
8×AGM-114A Hellfire anti-armour missiles

Air cavalry (Northern Europe)

In the cooler conditions of Northern Europe the Apache has a more sprightly performance, carrying this diverse load at 150 kts (278 km/h; 173 mph) with a vertical rate of climb of 860 ft (262 m) per minute.

■ 1×M230 Chain Gun 30-mm automatic cannon with 1,200 rounds of ammunition
76×2.75-in (69.85-mm) FFARs in four 19-round pods

Airmobile escort (Northern Europe)

The inner weapons pylons have had their usual complement of Hellfire missiles replaced by an additional pair of FFAR pods, this being the maximum permissable load for this mission profile at a maximum combat height of 2,000 ft (610 m). Mission endurance is about 2.5 hours.

e front cockpit houses the co-pilot/gunner
PG), with an uncluttered layout in front
d to the sides. The central unit is the multi-
pose sight system, including an optical
y tube linked to the TADS nose turret.
e left-hand section of the forward console
tains the integrated weapons controls,
ile the right-hand section contains basic
ng instruments. The latter, in conjunction
h a central control column, allow the CPG
ly the helicopter if necessary.

The pilot is seated in the rear cockpit, some 48 cm (19 in) above the CPG to enhance forward view. State-of-the-art technology results in a very neat layout of the forward console. The vertical strip instruments in the left-hand area cover engine and rotor information, while the central square is a Video Display Unit which covers items such as attitude, speed, altitude and hover. The VDU can also display information relating to the TADS and PNVS operations.

Clearly illustrating the higher seating position afforded to the pilot, this view of the crew area also shows the chunky but lightweight boron armour shields either side of the seats, their position helping to protect each crew member's torso. Shielding is also applied to the floor, sides and between the crew stations.

cDonnell Douglas AH-64 Apache
taway drawing key

Night systems sensor scanner
Pilot's Night Vision Sensor (PNVS) infra-red scanner
Electro-optical target designation and night sensor systems turret
Target acquisition and designation sight daylight scanner (TADS)
Azimuth motor housing
TADS/PNVS swivelling turret
Turret drive motor housing
Sensor turret mounting
Rear view mirror
Nose compartment access hatches
Remote terminal unit

12 Signal data converter
13 Co-pilot/gunner's yaw control rudder pedals
14 Forward radar warning antenna
15 M230A1 Chain Gun barrel
16 Fuselage sponson fairing
17 Avionics cooling air ducting
18 Boron armoured cockpit flooring
19 Co-pilot/gunner's 'fold-down' control column
20 Weapons control panel
21 Instrument panel shroud
22 Windscreen wiper
23 Co-pilot/gunner's armoured windscreen
24 Head-down sighting system viewfinder
25 Pilot's armoured windscreen panel
26 Windscreen wiper
27 Co-pilot/gunner's Kevlar armoured seat
28 Safety harness
29 Side console panel
30 Engine power levers
31 Avionics equipment bays, port and starboard
32 Avionics bay access door
33 Collective pitch control lever
34 Adjustable crash-resistant seat mountings
35 Pilot's rudder pedals
36 Cockpit side window panel

44 Pilot's Kevlar armoured seat
45 Collective pitch control lever
46 Side console panel
47 Engine power levers
48 Rear cockpit floor level
49 Main landing gear shock absorber mounting
50 Linkless ammunition feed chute
51 Forward fuel tank; total fuel capacity 1419 litres (375 US gal)
52 Control rod linkages
53 Cockpit ventilating air louvres

37 Pilot's instrument console
38 Inter-cockpit acrylic blast shield
39 Starboard side window entry hatches
40 Rocket launcher pack
41 Starboard wing stores pylons
42 Cockpit roof glazing
43 Instrument panel shroud

54 Display adjustment panel
55 Grab handles/maintenance steps
56 Control system hydraulic actuators (three)
57 Ventilating air intake
58 UHF aerial
59 Starboard stub wing
60 Main rotor blades
61 Laminated blade-root attachment joints
62 Vibration absorbers
63 Blade pitch bearing housing
64 Air data sensor mast
65 Rotor hub unit
66 Offset flapping hinges
67 Elastomeric lead/lag dampers
68 Blade pitch control rod
69 Pitch control swashplate
70 Main rotor mast
71 Air turbine starter/auxiliary powered unit (APU) input shaft
72 Rotor head control mixing linkages
73 Gearbox mounting plate
74 Transmission oil coolers, port and starboard
75 Rotor brake

76 Main gearbox
77 Gearbox mounting struts
78 Generator
79 Input shaft from port engine
80 Gearbox mounting deck
81 Tail rotor control rod linkage
82 Ammunition magazine, 1,200 rounds
83 Stub wing attachment joints
84 Engine transmission gearbox
85 Air intake
86 Engine integral oil tank
87 General Electric T700-GE-701 turboshaft
88 Intake particle separator
89 Engine accessory equipment gearbox
90 Oil cooler plenum
91 Gas turbine starter/auxiliary power unit
92 Starboard engine cowling panels/fold-down maintenance platform
93 Starboard engine exhaust ducts
94 APU exhaust
95 Pneumatic system and environmental control equipment
96 Cooling air exhaust louvres

97 Particle separator exhaust duct/mixer
98 'Black Hole' infra-red suppression engine exhaust ducts
99 Hydraulic reservoir
100 Gearbox/engine bay tail fairings
101 Internal maintenance platform
102 Tail rotor control rod
103 Spine shaft housing
104 Tail rotor transmission shaft
105 Shaft bearings and couplings
106 Bevel drive intermediate gearbox
107 Fin/rotor pylon construction
108 Tail rotor drive shafts
109 All moving tailplane
110 Tail rotor gearbox housing
111 Right-angle final drive gearbox
112 Fin tip aerial fairing
113 Rear radar warning antennae
114 Tail navigation light
115 Cambered trailing edge section (directional stability)
116 Tail rotor pitch actuator
117 Tail rotor hub mechanism
118 Asymmetric (noise attenuation) tail rotor blades

119 Tailplane construction
120 Castoring tailwheel
121 Castoring tailwheel
122 Tailwheel shock absorber
123 Tailwheel yoke attachment
124 Handgrips/maintenance steps
125 Tailplane control hydraulic jack
126 Fin/rotor pylon attachment joint
127 Chaff and flare dispenser
128 Tailboom ring frames
129 Ventral radar warning aerial
130 Tailcone frame and stringer construction
131 UHF aerial
132 ADF loop aerial
133 ADF sense aerial
134 Access hatch
135 Handgrips/maintenance steps
136 Radio and electronics equipment bay
137 Rear fuel tank
138 Reticulated foam fire suppressant tank bay linings

139 VHF aerial
140 Main rotor blade stainless steel spars (five)
141 Glassfibre spar linings
142 Honeycomb trailing edge panel
143 Glassfibre blade skins
144 Trailing edge fixed tab
145 Swept blade tip fairing
146 Static discharger
147 Stub wing trailing-edge flap
148 Stub wing rib construction
149 Twin spar booms
150 Port navigation and strobe lights
151 Port wing stores pylons
152 Rocket pack: 19 7-cm (2.75-in) FFAR rockets
153 Rockwell Hellfire AGM-114A anti-tank missiles
154 Missile launch rails
155 Fuselage sponson aft fairing
156 Boarding step
157 Port mainwheel
158 Main landing gear leg strut
159 Shock absorber strut
160 Boarding steps
161 Main landing gear leg pivot fixing
162 Ammunition feed and cartridge case return chutes
163 Gun swivelling mounting
164 Azimuth control mounting frame
165 Hughes M230A-1 Chain Gun 30-mm automatic cannon
166 Blast suppression cannon muzzle

AV-8B/Harrier GR. Mk 5 second-generation Jump Jet

The original Harrier was renowned for its versatility and manoeuvrability, but was severely hampered by its lack of range and extremely primitive navigation equipment. Pilots' prayers have been answered with the introduction of the McDonnell Douglas/BAe AV-8B Harrier II.

'Simplificate and add more lightness.' This well-known exhortation to the aircraft designer has, perhaps, been no more religiously observed than in the evolution of a second-generation Harrier. A fine example of transatlantic co-operation, the Harrier II is already being enthusiastically deployed by the US Marine Corps and is on the point of entering service with the RAF and Spanish navy. Modern constructional techniques, novel aerodynamic ideas, the latest in avionics and a new range of weapons have combined to transform the Harrier II into almost a new aircraft, while still retaining the best qualities of the old.

Whilst other air forces the world over remained obstinately committed to their vulnerable concrete runways, the USMC identified the Harrier as an ideal aircraft for its specialist requirements. It could operate from an assault carrier and also accompany troops ashore, providing virtually instant response to calls for close air support as the beach-head was being secured. McDonnell Douglas, which was the 'sister' firm to Hawker-Siddeley (later BAe), bought the rights to Harrier development in anticipation of the time when the original US model, the AV-8A, required replacement.

The British government opted out of joint development and later initiated its own project (known as the 'Big Wing Harrier') for local needs. Unfortunately, the American redesign, or AV-8B, ran into political flak and could only be saved by British participation in the programme (as a sub-contractor!) and the cancellation of the UK's own plans. Not quite what the RAF was asking for, the AV-8B was given the next free British mark number (Harrier GR.Mk 5) and prepared for production.

It has been the aim of the AV-8B programme approximately to double the first-generation Harrier's payload/radius capability. Usually such updates include a more powerful engine, but the cost of a radical redesign of the Rolls-Royce Pegasus vectored-thrust turbofan immediately ruled this out. Instead, the aircraft designers were doubly clever in reducing weight and adding lift-improvement devices, so that the dramatic enhancement of potential has been achieved with virtually the same installed power as that of the Harrier GR.Mk 3. In fact, the new model carries 70% more external ordnance (which it delivers with 200% greater accuracy), 50% more internal fuel, 400% more external fuel and requires 60% less maintenance man-hours.

Two for one

Viewed from above, the new Harrier shows a radically altered wing planform, having approximately 20% more span and 14.5% more area, but 10° less sweep. Marked anhedral is retained in the one-piece wing, though it is now of supercritical aerofoil section for improved efficiency at low speed and thicker (so holding more fuel). Only a closer inspection shows that construction relies largely upon carbonfibre and other composite materials for the torsion box, skins and ribs. Even ancillaries such as the single-slotted trailing-edge flaps, drooping ailerons, outrigger pods and fairings are of composites, as are the LERX

The last were originally proposed by BAe, and provide greater combat agility by improving both the instantaneous turn

The two YAV-8B prototypes retained the forward fuselage and kinked taileron leading edge shape of the AV-8A, and wore a garish red and white colour scheme. The American aircraft did not initially feature LERX.

rate and handling qualities at high angles of attack. That is being demonstrated conclusively by USMC Harrier IIs in simulated close air combat, during which they consistently achieve a 2:1 success rate against all-comers, including dedicated fighter types.

Holding 907 kg (2,000 lb) more fuel in its integral tanks, the wing is also more heavily loaded with weapons, having six attachment points for ordnance in the US version. The outrigger wheels are now well inboard, instead of at the tips, the reaction control valves remaining at the extremities and using engine bleed air to keep the aircraft stable at the hover. Large, positive-circulation flaps, it will be noted, are interlinked with the rotating engine nozzles for optimum STO performance, deflecting to a maximum of 60°. In the case of a 304 m (1,000 ft) ground roll, and with the assistance of 15° of aileron droop, they allow an increase in take-off weight of 3039 kg (6,700 lb) compared with that of the original Harrier.

The fuselage shares greater commonality with its predecessor, being of semi-monocoque aluminium alloy construction in its centre and rear sections. A

This neat formation of three lightly-armed AV-8Bs belong to VMA-331 'Bumblebees', the first front-line Harrier II squadron to form. The new aircraft gives a real improvement in capability over the AV-8A.

raised (30.5 cm/12 in) cockpit, as in the Sea Harrier, gives the pilot an improved outlook. The view inside is no less impressive to the former AV-8A/Harrier GR.Mk 3 flier, for the 1960s-style instrumentation has been replaced by modern displays, including a multi-function screen, and ergonomically-improved HOTAS controls.

Extra lift

Three hardpoints on the Harrier II's belly are available (as in the 'Harrier I') for weapon carriage. Cannon pods with added vertical fins fit on the shoulder positions and are replaced by large strakes when removed – but not for additional directional stability. In conjunction with a retractable transverse 'dam' which is lowered to interconnect the cannon pods on take-off and landing, these form a LID enclosure which captures the jet exhaust reflected upwards from the ground. The result is another 544 kg (1,200 lb) of 'free' extra lift which can be translated into greater weapon loads or a shortened STO run.

Rolls-Royce has been able to give the basic Pegasus a minor 'tweak' to uplift performance slightly. Trials and development AV-8Bs employed a model of the earlier Harrier's engine, known in the USA as the F402-RR-404, pending availability of the definitive and more reliable F402-RR-406. The latter is tailored specifically for the Harrier II and has changes such as improved high-pressure turbine cooling, a new shrouded low-pressure turbine and 'zero-scarf' front nozzles. Zero scarf (which adds 90 kg/198 lb to the thrust) describes nozzles which are not cut away at an angle to reveal the internal guide vanes. A further change, recently introduced (at the 64th aircraft, but to be retrofitted), is addition of a digital engine control system for more efficient power control, raising the designation to F402-RR-406A.

Looking to the future, Rolls-Royce is planning versions of the Pegasus delivering up to a further 1361 kg (3,000 lb) thrust, equivalent to an output of around 11340 kg (25,000 lb) thrust.

Even at this stage the list of Harrier II combat loads is impressive. Available attachment points are a fuselage centre-line pylon rated at 454 kg (1,000 lb), and three pylons beneath each wing with tolerances (working outwards) of 907, 907 and 281 kg (2,000, 2,000 and 620 lb). The two under-fuselage 'shoulder' pylons may be used to carry a General Electric GAU-12/U 25-mm cannon (port) and its 300 rounds of ammunition (starboard). The innermost four wing pylons are 'wet' and can each carry a 1136-litre (250-Imp gal) drop tank to augment the total of 4160 litres (915 Imp gal) in the fuselage and integral wing tanks. A retractable 'bolt on' refuelling probe is available for extra-long missions and an onboard oxygen generating system obviates the need for potentially hazardous pressurized storage of the gas.

Versatile weapons platform

On short missions close to the battle area, the AV-8B Harrier II can carry impressively large loads such as 16 500 lb (227 kg) general-purpose bombs, 12 Rock-eye cluster bombs, 10 Paveway laser-guided bombs, 10 LAU-3 rocket pods, four Hughes AGM-65 Maverick ASMs or a pair of 30-mm GEPOD gun pods underwing. AIM-9L Sidewinder AAMs are available as self-defence weapons, backed by extra chaff/flare dispensers (complementing the Goodyear ALE-39 unit in the rear fuselage) and, if necessary,

The AV-8B boasts an impressive array of Lift Improvement Devices, including a retractable transverse cross-dam between the cannon pods/LIDS strakes, positive circulation flaps, and drooping ailerons.

an ALQ-164 jamming pod on the centre-line. In a typical comparison with the popular McDonnell Douglas A-4 Sky-hawk it is replacing, the AV-8B will carry six 500 lb bombs over a 55% greater radius, and do so from a 366 m (1,200 ft) strip of road, instead of a 1280 m (4,200 ft) runway.

Assisting the pilot in accurate first-pass delivery of the above weaponry is an integrated, computer-controlled nav/attack system, including the Hughes ASB-19(V)2 Angle-Rate Bombing Set. ARBS comprises a nose-mounted TV/laser target seeker and tracker with which the pilot can identify the target for automatic weapon release whatever his chosen approach speed and angle. Alternatively, the target can be illuminated by a friendly ground or airborne laser designator, allowing the pilot to make a blind pass with equally high success probability.

Other important items of avionics are the Smiths SU-128/A HUD and Litton ASN-130A INS, whilst a Litton

The first Harrier GR.Mk 5 to be delivered to the Royal Air Force, flanked by a pair of Harrier GR.Mk 3s of No. 233 Operational Conversion Unit. No. 223 OCU is the RAF's first GR.Mk 5 operator.

ALR-67(V)2 RWR forms part of the self-defence suite. McDonnell Douglas is also developing a night attack (but not all-weather) version of the aircraft which is due to fly in 1987 with head-down FLIR presentation, a raster-scanning HUD with 1:1 presentation, a moving map display and cockpit lighting compatible with night vision goggles.

From 1989 onwards, the last 130 or so of the 328 AV-8Bs required by the USMC will be night-capable versions. However, within the larger total are 28 TAV-8B tandem-seat mission capable trainers, inserted into the production line at regular intervals, beginning in 1986. Some Marine Corps pilots are campaigning for an all-weather Harrier II, which could be fitted with a radar such as the Emerson Electric APG-69 at a weight penalty as low as 54 kg (120 lb), although that remains a long-term prospect.

Harrier GR.Mk 5

As the saying has it, the UK's Harrier II is 'the same, but different'. BAe makes 50% of the RAF model, compared to its 40% share of the AV-8B; assembly is at Dunsfold, not St Louis; and there are some changes in avionics and weaponry. Externally, with the obvious exception of markings, one of the most easily noted alterations is the addition of an extra weapon pylon ahead of each outrigger fairing specifically for a self-defence AIM-9L Sidewinder AAM. Weight is slightly increased, in part because of a thicker windscreen and strengthened forward-facing edges to meet birdstrike requirements.

Taking the Harrier GR.Mk 5 aloft is a Pegasus Mk 105 similar in all respects to the F402-RR-406, except that a DECS has been fitted from the outset. The engine will also be run at the slightly higher rating of 9979 kg (22,000 lb) in production form. The cockpit gives the pilot the same commanding view of the outside, so that he may fly lower with greater safety, one principal alteration being the circular screen of the Ferranti moving map display on the starboard side of the instrument panel. In an emergency, rapid departure is courtesy of Martin-Baker (Mk 12 seat) rather than Stencel, as for the USMC aircraft.

Other British systems are a Ferranti INS (FIN 1075) and a Marconi combined RWR/jammer (Zeus) in place of US counterparts, and a change in the rear-fuselage chaff/flare dispenser from the Tracor ALE-39 to ALE-40. Provision is made for undernose installation of a BAe miniature IR linescan reconnaissance system, based on the Panavia Tornado GR.Mk 1's equipment. At a later stage, a Philips dispenser may be fitted inside the Sidewinder pylons to augment or replace the ALE-40. Weapon delivery still involves the Hughes ARBS, complemented from 1990 by the FLIR/NVG additions being given to USMC aircraft for night attack capability.

The RAF has enough first-generation Harrier T.Mk 4/4As to obviate any requirement for an equivalent of the TAV-8B. Though at first feeling heavier to experienced V/STOL pilots, the Harrier II is generally easier to handle, especially during night and poor weather landings, and a remarkably steady weapons plat-

form. The precaution is being taken of accepting no first-tour pilots for the Harrier GR.Mk 5 until mid-1989, although there will be little difficulty in converting straight from Mk 4 to Mk 5 with the assistance of a simulator.

In the longer term the UK plans to replace the moving map display with a Video Map Generator which, whilst giving the same map picture, can also present other data. There are no plans for radar, but an all-weather potential might be obtained by fitting a Terrain Reference Navigation system which compares inputs from the INS and a terrain-profile sensor with a 'map' stored in the computer for remote and covert terrain-following. Not only is this more 'stealthy' than (say) the Tornado's active radar TF, but it gives a smoother ride and allows the aircraft to duck down more rapidly after crossing a ridge.

Continuing the traditions

RAF Harrier GR.Mk 5s will continue in the tradition established by their predecessors. Deployed both at home and in West Germany, they will be subjected to the rigours of low-level flying in the punishing European environment, and regularly stationed off-base to practise the Harrier's unique 'in the field' capability.

Rolling take-offs and vertical landings will remain the Harrier's modus operandi, with the advantage that the new model can return for a VL without having to jettison all unused weapons. The variation in useful loads (fuel, weapons, etc) is extremely wide, from about 3062 kg (6,750 lb) in VTO mode (less than the maximum internal fuel capacity) to almost 7710 kg (17,000 lb) with a short run. The last-mentioned figure represents full internal tanks and the maximum weapon (including drop-tanks) load of 4173 kg (9,200 lb),

Both the RAF and the USMC will receive dedicated night attack versions of the Harrier II, equipped with a FLIR. RAF aircraft will also have terrain reference navigation and terrain following equipment.

A careful process of innovation and refinement has 'added more lightness' to the Harrier II, giving it roughly twice the weapon potential of its predecessor, plus the up-coming ability to operate at night. Now far more complex in avionics terms, the aircraft can still claim to have been 'simplificated' in the view of flight-line servicing crews, having been designed to increase the ready-rate to 75% (although 86% is being achieved in practice) and improve mean time between failures from 1.5 hours to 2.38 hours. That will mean increased operational efficiency for a combat force already without equal.

Glossary
AAM Air-to-Air Missile
ARBS Angle-Rate Bombing Set
ASM Air-to-Surface Missile
DECS Digital Engine Control System
FLIR Forward-Looking Infra-Red
HOTAS Hands on Throttle And Stick
HUD Head-Up Display
INS Inertial Navigation System
IR Infra-Red
LERX Leading-Edge Root Extension
LID Lift-Improvement Device
NVG Night Vision Goggles
RWR Radar-Warning Receiver
STO Short Take-Off
TF Terrain Following
VL Vertical Landing
V/STOL Vertical/Short Take-Off and Landing
VTO Vertical Take-Off

An early AV-8B from the pilot production batch undertakes deck landing trials. Squadron aircraft have now conducted operations at sea, operating from the USS Belleau Wood near the Aleutians.

Harrier II in service

United States (Marine Corps)

Following successful evaluation of two AV-8As converted to YAV-8Bs, the US Navy (as purchasing authority for the Marine Corps) contracted with McDonnell Douglas for an initial four new-built AV-8Bs on 12 April 1979. From FY82, orders have been placed yearly against a requirement for an eventual 300 AV-8Bs and 28 TAV-8B trainers to equip a training unit and eight operational squadrons (four each on the east and west coasts). Horizons have been slightly lowered from the previously planned total of 336 aircraft, and the original date of 1989 for completion of this plan has been put back as a result of funding shortages and a consequent stretch-out of production. For example, quantities of 48 and 49 aircraft were to have been requested in FYs 88-89 but this has been reduced to 32 in each year, and even less may be approved by the Congress.

The first pre-production AV-8B was handed over to the USMC on 12 January 1984 for training, whilst the eight operational squadrons comprise three (VMA-231, -513 and -542) formerly with the AV-8A and its updated AV-8C derivative and five previously equipped with McDonnell Douglas A-4 Skyhawks. Complements are initially being restricted to 15 aircraft, with which the first unit, VMA-331 achieved IOC in August 1985 and full readiness in mid-1986, but the eventual total per squadron will be 20. Two-seat TAV-8Bs were introduced in 1987 to replace TAV-8As, and training unit VMAT-203 expects to train some 66 pilots per year. Ex-Skyhawk pilots fly about 65 conversion sorties, whilst those direct from training school fly 75-80 sorties. McDonnell Douglas produces 60% of the AV-8B's airframe and Pratt & Whitney has a 25% share in the Pegasus engine. Harrier IIs are available for deployment aboard USMC amphibious assault ships comprising the USS *Iwo Jima*, *Okinawa*, *Guadalcanal*, *Guam*, *Tripoli*, *New Orleans* and *Inchon* in the 'Iwo Jima' class; and the USS *Tarawa*, *Saipan*, *Belleau Wood*, *Nassau* and *Peleliu* in the 'Tarawa' class. A notional capability exists aboard dock landing ships of the 'Whidbey Island' class. From 1989 onwards, multi-purpose assault ships of the 'Wasp' class will be available for Harrier II operations.

VMAT-203 'Hawks'
Base: MCAS Cherry Point, North Carolina
Role: Pilot training
Equipped: 12 January 1984
Aircraft: 161573 '21', 161577 '23', 161578 '24', 161579 '31', 161581 '26' (AV-8B Harrier II), plus 159378 '06', 159379 '01', 159382 '04', 159383 '05', 159385 '03' (TAV-8A) coded 'KD'; TAV-8B Harrier II from 1987

VMA-211 'Wake Island Avengers'
Base: MCAS El Toro, California
Role: Light attack
Aircraft: Currently A-4M Skyhawk, coded 'CF'

VMA-214 'Black Sheep'
Base: MCAS El Toro, California
Role: Light attack
Aircraft: Currently A-4N Skyhawk, coded 'WE'

VMA-223 'Tomcats'
Base: MCAS Cherry Point, North Carolina
Role Light attack
Equipped: 1987
Aircraft: AV-8B Harrier II, coded 'WP'

VMA-231 'Ace of Spades'
Base: MCAS Cherry Point, North Carolina
Role: Light attack
Equipped: September 1985
Aircraft: 162084 '01', 162088 '05', 162725 '09', 162728 '12', 162730 '14' (AV-8B Harrier II), coded 'CG'

VMA-311 'Bulldogs'
Base: MCAS El Toro, California

Role: Light attack
Equipped: 1987
Aircraft: AV-8B Harrier II, coded 'WL'

VMA-331 'Bumblebees'
Base: MCAS Cherry Point, North Carolina
Role: Light attack
Equipped: 30 January 1985
Aircraft: 162069 '02', 162071 '04' 162074 '07', 162079 '12', 162082 '15' (AV-8B Harrier II), coded 'VL'

VMA-513 'Flying Nightmares'
Base: MCAS Yuma, Arizona
Role: Light attack
Equipped: January 1987
Aircraft: AV-8B Harrier II, coded 'WF'

VMA-542
Base: MCAS Cherry Point, North Carolina
Role: Light attack
Equipped: 1986
Aircraft: 162733 '01', 162735 '02', 162738 '04', 162741 '07', 162744 '10' (AV-8B Harrier II), coded 'WH'

VX-5 'Vampires'
Base: Naval Weapons Center, China Lake, California
Role: Experimental
Aircraft: 162721 '10' (AV-8B Harrier II), coded 'XE'

Naval Air Test Center
Base: NAS Patuxent River, Maryland
Role: Experimental
Aircraft: 161396 '623', 161399 '624' (AV-8B Harrier II), coded '7T'

This VMA 331 AV-8B wears the squadron's 'bumblebee with bomb' insignia under the windscreen. A triple cluster of real 500-lb slicks are carried on the mid-wing pylon.

This AV-8B Harrier II belongs to VMAT-203, the Cherry Point-based training and conversion unit.

The 'Vampires' of VX-5, based at the Naval Weapons Center, China Lake, are a composite unit, they have a handful of AV-8Bs on charge for experimental and trials purposes.

Groundcrew watch intently as a young pilot starts his AV-8B. The Ace of Spades insignia of VMA-231 is prominent on the aircraft's nose, and a row of spades are repeated on the pilot's helmet.

United Kingdom (Royal Air Force)

A memorandum of understanding between the UK and USA came into force on 24 August 1981 to cover the assembly by BAe at Dunsfold of up to 100 Harrier IIs, to be designated Harrier GR.Mk 5. Of these, two prototypes and 60 production aircraft were immediately taken up. BAe manufactures 50% of airframe and Rolls-Royce is responsible for 75% of the Pegasus engine. The first Harrier GR.Mk 5 (ZD318) flew on 30 April 1985 and was followed by ZD319 on 31 July 1985. The aircraft have been used for trials by BAe and the Aeroplane & Armament Experimental Establishment at Boscombe Down, the latter unit also receiving the first production aircraft (ZD320) late in 1986. At the same time, Singer Link Miles was authorized to produce two Harrier GR.Mk 5 simulators, to be installed at Wittering and Gütersloh (West Germany). Delivery of production Harrier GR.Mk 5s to the RAF begins in 1987. The aircraft will be assigned to No. 233 OCU, which currently operates Harrier GR.Mk 3s and T.Mk 4/4A trainers; to a new Operational Evaluation Unit, for development of combat techniques; and to No. 1 Squadron. The two Harrier GR.Mk 3 squadrons in RAF Germany will re-equip in 1989-90. The OCU and operational squadrons will retain their Harrier T.Mk 4s for dual instruction, four more of the type having been delivered in 1987 to increase RAF receipts to 27 (plus one funded by the Royal Navy).

No.233 Operational Conversion Unit
Base: RAF Wittering
Role: Pilot conversion
Equips: 1987
Aircraft: Harrier T.Mk 4/4A and GR.Mk 5

Harrier Operational Evaluation Unit
Base: RAF Wittering
Role: Operational assessment and trials
Equips: 1987
Aircraft: Harrier GR.Mk 5

No. 233 Operation Conversion Unit is responsible for conversion and refresher training of Harrier pilots, using Harrier GR.Mk 3s and T.Mk 4s. The GR.Mk 3s are being withdrawn in favour of GR.Mk 5s.

No. 1 Squadron
Base: RAF Wittering
Role: Close support
Equips: 1988
Aircraft: Harrier GR.Mk 5

No. 3 Squadron
Base: RAF Gütersloh
Role: Close support
Equips: 1989
Aircraft: Harrier GR.Mk 5

No. 4 Squadron
Base: RAF Gütersloh
Role: Close support and tactical recce
Equips: 1990
Aircraft: Harrier GR.Mk 5

Spain (Arma Aérea de la Armada)

Spanish naval aviation has operated first-generation Harriers of Escuadrilla 008 aboard the escort carrier *Dédalo* since 1976, assigning the local designation VA.1 Matador. In late 1982 Spain accepted a US offer of 12 Harrier IIs with the misleading US designation EAV-8B ('E' indicating *Español*, not Electronic). Originally planned for late 1986, deliveries will now begin a year later from the McDonnell Douglas assembly line in St Louis. BAe makes 25% of Spanish Matador II airframes and Rolls-Royce has a 75% share of the Pegasus engine. The new aircraft are expected to be shore-based at Rota and fly from the recently completed ASW carrier *Principe de Asturias*, which has been purpose-built for Harrier operation with a 12 'ski-jump' deck.

Above: The Harrier GR.Mk 5 differs from the AV-8B in, for example the gun and the ECM/EW system.

Left: The first EAV-8B, dubbed Matador II by the Spanish navy, made its maiden flight on 21 July 1987.

McDonnell Douglas/British Aerospace AV-8B cutaway drawing key

1 Starboard all-moving tailplane
2 Tailplane composite multi-spar construction
3 Tail navigation light
4 Rear radar warning antennae
5 Tail pitch control air valve
6 Yaw control air valves
7 Tail 'bullet' fairing
8 Reaction control system air ducting
9 Trim tab actuator
10 Rudder trim tab
11 Rudder composite construction
12 Rudder
13 Fin-tip antenna
14 Glassfibre aerial fairing
15 Upper broad-band communications aerial
16 Port tailplane
17 Graphite epoxy tailplane skin
18 Port side temperature probe
19 MAD compensator
20 Electro-luminescent formation lighting strip
21 Fin construction
22 Fin spar attachment joi
23 Tailplane pivot sealing plate
24 Tailplane attachment double frame
25 Ventral fin
26 Tail bumper

© Pilot Press Ltd

Harrier II variants

YAV-8B: two AV-8As converted as aerodynamic testbeds; 158394 flown 9 November 1978; 158395 flown 19 February 1979; preceded by full-scale wind-tunnel test vehicle built from AV-8A 158396, and demonstration mock up from AV-8A 159234; all with AV-8A low-set cockpit and original F402-RR-402 (Pegasus Mk 103) of 9752-kg (21,500-lb) thrust

AV-8B FSD: four Full-Scale Development aircraft ordered 12 April 1979, powered by interim F402-RR-404 Pegasus (-402 with zero-scarf front nozzles); double row of auxiliary doors on air inlets; 161396-161399 first flown 5 November 1981, 17 April 1982, 9 April 1982 and 4 June 1982, respectively; assigned to manufacturers and Naval Air Test Center, Patuxent River

AV-8B PP: 12 Pilot Production aircraft funded in Fiscal Year 1982 (FY82), powered by interim F402-RR-404A Pegasus and with double row of auxiliary doors; inlets later modified with single row of doors; 161573-161584 ordered in Fiscal Year 1983·

AV-8B: USMC requirement for 288 full production single-seat Harrier IIs, powered by definitive F402-RR-406 turbofan of 9979-kg (22,000-lb) thrust or similarly-rated F402-RR-406A (with DECS) from late 1986; single row of auxiliary inlet doors; empty weight 5936 kg (13,086 lb); funding allocations, including TAV-8Bs, comprise 21 aircraft (162068-162088) in FY83; 27 (162721-162747) in FY84; 32 (162942-162973) in FY85; 46 (163176-163207, 163419-163426, 163514-163519) in FY86; and 42 (163348-163389) in FY87; planned requests include 32 each in FY88-89, followed by 15 per annum in FYs 90-92

EAV-8B: export US-built Harrier II for Spanish navy; local name **Matador II**; deliveries during 1987-8; allocated USN serials 163101-163021

Harrier GR.Mk 5: British-built version of AV-8B with some UK avionics, chin-mounted IR reconnaissance system and additional two pylons ahead of outrigger fairings for AIM-9L Sidewinder AAMs; Pegasus Mk 105 engine of 9979-kg (22,000-lb) thrust; two development batch aircraft (ZD318-319 first flown 30 April 1985 and 31 July 1985) and 60 production aircraft beginning ZD320 built from 1986; re-order planned for 18-27 more

TAV-8B: two-seat operational trainer with stretched forward fuselage and 0.43 m (1 ft 5 in) extension to fin; USMC requirement for 28 aircraft included in AV-8B purchases, first nine being 162747, 162963, 162971, 163180, 163186, 163191, 163196, 163202 and 163207; initial flight 21 October 1986 (first US Harrier II with -406A engine)

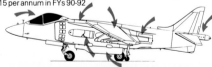

US Marine Corps aviators are Marines first and foremost. Here a pilot from VMA-231 marches smartly to his AV-8B during a deployment to Europe for Exercise 'Bold Guard'.

McDonnell Douglas/British Aerospace AV-8B Harrier II and Harrier GR.Mk 5

1. Lower broad-band communications aerial
2. Tailplane hydraulic actuator
3. Heat exchanger air exhaust
4. Aft fuselage frames
5. Rudder hydraulic actuator
6. Avionics equipment air conditioning plant
7. Reaction control air ducting
8. Avionics cooling air duct
9. Electrical system circuit breaker panels, port and starboard
10. Battery
11. Heat exchanger ram air intake
12. Fuselage frame and stringer construction
13. Avionics equipment racks
14. Avionics bay access door, port and starboard
15. Electro-luminescent formation lighting strip
16. Ventral airbrake, open
17. Airbrake hydraulic jack
18. Main undercarriage wheel bay
19. Wing root trailing edge fillet
20. Wing spar/fuselage attachment joint
21. Rear fuselage fuel tanks. Total internal capacity 4163 litres (1,100 US gal)
22. Water filler cap
23. Engine fire-extinguisher bottle
24. Anti-collision light
25. Water tank
26. Flap hydraulic actuator
27. Flap hinge fitting
28. Nimonic fuselage heat shield
29. Main undercarriage bay doors (closed after cycling of mainwheels)
30. Flap vane composite construction
31. Flap composite construction

Starboard slotted flap, lowered
Outrigger wheel fairing
Outrigger leg doors

Starboard aileron
Fuel tank tail fins

63. Aileron composite construction
64. Fuel jettison
65. Electro-luminescent wing-tip formation light
66. Roll control air valve
67. Wing-tip fairing
68. Starboard navigation light
69. Radar warning antenna
70. AIM-9L Sidewinder air-to-air missile
71. LAU-61 rocket launcher (19 FFAR)
72. LAU-10 rocket launcher (7 FFAR)
73. 69-mm Folding Fin Aircraft Rocket (FFAR)
74. Missile launch rail
75. Outboard pylon
76. Pylon attachment joint
77. Graphite epoxy composite wing construction
78. Aileron hydraulic actuator
79. Starboard outrigger wheel
80. External fuel tank, capacity 1135 litres (300 US gal)
81. Intermediate pylon
82. Reaction control air ducting

83. Aileron control rod
84. Outrigger hydraulic retraction jack
85. Outrigger leg strut
86. Leg pivot fixing
87. Multi-spar wing construction

88. Leading edge wing fence
89. Inboard pylon
90. Triple ejector rack
91. Snakeye retarded bombs
92. Aft retracting twin mainwheels
93. Inboard pylon attachment joint
94. Rear (hot stream) swivelling exhaust nozzle
95. Position of pressure refuelling connection on port side
96. Rear nozzle bearing
97. Centre fuselage flank fuel tank
98. Hydraulic reservoir
99. Nozzle bearing cooling air duct
100. Engine exhaust divider duct
101. Wing panel centre rib
102. Centre section integral fuel tank
103. Port wing integral fuel tank
104. Flap vane
105. Port slotted flap, lowered
106. Port outrigger wheel
107. Port outrigger wheel
108. Torque scissor links
109. Port aileron

110. Aileron hydraulic actuator
111. Aileron/air valve interconnection
112. Fuel jettison
113. Electro-luminescent wing-tip formation light
114. Port roll control air valve
115. Port navigation light
116. Radar warning antenna
117. TAV-8B two-seat training variant
118. Increased area tail fin
119. Instructor's cockpit enclosure
120. Student pilot's cockpit enclosure
121. Rockeye II cluster bomb
122. Port outboard pylon
123. Port wing reaction control air duct
124. Fuel pumps
125. Fuel system piping
126. Port wing leading-edge fence
127. Intermediate pylon
128. Port internal fuel tank
129. Paveway II (GBU-16) laser-guided bomb
130. General Electric GAU-12/U five-barrel, 25-mm rotary cannon (port gun pack fairing only)
131. Port leading-edge root extension (LERX)
132. Inboard stores pylon
133. Hydraulic pumps
134. APU intake

135. Gas turbine starter/auxiliary power unit (APU)
136. Alternator cooling air exhaust
137. APU exhaust
138. Engine fuel control unit
139. Engine bay venting ram air intake
140. Rotary nozzle bearing
141. Nozzle fairing construction
142. Ammunition feed chute
143. Fuel vent
144. Starboard gun pack fairing/ammunition magazine
145. Ventral strake
146. Zero-scarf forward (fan air) swivelling nozzle
147. Fuselage centreline pylon
148. Mk 83 447-kg (985-lb) HE bomb
149. AGM-65A Maverick laser-guided air-to-surface missile
150. Ammunition magazine, 300 rounds
151. Engine drain mast
152. Hydraulic system ground connections
153. Forward fuselage tank
154. Engine electronic control units
155. Engine accessory equipment gearbox
156. Gearbox-driven alternator
157. Rolls-Royce Pegasus F402-RR-406 vectored thrust turbofan engine
158. Electro-luminescent formation lighting strips
159. Engine oil tank
160. Bleed air spill duct
161. Air conditioning intake scoop
162. Cockpit air conditioning system heat exchanger
163. Engine compressor/fan face

170. Cross-dam hydraulic jack
171. Nosewheel, forward retracting
172. Nosewheel forks
173. Landing/taxiing lamp
174. Retractable boarding step
175. Nosewheel doors (closed after cycling of undercarriage)
176. Nosewheel door jack
177. Boundary layer bleed air duct
178. Nose undercarriage wheel bay
179. Kick-in boarding steps
180. Cockpit rear pressure bulkhead
181. Starboard side console panel
182. Stencel 'zero-zero' ejection seat
183. Safety harness
184. Ejection seat headrest
185. Port engine air intake
186. Probe air intake
187. Retractable in-flight refuelling probe (bolt-on pack)
188. Cockpit canopy cover
189. Miniature detonating cord (MDC) canopy breaker
190. Canopy frame
191. Engine throttle and nozzle angle control levers
192. Pilot's head-up display
193. Instrument panel
194. Moving map display
195. Control column
196. Central warning system panel
197. Cockpit pressure floor
198. Underfloor control runs
199. Electro-luminescent formation lighting strips
200. Aileron trim actuator
201. Rudder pedals
202. Cockpit section composite construction
203. Instrument panel shroud
204. One-piece wrap-around windscreen panel
205. Ram air intake (cockpit fresh air)

206. Front pressure bulkhead
207. Incidence vane
208. Air data computer
209. Pitot tube

210. Lower IFF aerial
211. Nose pitch control air valve
212. Pitch trim control actuator
213. Electrical system equipment
214. Yaw vane
215. Upper IFF aerial
216. Weapons system equipment

164. Heat exchanger discharge to intake duct
165. Nose undercarriage hydraulic retraction jack
166. Intake blow-in doors
167. Engine bay venting air scoop
168. Ammunition pack nose fairing
169. Lift augmentation retractable cross-dam

217. ARBS heat exchanger
218. Hughes Angle Rate Bombing Set (ARBS)
219. Composite construction nose cone
220. ARBS television/laser seeker/tracker glazed aperture

Harrier II warload

■ 1×25-mm General Electric five-barrelled cannon in port underfuselage pod, with 300 rounds of linkless ammunition in starboard underfuselage pod
4×AGM-65 Maverick air-to-surface guided missiles on inboard and middle underwing pylons

■ 1×25-mm General Electric five-barrelled cannon in port underfuselage pod, with 300 rounds of linkless ammunition in starboard underfuselage pod
6×500-lb Mk 82 GP bombs on middle and outboard underwing pylons
■ 2×1136-litre (300-US gal) fuel tanks on inboard underwing pylons

■ 1×25-mm General Electric five-barrelled cannon in port underfuselage pod, with 300 rounds of linkless ammunition in starboard underfuselage pod
12×CBU Rockeye cluster bombs, carried singly on outer pylons, in pairs on middle pylons and in triple clusters inboard
■ 1×ALQ 164 ECM pod on centreline, between gun and ammunition pods

■ 1×25-mm General Electric five-barrelled cannon in port underfuselage pod, with 300 rounds of linkless ammunition in starboard underfuselage pod
■ 2×1136-litre (300-US gal) fuel tanks on inboard underwing pylons
4×AIM-9L Sidewinders on middle and outboard underwing pylons

■ 2×25-mm Royal Ordnance Factories revolver cannon based on the 30-mm Aden, each with 100 rounds, in port and starboard underfuselage pods
■ 2×AIM-9L Sidewinder IR-Homing AAM's on additional outrigger pylons
■ 7×Hunting BL755 cluster bombs, one underfuselage and one under each underwing pylon
□ BAe Dynamics miniature infra-red linescanner (MIRLS) in nose

■ 2×25-mm Royal Ordnance Factories revolver cannon based on the 30-mm Aden, each with 100 rounds, in port and starboard underfuselage pods
4×AIM-9L Sidewinder IR-homing AAM's in pairs on additional outrigger pylons
4×Matra SNEB 155 rocket pods, each containing 18×68-mm RP's, on middle and outboard underwing pylons
■ 2×1136-litre (300-US gal) fuel tanks on inboard underwing pylons
□ BAe Dynamics miniature infra-red linescanner (MIRLS) in nose

US Marine Corps, Precision Attack
The AGM-65 Maverick is available with imaging infra-red, television or laser seekers giving a genuine night/all-weather capability. The missile allows attacks to be made against small heavily armoured targets, such as tanks and pillboxes. Maverick can be carried on a single-rail or triple-round launcher. The obsolescent AGM-62 Walleye, a TV-guided bomb utilising the Maverick's TV seeker head, can also be carried by the AV-8B.

US Marine Corps, interdiction
In this configuration a development AV-8B has demonstrated a 917-km (570-mile) radius of action, including a 93-km (58-mile) low-level dash. Up to 16 Mk 82's can be carried, albeit with a substantial range penalty, with triple clusters on four wing pylons. A wide range of guided and unguided free fall ordnance can be carried by the AV-8B, including the Paveway laser-guided bomb and the GBU-15 cruciform-wing weapon.

US Marine Corps, airfield denial
The AV-88 can carry twice the payload of the AV-8A over a given range or the same payload over twice the range. It carries 50 per cent more internal fuel, and can carry up to 400 per cent more external fuel or 70 per cent more ordnance. Vertical take-offs are still not possible with maximum bombloads since the maximum load, including fuel, is 3062 kg (6,750 lb) for VTOL operation, or 7711 kg (17,000 lb) for short rolling take-offs.

Spanish Navy, air defence
The AV-8B has inherited the superb manoeuvrability of the earlier Harrier, but can carry twice as many air-to-air missiles; it has leading edge root extensions to improve turning performance and handling at high angles of attack. Spanish Navy AV-8B's will be employed in the air defence and close support roles. The aircraft may eventually be cleared to carry the AGM-84 Harpoon and BAe Sea Eagle anti-ship missiles.

Royal Air Force, interdiction
Harrier GR.Mk 5's have two indigenously designed cannon in place of the single gun of the AV-8B. Seven hardpoints are available to carry one BL755 each, although the inboard pylons could theoretically carry two bombs each, and RAF Harrier GR. Mk 5's have an extra pylon in line with the outriggers for the carriage of Sidewinder missiles.

Royal Air Force, ground attack
The Harrier GR. Mk 5 is certain to receive eventually the BAe/Bodenseewerk ASRAAM to replace its Sidewinders. 300 US-gallon fuel tanks are carried since the ordinary Harrier 455-litre (100-Imp gal) and 864-litre (190-Imp gal) tanks not being compatible with the new pylon.

Specification: Harrier GR.Mk 5

Wings
Span	9.25 m	(30 ft 4 in)
Area (including LERX)	22.18 m²	(238.7 sq ft)

Fuselage and tail unit
Accommodation	pilot, on Martin-Baker Mk 12 zero-zero ejector seat	
Length overall	14.12 m	(46 ft 4 in)
Height overall	3.55 m	(11 ft 7.75 in)

Weights
Empty	6259 kg	(13,798 lb)
Maximum, vertical take-off	8596 kg	(18,950 lb)
short take-off	14061 kg	(31,000 lb)
Maximum external load	4173 kg	(9,200 lb)
Internal fuel load	3519 kg	(7,759 lb)

Powerplant
One Rolls-Royce Pegasus Mk 105 vectored thrust turbofan		
Static thrust	9866 kg	(21,750 lb)

AV-8B recognition features

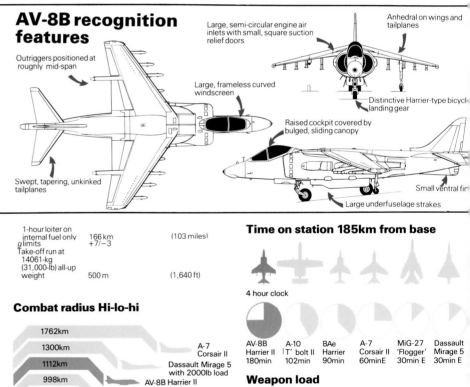

Outriggers positioned at roughly mid-span

Large, frameless curved windscreen

Swept, tapering, unkinked tailplanes

Large, semi-circular engine air inlets with small, square suction relief doors

Anhedral on wings and tailplanes

Distinctive Harrier-type bicycle landing gear

Raised cockpit covered by bulged, sliding canopy

Small ventral fin

Large underfuselage strakes

Performance

Maximum speed, at altitude Mach 0.91		
at sea level	522 kts; 967 km/h	(601 mph)
Mach 0.85	562 kts; 1041 km/h	(647 mph)
Service ceiling	not available	
Combat radius with 2722-kg (6,000lb) bomb load and		
1-hour loiter on internal fuel only g limits	166 km +7/−3	(103 miles)
Take-off run at 14061-kg (31,000-lb) all-up weight	500 m	(1,640 ft)

Speed at sea level
Dassault Mirage 5	750kt
MiG-27 'Flogger-D'	677kt E
BAe Harrier	634kt
A-7 Corsair II	600kt
AV-8B Harrier II	590kt
A-10	381kt

Take off run
1000ft	BAe Harrier at max weight
1200ft	AV-8B Harrier II at max weight
2625ft clean E	MiG-27 'Flogger-D'
4000ft at max weight	A-10
5250ft at max weight	Dassault Mirage 5
6000ft at max weight	A-7 Corsair II

Combat radius Hi-lo-hi
1762km	A-7 Corsair II
1300km	Dassault Mirage 5 with 2000lb load
1112km	AV-8B Harrier II
998km	A-10 Thunderbolt II with 20 min reserves
950km	MiG-27 'Flogger-D' with external fuel
666km	BAe Harrier

Combat radius lo-lo-lo
885km	A-7 Corsair II
650km with 2000-lb load	Dassault Mirage 5
463km	A-10 Thunderbolt II with 20 min reserves
390km	MiG-27 with 6400-lb load
370km	BAe Harrier with external payload
278km	AV-8B Harrier II

Time on station 185km from base

4 hour clock

AV-8B Harrier II 180min	A-10 'T' bolt II 102min	BAe Harrier 90min	A-7 Corsair II 60minE	MiG-27 'Flogger' 30min E	Dassault Mirage 5 30min E

Weapon load

A-10 Thunderbolt II 16000-lb	A-7 Corsair II 15000-lb	AV-8B Harrier II 9200-lb	Dassault Mirage 5 8900-lb	BAe Harrier 8000-lb	MiG-27 'Flogger-D' 6615-lb

Northrop F-5E Tiger II

Bahrain · Brazil · Chile · Indonesia · Iran · Jordan · South Korea · Malaysia · Mexico · Saudi Arabia · Singapore · Sudan · Switzerland · Taiwan

Thailand · Tunisia · United States · Vietnam · Yemen

In November 1970 the US government chose the **Northrop F-5E Tiger II** as winner of its International Fighter Aircraft (IFA) competition to replace the outdated F-5A; contenders for the new type had included the Lockheed CL-1200 Lancer, Vought V-1000 and a stripped-down variant of the McDonnell Douglas F-4 Phantom II. A combination of increased engine power and a two-position extending nosewheel unit gave the F-5E an improvement of some 30 per cent in take-off performance over earlier versions, while the provision of arrester gear permitted operation from very short runways. The fuselage of the Tiger II is widened, which increases the wing span of the aircraft, and the wing loading on the F-5E is thus maintained at approximately the same value as that of the F-5A.

First flight of a production F-5E took place on 11 August 1972, and first deliveries were made on 4 April 1973 to the USAF's 425th Tactical Fighter Training Squadron. In the design and construction of the aircraft there was considerable emphasis on aerial agility rather than on high speed, particularly through the use of manoeuvring flaps. Powered by two General Electric J85-GE-21 turbojet engines, the Tiger II nonetheless has

very useful performance in terms of speed, rate of climb and ceiling. As well as serving in the tactical fighter role with many countries in the US political orbit, the F-5E also operates in the 'aggressor' role at US combat training stations based in the USA, UK and Philippines. The 64th and 65th Aggressor Squadrons operate at Nellis AFB in the USA as part of the 57th Fighter Weapons Wing, and the 527th AS operates at RAF Alconbury in the UK, flying training missions for NATO. The Philippines-based squadron, the 26th AS, is stationed at Clark AFB and performs training missions for Far East squadrons.

A two-seat trainer version of the F-5E is also produced with the designation **F-5F**, and this is also capable of carrying out combat duties. It has a fuselage lengthened by 1.02 m (3 ft 4 in) and its development was approved by the USAF in early 1974, the first flight taking place on 25 September 1974. Deliveries of 118 aircraft began in the summer of 1976. Export orders for the F-5E are numerous. The variant delivered to the Brazilian air force has a large dorsal fin to accommodate an ADF antenna, and those delivered to the Royal Saudi air force have a Litton LN-33 INS and inflight refuelling capability.

This F-5E serves with the US Navy Fighter Weapons School at NAS Miramar, providing adversary aircraft for the 'Top Gun' programme.

Northrop F-5E Tiger II

A Force Aérienne de la Republique de Tunisie Northrop F-5F Tiger II is seen on its delivery flight, staging through RAF Alconbury, carrying a long range ferry tank.

This F-5E of No. 14 Skwadron, 300 Wing, Tentara Nasional Indonesia-Angkatan Udara (Indonesian air force) is based at Meidun and operates primarily in the air defence role.

Specification: Northrop F-5E Tiger II
Origin: USA
Type: single-seat light tactical fighter
Powerplant: two 2268-kg (5,000-lb) General Electric J85-GE-21B turbojet engines
Performance: maximum speed at 36,000 ft (10975 m) Mach 1.64 or 940 kts (1741 km/h; 1,082 mph); initial climb rate 34,500 ft (10516 m) per minute; service ceiling 51,800 ft (15790 m); combat radius with maximum load 306 km (190 miles); ferry range 3724 km (2,314 miles)
Weights: empty 4410 kg (9,723 lb); maximum take-off 11214 kg (24,722 lb)
Dimensions: span 8.13 m (26 ft 8 in); length 14.45 m (47 ft 4.75 in); height 4.07 m (13 ft 4.25 in); wing area 17.28 m² (186.0 sq ft)
Armament: two AIM-9 Sidewinders on wingtip launchers, two 20-mm cannon with 280 rounds per gun in the nose and five hardpoints (one under the fuselage and four under the wings) for a maximum disposable load of 3175 kg (7,000 lb) of bombs, missiles, rocket-launcher pods, drop tanks and other stores.

Role
Fighter
Close support
Counter-insurgency
Tactical strike
Strategic bomber
Tactical reconnaissance
Strategic reconnaissance
Maritime patrol
Anti-ship strike
Anti-submarine warfare
Search and rescue
Assault transport
Transport
Liaison
Trainer
Inflight-refuelling tanker
Specialized

Performance
All-weather capability
Rough field capability
STOL capability
VTOL capability
Airspeed 0-250 mph
Airspeed 250 mph-Mach 1
Airspeed Mach 1 plus
Ceiling 0-20,000 ft
Ceiling 20,000-40,000 ft
Ceiling 40,000ft plus
Range 0-1,000 miles
Range 1,000-3,000 miles
Range 3,000 miles plus

Weapons
Air-to-air missiles
Air-to-surface missiles
Cruise missiles
Cannon
Trainable guns
Naval weapons
Nuclear-capable
Rockets
'Smart' weapon kit
Weapon load 0-4,000 lb
Weapon load 4,000-15,000 lb
Weapon load 15,000 lb plus

Avionics
Electronic Counter Measures
Electronic Support Measures
Search radar
Fire control radar
Look-down/shoot-down radar
Terrain-following radar
Forward-looking infra-red
Laser
Television

Northrop T-38 Talon

Role
- Fighter
- Close support
- Counter-insurgency
- Tactical strike
- Strategic bomber
- Tactical reconnaissance
- Strategic reconnaissance
- Maritime patrol
- Anti-ship strike
- Anti-submarine warfare
- Search and rescue
- Assault transport
- Transport
- Liaison
- Trainer
- Inflight-refuelling tanker
- Specialized

Performance
- All-weather capability
- Rough field capability
- STOL capability
- VTOL capability
- Airspeed 0-250 mph
- Airspeed 250 mph-Mach 1
- Airspeed Mach 1 plus
- Ceiling 0-20,000 ft
- Ceiling 20,000-40,000 ft
- Ceiling 40,000 ft plus
- Range 0-1,000 miles
- Range 1,000-3,000 miles
- Range 3,000 miles plus

Weapons
- Air-to-air missiles
- Air-to-surface missiles
- Cruise missiles
- Cannon
- Trainable guns
- Naval weapons
- Nuclear-capable
- Rockets
- 'Smart' weapon kit
- Weapon load 0-4,000 lb
- Weapon load 4,000-15,000 lb
- Weapon load 15,000 lb plus

Avionics
- Electronic Counter Measures
- Electronic Support Measures
- Search radar
- Fire control radar
- Look-down/shoot-down
- Terrain-following radar
- Forward-looking infra-red
- Laser
- Television

Initial development of the **Northrop T-38 Talon** resulted from studies carried out by the company which showed that the most significant cost factors in the life of an aircraft were those of maintenance and operation rather than those associated with research, development and production. The original outcome of these studies was the completion of designs, by Northrop, for a tactical fighter-bomber designated N-156F (developed as the F-5) and a two-seat trainer version designated **N-156T**. Development of these types was continued as a private venture until the USAF issued a General Operational Requirement for a supersonic basic trainer support system. Northrop met this requirement with a variant of the N-156T design, and was awarded a contract in 1956. During the next two years production of the trainer aircraft, designated **T-38A**, took precedence over that of the fighter.

The T-38 first flew on 10 April 1959, powered by two non-afterburning General Electric YJ85-GE-5 engines each rated at 953-kg (2,100-lb) thrust, and a second aircraft was flown on 12 June 1959. The first production aircraft was flown in January 1960, powered by two afterburning engines each giving a thrust of 1633 kg (3,600 lb); later production aircraft used the 1746-kg (3,850-lb) afterburning thrust J85-GE-5. The first supersonic aircraft designed from the outset specifically to fulfil the training role, the Talon entered service on 17 March 1961 with the USAF's Air Training Command Instructors School at Randolph AFB as a successor to the subsonic Lockheed T-33A; the first group of students began basic training in the aircraft in September 1961.

Excluding prototype and pre-production aircraft, 1,139 Talons were produced, and although the aircraft served primarily with the USAF, the type was exported to West Germany, among other countries. A number of performance records set by the T-38 reflects the high quality of its design, and the aircraft (together with its combat counterpart, the F-5 series) will remain operational for many years to come.

Specification: Northrop T-38A Talon
Origin: USA
Type: two-seat supersonic basic trainer aircraft
Powerplant: two 1746-kg (3,850-lb) General Electric J85-GE-5 turbojet engines
Performance: maximum speed at 36,000 ft (10975 m) Mach 1.3 or 745 kts (1381 km/h; 858 mph); initial climb rate 33,600 ft (10241 m) per minute; service ceiling 53,600 ft (16340 m); range with maximum fuel 1759 km (1,093 miles)
Weights: empty 3254 kg (7,174 lb); maximum take-off 5361 kg (11,820 lb)
Dimensions: span 7.70 m (25 ft 3 in); length 14.14 m (46 ft 4.5 in); height 3.92 m (12 ft 10.5 in); wing area 15.79 m² (170.0 sq ft)
Armament: none

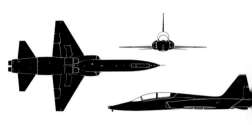

A Northrop T-38 Talon of the Forca Aérea Portuguesa.

Northrop T-38 Talon

This Talon serves with the Air Force Flight Test Center, for a variety of duties. The Talons sometimes act as chase aircraft, and are used by Shuttle pilots for training purposes.

In Turkish air force service, the T-38 Talon serves with the Izmir-Cigli based 121 Filo for advanced pilot training. About 30 were delivered, and most remain in use.

A Rockwell B-1B

influential members of Congress and the media are increasingly concerned that the failure to correct these alleged deficiencies will result in a serious gap in the USA's defences and an unparalleled waste of taxpayers' money.

The first of these criticisms, excessive weight and resultant degradation of cruise altitude, is undoubtedly the least deserved of all and reflects the critics' lack of understanding of the B-1B's mission as, since high-flying aircraft are too vulnerable, it was purposely optimized for low-altitude penetration below enemy radar.

Cannibalization

More valid but overstated, the claim that the flight controls are deficient will hopefully be unfounded as soon as the effectiveness of a recently developed stall inhibitor system can be demonstrated. Similarly, leaks in the fuel and hydraulic systems are, almost, problems of the past as improved manufacturing methods and better maintenance have reduced these leaks to levels equivalent to those experienced with other aircraft types. On the other hand, inadequate spare parts provisioning (a problem not specific to the B-1B as the Department of Defense is frequently forced to save on spare parts procurement in order to remain within budget) will take longer to solve and continues to force the Air Force to cannibalize parts, using a few B-1Bs as expensive 'spare part warehouses'.

The haste with which the B-1B was placed in service meant that its OAS, albeit developed from that already used by B-52G/Hs and thus expected to require shorter than normal flight evaluation, could not be fully validated during abbreviated flight trials. Consequently, when the 96th BW achieved IOC, its crews were not authorized to make automatic terrain-following flights below 1,000 ft (305 m) above ground level and at speeds in excess of Mach 0.85, whereas the aircraft had been designed for flights down to 200 ft (60 m) at Mach 0.92. Progressively, these limits have been brought down to 500 ft (150 m) and Mach 0.90 and will soon reach design values, thus wiping out the validity of this criticism.

Problems with interferences between the offensive and defensive avionics systems and with the unreliability of the

CITS are so far proving the most serious difficulties faced by the B-1B. Although CITS false alarms dropped from some 115 per flight at the end of 1986 to 75 per flight in the spring of 1987, the unreliability of this self-diagnostic test equipment remains alarmingly poor and far exceeds the contractually required level of three false alarms per flight. True, this deficiency does not impact on flight safety but it does lead to excessive 'down time' due to the need to check whether CITS-reported failures are genuine or false.

Electronic defence

Developed by the AIL Division of Eaton Corporation from its ALQ-161 originally planned for the B-1A and first tested in the model's fourth prototype (76-0174), the B-1B's defensive avionics system consists of four primary sub-systems: the radio frequency surveillance/electronics countermeasures system (RFS/ECMS); the tail-warning function (TWF); the defensive management system (DMS); and the expendable countermeasures system (EXCM). In service both the passive detection subsystem and the EXCM system, which is fairly conventional and comprised of eight dispensers each containing either 120 chaff cartridges or 12 IRCM flares, have proved to be effective and reliable.

Currently, the active function of the ALQ-161A continues to be the source of major developmental problems, as the B-1B defensive avionics system is not capable of coping with all known electronic threats and its use may result in interferences with the aircraft's terrain-following system. Consequently, much of the

The second B-1A prototype was used for trials of the B-1B flight control system, and for weapons release trials. It was eventually lost in September 1984, killing Rockwell's chief test pilot and seriously injuring two of the crew.

activities of the Combined Test Force at Edwards AFB is now devoted to getting the active jammers to work as advertised, and in the spring of 1987 the Air Force was forced to admit that this may not be achieved for another 1.5 to 2 years.

Only time will tell if the B-1B can mature into a worthy B-52 successor and will have as long an operational career as the Stratofortress. In the meantime, while answering ever more pointed criticisms from Congress and the media, Rockwell International and SAC can take some comfort in the knowledge that Tupolev and the Aviatsiya Dal'nevo Deistviya appear to have even greater difficulties with their 'Blackjack', the Soviet equivalent of the B-1B.

Glossary
AFB Air Force Base
ALCM Air-Launched Cruise Missile
BW Bombardment Wing
CITS Central Integrated Test System
ECM Electronic CounterMeasures
IOC Initial Operational Capability
IRCM Infra-Red CounterMeasures
OAS Offensive Avionics System
SAC Strategic Air Command
SRAM Short-Range Attack Missile
TFR Terrain-Following Radar

A production B-1B taxis out at Palmdale, showing off its sinister dark green and grey colour scheme. The paint almost certainly incorporates some degree of 'stealth' technology, giving it a low infra-red and radar signature.

Rockwell B-1B in service

Born out of the US Air Force's Advanced Manned Strategic Aircraft (AMSA) programme of the mid-1960s, the Rockwell B-1B has suffered a bumpy ride on its way to front-line operational service with Strategic Air Command. Initial contracts in 1970 covered five flying prototypes, two static test airframes and 240 production standard B-1s, the last of which was to be delivered during 1981. The first prototype took to the air in December 1974 and the fourth (the number having been cut back by one) in August 1975 as part of the extensive flight test programme. Cancellation by the Carter Administration during 1977 was a severe blow, but two prototypes continued limited flying, and the emergence of a strategic air-launched missile carrier requirement brought the aircraft back into the running. The Reagan Administration's hardline defence led to the programme being reactivated on 2 October 1981 with an order for 100 B-1Bs (this figure including two for permanent testing). The Fiscal Year allocations allow for the following construction programme:

Deliveries to Strategic Air Command began on 7 July 1986 with the second production B-1B going to the 4018th Combat Crew Training Squadron (since redesignated 338th Strategic Bombardment Training Squadron), 96th Bomb Wing at Dyess AFB for work-up. The last aircraft is scheduled to enter service during 1988. The aircraft allocation per wing is as follows:

28th Bombardment Wing
Squadrons: 37th and 77th BS
Base: Ellsworth AFB, South Dakota
Example aircraft: 50071

96th Bombardment Wing
Squadrons: 337th BS and 338th SBTS
Base: Dyess AFB, Texas
Example aircraft: 30069, 40052, 50064, 50075

319th Bombardment Wing
Squadron: 46th BS
Base: Grand Forks AFB, North Dakota
Example: none yet assigned

384th Bombardment Wing
Squadron(s): not yet confirmed
Base: McConnell AFB, Kansas
Example aircraft: none yet assigned

Air Force Systems Command
The first and ninth B-1Bs are permanently assigned to the 6512nd TS as part of a continuing research, test and development programme. The aircraft fly as part of a combined test force.

6512nd Test Squadron/Air Force Flight Test Center
Base: Edwards AFB, California
Example aircraft: 20001, 40049

The first production B-1B was rolled out at Palmdale on 4 September 1984, and was eventually delivered to the 96th Bomb Wing at Dyess AFB during June 1985.

The main fault experienced by the B-1B in USAF service has been the vulnerability of the terrain-following radar to interference from the active ECM jamming system.

This B-1B is seen plugging into a Boeing KC-135 Stratotanker during its journey to Dyess AFB from Le Bourget, where it had been visiting the Paris Air Show.

Performance

Maximum level speed at 50,000 ft (15240 m)	Mach 1.25 or 716 kts; 1328 km/h (825 mph)	
Combat cruising speed at 500 ft (150 m)	Mach 0.92 or 607 kts; 1125 km/h (699 mph)	
Service ceiling at reduced weights over	60,000 ft	(18290 m)
Maximum unrefuelled range	11990 km	(7,450 miles)

Weapon load

- Rockwell International B-1B 29030 kg typical
- General Dynamics FB-111A 17000 kg
- Tupolev Tu-26 'Backfire' 12000 kg E
- Sukhoi Su-24
- 'Fencer' 11000 kg E
- Panavia Tornado GR.Mk1 9000 kg
- British Aerospace (HS) S.Mk 2 Buccaneer 7257 kg
- Dassault-Breguet Mirage IVA 4000 kg

Service ceiling

- Dassault-Breguet Mirage IVA 65,600 ft
- General Dynamics FB-111A 60,000 ft +
- Tupolev Tu-26 'Backfire' 55,000 ft E
- Sukhoi Su-24 'Fencer' 54,135 ft E
- Rockwell International B-1B 50,000 ft E
- Panavia Tornado GR.Mk1 50,000 ft +
- British Aerospace Buccaneer (HS) S.Mk 2 40,000 ft + E

Maximum speed at high altitude

- Dassault-Breguet Mirage IVA Mach 2.2
- General Dynamics FB-111A Mach 2.2
- Panavia Tornado GR.Mk1 Mach 2.2 'clean'
- Sukhoi Su-24 'Fencer' Mach 2.18 E
- Tupolev Tu-26 'Backfire' Mach 1.92 E
- Rockwell International B-1B Mach 1.25 E
- British Aerospace S.Mk 2 Buccaneer Mach 0.85

Maximum speed at low altitude

- Sukhoi Su-24 'Fencer' Mach 1.2 E
- General Dynamics FB-111A Mach 1.1
- Dassault-Breguet Mirage IVA Mach 1.1 E
- British Aerospace (HS) S.Mk 2 Buccaneer Mach 0.92
- Tupolev Tu-26 'Backfire' Mach 0.9 E
- Rockwell International B-1B Mach 0.8 E

Range

- Rockwell International B-1B 12000 km E
- Tupolev Tu-26 'Backfire' 11000 km E
- General Dynamics FB-111A 5000 km E
- Sukhoi Su-24 'Fencer' 3900 km E
- British Aerospace (HS) S.Mk 2 Buccaneer 3700 km E
- Dassault-Breguet Mirage IVA 3200 km E
- Panavia Tornado GR.Mk1 3000 km E

B-1 recognition features

Specification: Rockwell B-1B

Wings
Span, unswept	41.67 m	(136 ft 8.5 in)
swept	23.84 m	(78 ft 2.5 in)
Area	181.16 m²	(1,950 sq ft)

Fuselage and tail unit
Accommodation	pilot, co-pilot, offensive and defensive systems officers	
Length overall	44.81 m	(147 ft 0 in)
Height overall	10.24 m	(33 ft 7.25 in)
Tailplane span	13.67 m	(44 ft 10 in)

Landing gear
Retractable tricycle landing gear with four-wheeled main bogies and twin nosewheels
Wheel track	4.42 m	(14 ft 6 in)
Wheelbase	17.53 m	(57 ft 6 in)

Weights
Empty	87090 kg	(192,000 lb)
Maximum take-off	216364 kg	(477,000 lb)

Powerplant
Four General Electric F101-GE-102 afterburning turbofans
Thrust rating, each
with reheat	13948 kg	(30,750 lb)
Available fuel	740237 litres	(195,550 US gal)
Available fuel (with bomb bay tanks)	845528 litres	(223,365 US gal)

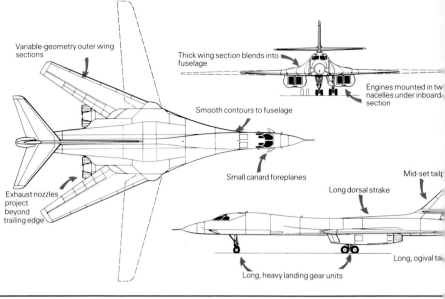

Variable-geometry outer wing sections

Thick wing section blends into fuselage

Engines mounted in two nacelles under inboard section

Smooth contours to fuselage

Exhaust nozzles project beyond trailing edge

Small canard foreplanes

Mid-set tailplane

Long dorsal strake

Long, ogival tailcone

Long, heavy landing gear units

© Pilot Press Ltd

B-1B warload

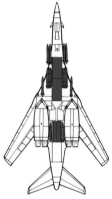

38×AGM-69A Short Range Attack Missiles (24 on three rotary launchers in the internal weapons bay and 14 on the eight external hardpoints)

32×B-83 free-fall nuclear bombs (24 on three rotary launchers in the internal weapons bays and eight on the eight external hardpoints)

22×AGM-86B/C ALCMs (eight on a rotary launcher in the forward weapons bay and 14 on the eight external hardpoints)
1×18170-litre (4,800-US gal) auxiliary fuel tank ahead of the ALCMs in the forward weapons bay
1×32080-litre (8,475-US gal) auxiliary fuel tank in the rear weapons bay

128×500-lb (227 kg) Mk 82 free-fall 'iron' bombs in the internal weapons bays and 44 on the eight external hardpoints)

Nuclear penetration (SRAM)
The SRAMs have warheads in the 170-200 kiloton range and can be launched at distances up to 220 km (137 miles). Three types of rotary launcher are used for the delivery of nuclear weapons

Nuclear penetration (free-fall)
The B-83 is the primary free-fall nuclear bomb for use by the B-1B force, though the smaller, less powerful B-61 can also be carried. Earlier models such as the B-28 and B-43 are being retired.

Cruise missile platform
The dimensions of the ALCM mean that the bulkhead dividing the two forward weapons bays has to be repositioned to provide a larger aft section.

Conventional bombing
An awesome capability is provided by this warload, which would devastate a large area in a similar manner to the B-52 saturation bombing missions during the Vietnam war.

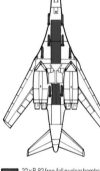

B-1 variants

B-1 no. 1 (74-0158): first of the four flying prototypes for B-1 RDT&E programme; first flown on 23 December 1974 and used specifically for flight qualification tests; total of 79 flights completed; features include a long nose test boom, short forward fuselage, crew escape module, two-dimensional engine inlets, pre-production long engine nozzles and pointed tailcone; powered by four General Electric YF101-GE-100 turbofan engines; retroactively designated B-1A when the B-1B production order was announced (as were the second, third and fourth B-1 prototypes); now withdrawn from use
B-1 no. 2 (74-0159): used for evaluation of structural load parameters in ground and air tests; first flown on 14 June '74; 60 flights completed; distinguishing features as per B-1 no. 1; received interim modifications to act as test aircraft for B-1B programme; duties include weaponry release and separation, engine and systems evaluation; also received B-1B flight control system configuration; aircraft crashed and written off on 29 August '84
B-1 no. 3 (74-0160): assigned to offensive/defensive weapons systems trials; first flew on 1 April '76, completing 138 flights; distinguishing features as per B-1 no. 1, but spine fairing added during ECM tests; navigation lights removed during test programme and 'Crosseye' ECM equipment fitted (though later partially removed); aircraft now withdrawn from use
B-1 no. 4 (76-0174): tasked with ECM/ESM/ECCM systems evaluation but with more comprehensive systems integration; 70 flights completed as part of the original programme; first flown 14 February '79; aerodynamically more similar to the production standard B-1B, features including a blunt tailcone and rear sensor cut-outs, shorter, more ogival nose radome, longer forward fuselage and ejection seats; brought up to B-1B standard and first

flown as such on 30 July '84 with full offensive/defensive avionics systems; two-dimensional engine inlets and longer nozzles retained; fuselage spine fitted but later removed
B-1B: full production standard model for service with US Air Force; powered by four General Electric F101-GE-102 turbofan engines each rated at 13608 kg (30,000 lb st); externally very similar to the B-1As, but changes include the replacement of variable geometry engine inlets by fixed inlets, shorter engine nacelles, blunt tailcone replacing sharper example on B-1As, a new, shorter ogival radome, forward fuselage has been lengthened in similar manner to B-1A no. 4; internal changes include the replacement of the crew escape capsule by four Weber ACES II ejector seats, structural strengthening and increase in overall gross weights, strengthened landing gear and up to eight external hardpoints for ordnance or fuel; a movable bulkhead dividing the two forward weapons bays has been incorporated from the ninth production B-1B and will be retrofitted to the first eight examples; small sweptback vanes with 30° anhedral each side of the nose

Radome
Multi-mode phased array radar scanner
Low-observable shrouded scanner tracking mechanism
Radar mounting bulkhead
Radome hinge joint
Inflight-refuelling receptacle, open
Nose avionics equipment bays
APQ-164 offensive radar system
Dual pitot heads
Foreplane hydraulic actuator
Structural mode control system (SMCS) ride control foreplane
Foreplane pivot fixing
Front pressure bulkhead
Nose landing gear wheel bay
Nosewheel doors
Control cable runs
Cockpit floor level
Rudder pedals
Control column, quadruplex automatic flight control system
Instrument panel shroud
Windscreen panels
Detachable nuclear flash screen, all window positions
Co-pilot's ejector seat
Co-pilot's emergency escape hatch
Overhead switch panel
Pilot's emergency escape hatch
Cockpit eyebrow window
Ejector seat launch/mounting rails
Pilot's Weber ACES 'zero-zero' ejector seat
Wing sweep control lever
Cockpit section framing
Toilet
Nose landing gear drag brace
Twin landing lamps
Taxiing lamp
Shock absorber strut

46 Radar hand controller
47 Crew cabin side window panel
48 Offensive Systems Operators' ejector seat (OSO)
49 Cabin roof escape hatches
50 Defensive Systems Operators' ejector seat (DSO)
51 Rear pressure bulkhead
52 External emergency release handle
53 Underfloor air conditioning ducting
54 Air system ground connection
55 External access panels
56 Avionics equipment racks, port and starboard
57 Cooling air exhaust duct
58 Astro navigation antenna
59 Forward fuselage joint frame
60 Air system valves and ducting
61 Dorsal systems and equipment duct
62 Weapons bay extended range fuel tank
63 Electric cable multiplexes
64 Forward fuselage integral fuel tank
65 Electronics equipment bay
66 Ground cooling air connection
67 Defensive avionics system transmitting antennas
68 Weapons bay door hinge mechanism
69 Forward weapons bay
70 Weapons bay doors, open
71 Retractable spoiler
72 Movable (non-structural) weapons bay bulkhead to suit varying load sizes
73 Rotary dispenser hydraulic drive motor
74 Fuel system piping
75 Communications antennas, port and starboard

76 Starboard lateral radome
77 ALQ-161 defensive avionics system equipment
78 Forward fuselage fuel tanks
79 Control cable runs
80 Rotary weapons dispenser
81 AGM-69 SRAM short-range air-to-surface missiles
82 Weapons bay door and hinge links
83 Port defensive avionics system equipment

84 Fuselage flank fuel tanks
85 Defensive avionics system transmitting antennas
86 Port lateral radome
87 Port navigation light
88 Wing sweep control screw jack
89 Wing pivot hinge fitting
90 Lateral longeron attachment joints
91 Wing pivot box carry-through
92 Wing sweep control jack hydraulic motor
93 Carry-through structure integral fuel tank
94 Upper longeron/carry-through joints
95 Starboard wing sweep control hydraulic motor
96 Wing sweep control screw jack
97 Starboard navigation light
98 Wing sweep pivot fixing
99 Wing root flexible seals
100 Aperture closing horn fairing
101 Flap/slat interconnecting drive shaft
102 Fuel pump
103 Fuel system piping
104 Starboard wing integral fuel tanks
105 Leading edge slat drive shaft
106 Slat guide rails
107 Slat screw jacks
108 Leading edge slat segments (seven), open
109 Wing tip strobe light
110 Fuel system vent tank
111 Wing tip fairing
112 Static dischargers
113 Fuel jettison
114 Fixed portion of trailing edge
115 Starboard spoilers, open
116 Spoiler hydraulic jacks
117 Single-slotted Fowler-type flap, down position
118 Flap screw jacks
119 Flap guide rails
120 Wing root housing fairings
121 Dorsal spine fairing
122 Wheel bay dorsal fuel tank
123 Main landing gear leg strut
124 Port main landing gear stowed position
125 Wheel bay avionics equipment racks
126 Fuselage lateral longeron
127 Wing root housing
128 Engine bleed air ducting
129 Ventral retractable air scoop
130 Fuel cooling heat exchanger
131 Heat exchanger spill air louvres
132 Rear rotary weapons dispenser
133 Control ducting
134 Tailplane longeron
135 Wing glove section tail fairing
136 Starboard wing fully swept position

137 Starboard engine exhaust nozzles
138 Longeron joint
139 Automatic stability and control system equipment (SCAS)
140 Tailplane control linkages
141 Fin root support structure
142 Fin/tailplane frames
143 Fin spar attachment joint
144 Tailplane tandem hydraulic control jacks
145 All-moving tailplane pivot fixing
146 Fin multi-spar construction
147 Fin leading edge ribs
148 Starboard all-moving tailplane
149 Static dischargers
150 Fin tip antenna fairing
151 Defensive avionics system receiving antennas
152 Rudder honeycomb construction
153 Rudder powered hinges
154 Two-segment upper rudder
155 Port automatic stability and control system equipment (SCAS)
156 Tail warning radar equipment
157 Tailcone radome fairing
158 Lower rudder segment
159 Tail radome
160 Defensive avionics system transmitting antennas
161 Tailplane trailing edge rib construction
162 Static dischargers

163 Tailplane tip fairing
164 Multi-spar tailplane construction
165 Port all-moving tailplane
166 Tailplane skin panelling

167 ALQ-161 defensive avionics system equipment racks
168 Vortex generators
169 Ventral communications antennas
170 Fin attachment fuselage main frames
171 Rear fuselage integral fuel tank
172 Tank pressurization nitrogen bottle
173 Rear fuselage lower longeron
174 Rear weapons bay bulkhead
175 Weapons bay doors
176 Engine nacelle mounting beam
177 Radar absorbent material (RAM) coated skin panelling
178 Trailing edge wing root fairing
179 Aft external cruise missile carriage
180 Port engine afterburner nozzles
181 Wing glove section tail fairing
182 Afterburner ducting
183 Variable area afterburner nozzle control jacks
184 General Electric F101-GE-102 afterburning turbofan engines

185 Engine bleed air trappings
186 Bleed air pre-cooler
187 Inlet compressor faces
188 Wing glove articulated sealing plates
189 Nacelle duct framing
190 Hydraulic reservoirs
191 Engine fire suppression bottles

192 Garrett Auxiliary Power Unit (APU), port and starboard
193 Airframe mounted engine accessory equipment gearbox
194 Electrical system generator
195 Engine fuel system equipment, fully automatic digital engine control
196 Engine cowling panels
197 Port single-slotted Fowler-type flaps
198 Port spoiler panels (four)
199 Spoiler hydraulic jacks
200 Flap rib construction
201 Port wing fully swept position
202 Flap down position
203 Trailing edge ribs
204 Fixed portion of trailing edge
205 Static dischargers
206 Fuel jettison
207 Port wing tip fairing
208 Wing tip strobe light
209 Fuel vent tank
210 Port leading edge slat segments
211 Slat open position
212 Slat rib construction
213 Port wing integral fuel tank
214 Rear spar

215 Lower wing skin/stringer panel
216 Wing rib construction
217 Front spar
218 Leading edge slat guide rails
219 Slat screw jacks
220 Slat drive shaft
221 Wing skin panelling

222 Nacelle inlet S-duct
223 Inlet anti-radar reflection internal vanes
224 Boundary layer spill duct
225 Port engine air inlets
226 Hinged inlet side panel variable capture area
227 Four-wheel main landing gear bogie, inward and aft retracting
228 Engine inlet central divider
229 External carriage 14 x ALCM maximum
230 Missile pylons
231 AGM-86B Air Launched Cruise Missile (ALCM) deployed configuration, maximum of eight missiles internally
232 AGM-69 SRAM air-to-surface missiles, 24 internally
233 B-28 or B-43 free fall nuclear weapons (eight)

234 B-61 or B-83 free fall nuclear weapons (24)
235 Mk 84 907-kg (2000-lb) HE bombs (24)
236 Mk 82 227-kg (500-lb) HE bombs (84)

Twin nosewheels, forward retracting
Torque scissor links
Hydraulic steering control unit
Nosewheel leg door
Retractable boarding ladder
Ventral crew entry hatch, open
Nose landing gear pivot
Hydraulic retraction jack
Systems Operators' instrument console

Rockwell International OV-10 Bronco

West Germany   Indonesia   Morocco   Thailand   United States   Venezuela

In the early 1960s the US Marine Corps realized its need for a purpose-built counter-insurgency (COIN) aircraft and drew up the specification for what it identified as a LARA (Light Armed Reconnaissance Airplane). The procurement process was initiated by a design competition, with North American's NA-300 proposal being selected as the winner in August 1964. The initial contract covered seven **YOV-10A** prototypes, the first of them flown on 16 July 1965 on the power of two 492-kW (660-shp) Garrett T76 turboprop engines, but development testing revealed some shortcomings. These were rectified by a 3.05-m (10-ft) increase in wing span, and the introduction of an uprated version of the T76 engine in nacelles that were moved outboard slightly to reduce engine noise in the cabin. The increased span was introduced on a prototype first flown on 15 August 1966 and the seventh prototype was given alternative Pratt & Whitney Canada T74 engines (military designation for PT6A turbo-prop) for comparative evaluation. The **Rockwell OV-10 Bronco** is of distinctive configuration with a shoulder-mounted constant-chord wing, and twin booms extending aft from the engine nacelles to terminate in

vertical tail surfaces that are linked by a fixed-incidence tailplane with inset elevator. The landing gear is of retractable tricycle type and the slender pod-type fuselage accommodates the crew of two in tandem.

Procurement of the initial **OV-10A** covered 114 aircraft for the US Marine Corps, the first of them flown on 6 August 1967, and this service used the type for forward air control and helicopter escort in addition to the intended role of light armed reconnaissance. The USAF acquired 157, primarily for forward air control, but with a secondary limited ground-support role in the absence of tactical fighters. Six generally similar **OV-10B** aircraft were supplied to West Germany for use as target tugs, followed by 12 higher-performance **OV-10B(Z)** aircraft with a 1338-kg (2,950-lb) thrust General Electric J85-GE-4 turbojet pylon-mounted above the wing. Production of versions generally similar to the OV-10A also included the **OV-10C** (40 built) for the Royal Thai air force, the **OV-10E** (16) for the Venezuelan air force and the **OV-10F** (16) for the Indonesian air force. The remaining version, the OV-10D, is the subject of a separate entry.

A Rockwell OV-10E Bronco of the Fuerza Aérea Venezuela.

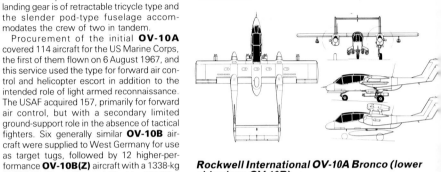

Rockwell International OV-10A Bronco (lower side view: OV-10B)

This US Marine Corps OV-10A belongs to Marine Observation Squadron (VMO-) 2, the Atlanta-based reserve squadron. The Bronco's main roles are FAC and COIN.

This OV-10A Bronco is seen in the markings of the 601st Tactical Control Wing, based at Sembach in West Germany. The wing's Broncos have been passed on to the George-based 27th TASS.

Specification: Rockwell International OV-10A Bronco
Origin: USA
Type: multi-purpose counter-insurgency aircraft
Powerplant: two 533-ekw (715-eshp) Garrett T76-G-416/417 counter-rotating turboprop engines
Performance: maximum speed, clean at sea level 244 kts (452 km/h; 281 mph); initial climb rate 2,600 ft (792 m) per minute; service ceiling 24,000 ft (7315 m); combat radius with maximum weapon load and no loiter 367 km (228 miles)
Weights: empty 3127 kg (6,893 lb); maximum take-off 6552 kg (14,444 lb)
Dimensions: span 12.19 m (40 ft 0 in); length 12.67 m (41 ft 7 in); height 4.62 m (15 ft 2 in); wing area 27.03 m² (291.0 sq ft)
Armament: one underfuselage station, plus four weapon attachment points on short sponsons for a combined weapon load of 1633 kg (3,600 lb) suitable for a wide range of bombs, rockets, machine-gun and cannon pods, flares and smoke tanks; each sponson also houses two 7.62-mm (0.3-in) M60C machine-guns, each with 500 rounds

Rockwell International OV-10D Bronco

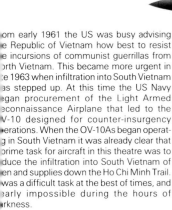

United States

om early 1961 the US was busy advising e Republic of Vietnam how best to resist e incursions of communist guerrillas from orth Vietnam. This became more urgent in te 1963 when infiltration into South Vietnam as stepped up. At this time the US Navy egan procurement of the Light Armed econnaissance Airplane that led to the V-10 designed for counter-insurgency erations. When the OV-10As began operat g in South Vietnam it was already clear that rime task for aircraft in this theatre was to duce the infiltration into South Vietnam of en and supplies down the Ho Chi Minh Trail. was a difficult task at the best of times, and early impossible during the hours of rkness.

The OV-10, suitably equipped, seemed eal to fulfil a night forward air control and rike designation role, and in the early 1970s OV-10As were modified under the USAF's ave Nail' programme. Specialized equip ent given to these aircraft included a mbined laser rangefinder/target illumina r, a Loran receiver and a Loran co-ordinate nverter. After the withdrawal from Vietnam ese 'Pave Nail' OV-10s reverted to standard nfiguration. The US Navy had been slightly ead of the USAF in considering the OV-10A r such a task, and in 1970 two Navy

OV-10As were converted as **Rockwell YOV-10D Night Observation/Gunship System** prototypes. They were equipped with an undernose turret for installation of FLIR and a laser target designator, a rear underfuselage turret to mount a 20-mm cannon, and two underwing pylons carrying extra stores. By the time that evaluation was complete the USA had withdrawn its forces from Vietnam, but in 1974 the US Navy contracted Rockwell to establish and test an **OV-10D** production configuration. This resulted in 17 of the US Marine Corps' OV-10As being converted as OV-10Ds for a NOS (Night Observation Surveillance) role, all of them being redelivered to the USMC during 1979-80. They are equipped with an AAS-37 pod which incorporates a FLIR sensor, laser target designator and automatic video tracker, and can be armed with an M197 20-mm three-barrel cannon with 1,500 rounds of ammunition (in place of the OV-10A's conventional armament) which can be directed by the AAS-37 system. These OV-10Ds also have uprated engines, and additional under-wing pylons suitable for weapons or auxiliary fuel. It has been rumoured that Rockwell's production line may be reopened to build 24 OV-10D NOS aircraft for South Korea.

A Rockwell International OV-10D of the US Marine Corps.

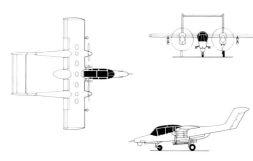

Rockwell International OV-10D NOGS

This OV-10D Bronco serves with VMO-1, based at New River Marine Corps Air Station, North Carolina, for night observation and surveillance duties.

The Rockwell International YOV-10D NOGS (Night Observation/Gunship System) prototype, complete with FLIR, laser designator and video tracker. A gun turret can be installed under the belly.

pecification: Rockwell International OV-10D

rigin: USA

ype: night surveillance aircraft

owerplant: two 776-ekw (1,040-eshp) Garrett T76-G-420/421 counter-rotating turboprop gines

erformance: maximum speed, clean at sea level 250 kts (463 km/h; 288 mph); initial mb rate 3,020 ft (920 m) per minute; service ceiling 30,000 ft (9145 m); combat radius with aximum weapons load and no loiter 367 km (228 miles)

eights: empty 3127 kg (6,893 lb); maximum take-off 6552 kg (14,444 lb)

imensions: span 12.19 m (40 ft 0 in); length 13.41 m (44 ft 0 in); height 4.62 m (15 ft 2 in); ng area 27.03 m² (291.0 sq ft)

rmament: generally as for OV-10 Bronco, plus two underwing pylons with combined pacity of 544 kg (1,200 lb) and suitable for the carriage of cluster bombs, flares, laser guided mbs and rocket pods; an M197 20-mm cannon with 1,500 rounds can be installed on the entreline underfuselage station if no weapons are carried on the sponsons

Role

Fighter
Close support
Counter-insurgency
Tactical strike
Strategic bomber
Tactical reconnaissance
Strategic reconnaissance
Maritime patrol
Anti-ship strike
Anti-submarine warfare
Search and rescue
Assault transport
Transport
Liaison
Trainer
Inflight-refuelling tanker
Specialized

Performance

All-weather capability
Rough field capability
STOL capability
VTOL capability
Airspeed 0-250 mph
Airspeed 250 mph-Mach 1
Airspeed Mach 1 plus
Ceiling 0-20,000 ft
Ceiling 20,000-40,000 ft
Ceiling 40,000 ft plus
Range 0-1,000 miles
Range 1,000-3,000 miles
Range 3,000 miles plus

Weapons

Air-to-air missiles
Air-to-surface missiles
Cruise missiles
Cannon
Trainable guns
Naval weapons
Nuclear-capable
Rockets
'Smart' weapon kit
Weapon load 0-4,000 lb
Weapon load 4,000-15,000 lb
Weapon load 15,000 lb plus

Avionics

Electronic Counter Measures
Electronic Support Measures
Search radar
Fire control radar
Look-down/shoot-down
Terrain-following radar
Forward-looking infra-red
Laser
Television

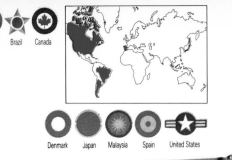

Argentina Brazil Canada

Denmark Japan Malaysia Spain United States

Sikorsky S-61 (SH-3/VH-3 Sea King)

Role

Fighter
Close support
Counter-insurgency
Tactical strike
Strategic bomber
Tactical reconnaissance
Strategic reconnaissance
Maritime patrol
Anti-ship strike
Anti-submarine warfare
Search and rescue
Assault transport
Transport
Liaison
Trainer
Inflight-refuelling tanker
Specialized

Performance

All-weather capability
Rough field capability
STOL capability
VTOL capability
Airspeed 0-250 mph
Airspeed 250 mph-Mach 1
Airspeed Mach 1 plus
Ceiling 0-20,000 ft
Ceiling 20,000-40,000 ft
Ceiling 40,000ft plus
Range 0-1,000 miles
Range 1,000-3,000 miles
Range 3,000 miles plus

Weapons

Air-to-air missiles
Air-to-surface missiles
Cruise missiles
Cannon
Trainable guns
Naval weapons
Nuclear-capable
Rockets
'Smart' weapon kit
Weapon load 0-4,000 lb
Weapon load 4,000-15,000 lb
Weapon load 15,000 lb plus

Avionics

Electronic Counter Measures
Electronic Support Measures
Search radar
Fire control radar
Look-down/shoot-down
Terrain-following radar
Forward-looking infra-red
Laser
Television

US Navy experience with the Sikorsky S-58 (USN designation HSS-1 Seabat) highlighted the shortcomings of hunter/killer pairs of helicopters used in the ASW role. On 24 December 1957 a contract was finalized with Sikorsky Aircraft for the development of a helicopter to combine the hunter and killer roles, the resulting **Sikorsky S-61** prototype (USN designation **XHSS-2**) recording the type's maiden flight on 11 March 1959. Ten **YHSS-2** pre-production aircraft were built, seven of them being used for service trials, leading to initial deliveries of production **HSS-2 Sea King** helicopters in September 1961 to Navy squadrons VHS-10 and VHS-3, based respectively at Ream Field, California, and Norfolk, Virginia.

Features of this new, large helicopter included five-blade main and six-blade tail rotors, two 932-kW (1,250-shp) General Electric T58-GE-8B turboshafts mounted above the cabin and adjacent to the main rotor shaft, a rugged fuselage structure incorporating a watertight hull, and stabilizing floats on each side of the fuselage into which the main units of the tailwheel landing gear could retract, thus giving the Sea King true amphibious capability.

In September 1962 the HSS-2 was redesignated **SH-3A**. Operated by a crew of four (pilot, co-pilot and two sonar operators) it was equipped for the ASW role with Bendix AQS-10 or AQS-13 sonar and had a system to hold

automatic hover in conjunction with APN-130 Doppler and a radar altimeter; for true all-weather capability an auto-stabilization system was provided. A total of 245 SH-3As was produced for the Navy, and after token deliveries the type was built by Mitsubishi in Japan as the HSS-2 for the JMSDF and by United Aircraft Corporation in Canada for the CAF, which designated the helicopter **CH-124**. The following **Sikorsky SH-3D** (72 built) had more powerful turboshafts, increased fuel capacity and improved sonar, and this was the last new-build SH-3 variant. Subsequent SH-3A conversions include nine for mine countermeasures use with the US Navy, redesignated **RH-3A**; 105 conversions of SH-3A/SH-3D for a utility role under the designation **SH-3G**; and 112 SH-3A/SH-3D and SH-3G conversions to an **SH-3H** improved ASW configuration. This last variant, based on the SH-3D, has advanced radar and MAD gear plus updated avionics. Ten SH-3As with VIP interiors were operated jointly by the US Army and Marine Corps under the designation **VH-3A** for VIP transport and based with the Executive Flight Detachment at Andrews AFB, Washington; they were replaced subsequently by 11 **VH-3D** aircraft based on the improved SH-3D. Sikorsky export versions based on the SH-3A/SH-3D include the **S-61A**, the **S-61A-4 Nuri** for the Royal Malaysian air force and the **S-61D-4** for the Argentine navy.

A Sikorsky S-61A-4 of the Malaysian air force.

Sikorsky SH-3H Sea King

The SH-3A is known as the CH-124 in Canadian service and serves with the Shearwater-based 42 and 443 Squadrons on anti-submarine and search and rescue duties.

This SH-3H belongs to HS-11, 'Sea Seekers', and is seen on board the USS America Shortly before the squadron's participation in Operation Eldorado Canyon.

Specification: Sikorsky SH-3D
Origin: USA
Type: amphibious all-weather ASW helicopter
Powerplant: two 1044-kW (1,400-shp) General Electric T58-GE-10 turboshaft engines
Performance: maximum speed 144 kts (267 km/h; 166 mph); economic cruising speed 118 kts (219 km/h; 136 mph); initial climb rate 2,200 ft (671 m) per minute; service ceiling 14,700 ft (4480 m); range with maximum fuel and 10 per cent reserves 1006 km (625 miles)
Weights: empty 5382 kg (11,865 lb); maximum take-off 9752 kg (21,500 lb)
Dimensions: main rotor diameter 18.90 m (62 ft 0 in); length, rotors turning 22.15 m (72 ft 8 in); height 4.72 m (15 ft 6 in); main rotor disc area 280.47 m² (3,019.08 sq ft)
Armament: provision to carry 381 kg (840 lb) of depth bombs, homing torpedoes or other stores

Sikorsky S-61R (CH-3/HH-3)

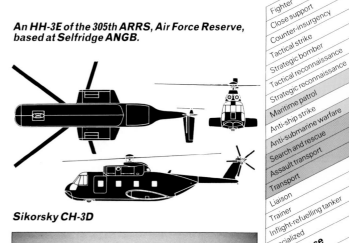

The first HH-3 designation was that applied to a search-and-rescue version of the SH-3A for US Navy service in combat areas. The first conversion from SH-3A to **HH-3A** configuration was completed by Sikorsky, the Navy's repair and overhaul base at Quonset Point, Rhode Island, then making 11 more conversions from kits supplied by Sikorsky. These added to the basic SH-3A two 7.62-mm (0.3-in) barbettes in each sponson, a fast refuelling and fuel jettison system, and provision for auxiliary fuel tanks, armour protection for the crew, a high-speed rescue hoist, a revised avionics package, and 1019-kW (1,350-shp) General Electric T58-GE-8F turboshafts.

US Air Force interest in the S-61 for use in a transport role resulted in six SH-3As being loaned by the US Navy, under the designation **VH-3B**, primarily for missile site support and drone recovery duties. These were used pending initial USAF procurement of a long-range transport version. Specific USAF requirements meant these transports incorporated some important changes (resulting in the revised company designation **Sikorsky S-61R**), including advanced main and tail rotors; retractable tricycle landing gear, the main units housed in sponsons when retracted; an internal cargo handling winch with a capacity of 907 kg (2,000 lb); and a hydraulic-

ally-actuated tail loading ramp to give direct access for vehicles. These entered service under the designation **CH-3C**, the first being delivered on 30 December 1963. A total of 41 was built with 981-kW (1,300-shp) T58-GE-1 engines before production switched to 42 **CH-3E** helicopters with uprated T58-GE-5 turboshafts, the 41 earlier aircraft later being converted to CH-3E standard. Both variants gave valuable service, and were able to carry up to 25 fully equipped troops, or 15 stretchers, or 2268 kg (5,000 lb) of cargo.

The final USAF variant was the **HH-3E**, an armed rescue version of the CH-3E for service with the Aerospace Rescue and Recovery Service. About 50 were completed as a mix of newly-built aircraft and conversions from CH-3Es. These had additional armour, a high-speed rescue hoist, self-sealing fuel tanks and a retractable inflight-refuelling probe. The HH-3E gave valuable service in Vietnam where, with the nickname **Jolly Green Giant**, its long-range rescue operations into enemy airspace have become part of USAF legend. In 1968 the US Coast Guard received the first of 40 **HH-3F Pelican** rescue aircraft, and these were similar to the HH-3E but without armament, armour or self-sealing tanks.

An HH-3E of the 305th ARRS, Air Force Reserve, based at Selfridge ANGB.

Sikorsky CH-3D

The HH-3 forms the backbone of the US Coast Guard helicopter fleet, having sufficient range, endurance and payload to be a very useful search and rescue tool.

This HH-3E serves with Detachment 14 of the 67th ARRS at Keflavik, Iceland. The squadron's various detachments provide SAR and combat rescue cover for the USAF in Europe.

Specification: Sikorsky CH-3E
Origin: USA
Type: amphibious transport helicopter
Powerplant: two 1132-kW (1,500-shp) General Electric T58-GE-5 turboshaft engines
Performance: maximum speed 141 kts (261 km/h; 162 mph) at sea level; economic cruising speed 125 kts (232 km/h; 144 mph); initial climb rate 1,310 ft (399 m) per minute; service ceiling 11,100 ft (3385 m); range with maximum fuel and 10 per cent reserves 748 km (465 miles)
Weights: empty 6012 kg (13,255 lb); maximum take-off 10002 kg (22,050 lb)
Dimensions: main rotor diameter 18.90 m (62 ft 0 in); length, rotors turning 22.25 m (73 ft 0 in); height 4.90 m (16 ft 1 in); main rotor disc area 280.47 m² (3,019.08 sq ft)
Armament: pod-mounted turret at each sponson, each housing a six-barrel 7.62-mm (0.3-in) General Electric Minigun and 8,000 rounds of ammunition

Role	
Fighter	
Close support	
Counter-insurgency	
Tactical strike	
Strategic bomber	
Tactical reconnaissance	
Strategic reconnaissance	
Maritime patrol	
Anti-ship strike	
Anti-submarine warfare	
Search and rescue	■
Assault transport	
Transport	■
Liaison	
Trainer	
Inflight-refuelling tanker	
Specialized	

Performance	
All-weather capability	
Rough field capability	■
STOL capability	
VTOL capability	■
Airspeed 0-250 mph	■
Airspeed 250 mph-Mach 1	
Airspeed Mach 1 plus	
Ceiling 0-20,000 ft	■
Ceiling 20,000-40,000 ft	
Ceiling 40,000 ft plus	
Range 0-1,000 miles	■
Range 1,000-3,000 miles	
Range 3,000 miles plus	

Weapons	
Air-to-air missiles	
Air-to-surface missiles	
Cruise missiles	
Cannon	
Trainable guns	■
Naval weapons	
Nuclear-capable	
Rockets	
'Smart' weapon kit	
Weapon load 0-4,000 lb	■
Weapon load 4,000-15,000 lb	
Weapon load 15,000 lb plus	

Avionics	
Electronic Counter Measures	
Electronic Support Measures	
Search radar	
Fire control radar	
Look-down/shoot-down	
Terrain-following radar	
Forward-looking infra-red	
Laser	
Television	

Sikorsky S-64 Skycrane (CH-54 Tarhe)

Development by Sikorsky of a flying-crane helicopter, intended to lift heavy slung loads rather than carry them internally, began in 1958 when an aircraft designated S-60 was developed from the S-56 transport helicopter. The S-60 (N807) was first flown on 25 March 1959 and used for test, evaluation and development before it crashed in 1961. By then the company had completed the design of and started to build an enlarged **Sikorsky S-64** which it later named **Skycrane**.

First flown on 9 May 1962, the **S-64A** prototype (N325Y) had a pod-and-boom fuselage structure, the comparatively small pod incorporating the nosewheel of the landing gear and seating a pilot and co-pilot forward, a third (rearward-facing) seat with flying controls being provided to allow a pilot to take full control during loading/unloading operations. The long and strong boom served to mount all other features of the S-64: its two turboshaft engines forward of the six-blade main rotor, two outriggers for the main units of the fixed tricycle landing gear (giving a wheel track of 6.02 m/19 ft 9 in to clear wide loads), a removable hoist of 9072-kg (20,000-lb) capacity, and a pylon for the four-blade tail rotor (port) and horizontal stabilizer (starboard). Attachments were provided on the landing gear outriggers and fuselage boom to mount

bulky loads, including specially developed pods or vans to house, for example, 67 troops, or 48 stretchers, or a field hospital unit, or 10383 kg (22,890 lb) of cargo.

Following evaluation of the first of the three prototypes, the US Army ordered six S-64As, designating them **CH-54A** and naming them **Tarhe**. Five were delivered during 1964-5, equipping initially the 478th Aviation Company of the US Army's 1st Cavalry Division in Vietnam, where they quickly proved to be immensely valuable. They were soon airlifting such items as bulldozers and road graders weighing up to 9072 kg (20,000 lb), retrieving damaged aircraft from enemy territory and, in one instance, lifting its crew of three and 87 troops in a detachable van. Additional orders soon followed and CH-54A procurement totalled 54, being followd by 37 **CH-54B** helicopters which differed by having structural strengthening, 3579-kW (4,800-shp) Pratt & Whitney T73-P-700 turboshaft engines, heavy-lift rotor blades, twin wheels on the main gear units, an improved automatic flight control system, and detail improvements.

In addition to its manufacture of CH-54A/B aircraft for the US Army, Sikorsky also built small numbers for commercial use.

Specification: Sikorsky CH-54A
Origin: USA
Type: flying-crane helicopter
Powerplant: two 3356-kW (4,500-shp) Pratt & Whitney T73-P-1 turboshaft engines
Performance: maximum speed 109 kts (203 km/h; 126 mph) at sea level; maximum cruising speed 91 kts (169 km/h; 105 mph); initial climb rate 1,330 ft (405 m) per minute; service ceiling 9,000 ft (2745 m); range with maximum fuel and 10 per cent reserves 370 km (230 miles)
Weights: empty 8724 kg (19,234 lb); maximum take-off 19051 kg (42,000 lb)
Dimensions: main rotor diameter 21.95 m (72 ft 0 in); length, rotors turning 26.97 m (88 ft 6 in); height 7.75 m (25 ft 5 in); main rotor disc area 378.24 m² (4,071.5 sq ft)
Armament: none

A Sikorsky CH-54B Tarhe of the US Army.

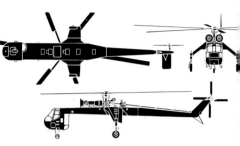

Sikorsky CH-54A Tarhe

The CH-54 Tarhe has built up an impressive record as a flying crane and saw active service during the Vietnam war. The helicopter has now been withdrawn to second-line units.

In its day the Tarhe was a powerful flying crane, but now that the CH-47D version of the Chinook can lift heavier weights the Tarhe has been relegated to ANG units.

Sikorsky S-65 (CH-53 Sea Stallion)

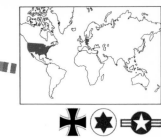

West Germany   Israel   United States

korsky started design and development of rge transport helicopters at the beginning of e 1950s, and its S-56 which saw service vith the US Army, Navy and Marine Corps om 1955 was, for almost a decade, the rgest helicopter flying outside the USSR. In e late 1950s the company began work on rge flying-crane helicopters and then drew p its proposals to meet a US Marine Corps quirement for a ship-based heavy assault ansport. Identified as the **Sikorsky -65A**, this was selected by the USMC in ugust 1962 to fill this role, being allocated e service designation **CH-53A** and named ea Stallion.

The S-65A was something of a hybrid, with atures of the S-64 Skycrane developed at bout the same time and a watertight hull that enefited from experience with the S-61 mily. The S-65 was much larger than the tter, however, with sufficient volume in a selage structure which equated with that of conventional fixed-wing aircraft to accommodate a crew of three and up to 38 equipped oops. Alternative loads included 24 stretchers, or some 3629 kg (8,000 lb) of cargo or, via rear door/ramp, such military loads as a 5-ton truck and its trailer, a 105-mm (4.13-) howitzer, a HAWK SAM system or an onest John SSM on its trailer. Alternatively, n external slung load of 5897 kg (13,000 lb) ould be carried. The configuration includes

six-blade main and four-blade tail rotors, stabilizing sponsons on each side of the fuselage for on-water operations and into which the main units of the tricycle landing gear retract, and twin-turbine powerplant mounted above the cabin. In the initial CH-53A, first flown on 14 October 1964 and entering service in mid-1966, the powerplant consisted of two 2125-kW (2,850-shp) General Electric T64-GE-6 turboshafts, but the alternative T64-GE-1 of 2297 kW (3,080 shp) or T64-GE-16 (mod) of 2561 kW (3,435 shp) could be installed without modification.

An improved version designated **CH-53D** was introduced on the production line late in 1968, with initial deliveries made on 3 March 1969. The major changes involved were internal revisions to make it possible to seat up to 55 troops, the installation of either 2755-kW (3,695-shp) T64-GE-412 or 2927-kW (3,925-shp) T64-GE-413 turboshafts, and the incorporation of automatic folding of the main and tail rotors to simplify stowage on board aircraft-carriers. Production for the USMC ended in January 1972 after 139 CH-53A and 126 CH-53D Sea Stallions had been completed. Two **CH-53G** helicopters, of a type basically similar to the CH-53D, were built as sample aircraft for West Germany, where VFW-Fokker assembled under licence an additional 110.

A CH-53G of West German army aviation (Heeresflieger).

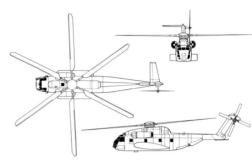

Sikorsky CH-53 Sea Stallion

Specification: Sikorsky CH-53D Sea Stallion
rigin: USA
ype: assault transport helicopter
owerplant: two 2927-kW (3,925-shp) General Electric T64-GE-413 turboshaft engines
erformance: maximum speed 170 kts (315 km/h; 196 mph) at sea level; cruising speed 50 kts (278 km/h; 173 mph); initial climb rate 2,180 ft (664 m) per minute; service ceiling 1,000 ft (6400 m); range with maximum standard fuel and 10 per cent reserves 414 km 57 miles)
Weights: empty 10653 kg (23,485 lb); mission take-off 16511 kg (36,400 lb); maximum ke-off 19051 kg (42,000 lb)
imensions: main rotor diameter 22.02 m (72 ft 3 in); length, rotors turning 26.90 m 8 ft 3 in); height 7.59 m (24 ft 11 in); main rotor disc area 380.87 m² (4,099.8 sq ft)
rmament: none

This elderly CH-53A serves with the shore-based heavy transport squadron HMT-301 at MCAS Tustin, California, a composite unit which also operates the CH-46E, and the CH-53E.

Over 100 CH-53Gs were delivered to the Heeresflieger, and most remain in front-line service. The CH-53G is essentially similar to the CH-53D.

Role	
Fighter	
Close support	
Counter-insurgency	
Tactical strike	
Strategic bomber	
Tactical reconnaissance	
Strategic reconnaissance	
Maritime patrol	
Anti-ship strike	
Anti-submarine warfare	
Search and rescue	
Assault transport	■
Transport	
Liaison	
Trainer	
Inflight-refuelling tanker	
Specialized	

Performance	
All-weather capability	
Rough field capability	■
STOL capability	
VTOL capability	■
Airspeed 0-250 mph	■
Airspeed 250 mph-Mach 1	
Airspeed Mach 1 plus	
Ceiling 0-20,000 ft	■
Ceiling 20,000-40,000 ft	
Ceiling 40,000ft plus	
Range 0-1,000 miles	■
Range 1,000-3,000 miles	
Range 3,000 miles plus	

Weapons	
Air-to-air missiles	
Air-to-surface missiles	
Cruise missiles	
Cannon	
Trainable guns	
Naval weapons	
Nuclear-capable	
Rockets	
'Smart' weapon kit	
Weapon load 0-4,000 lb	
Weapon load 4,000-15,000 lb	
Weapon load 15,000 lb plus	

Avionics	
Electronic Counter Measures	
Electronic Support Measures	
Search radar	
Fire control radar	
Look-down/shoot-down	
Terrain-following radar	
Forward-looking infra-red	
Laser	
Television	

Sikorsky S-65 (CH-53E/MH-53E)

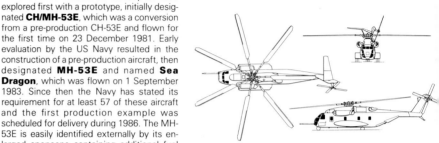

United States

Although both the US Navy and Marine Corps had gained good service in heavy transport and minesweeping roles from the Sikorsky CH-53D and RH-53D, it was clear by the early 1970s that an even more capable helicopter could be built to fulfil such tasks. In 1973 the Sikorsky S-65 was selected for development, and in May of that year the construction of two **YCH-53E** prototypes was initiated, the first of them flying on 1 March 1974. The first of two pre-production aircraft flew on 13 December 1980, and initial production deliveries of the **Sikorsky CH-53E Super Stallion** to Marine Corps squadron HMH-464, at New River, North Carolina, began on 16 June 1981. The US Navy plans to procure ultimately at least 300 of these helicopters, and about 100 had been delivered in mid-1986. By comparison with the CH-53D, the new helicopter has a lengthened fuselage, three turboshaft engines, an increased diameter seven-blade main rotor and an uprated transmission, giving double the lift capability of the twin-turbine H-53s with only 50 per cent more engine power. With a single-point cargo hook rated at 16329 kg (36,000 lb), the CH-53E is suitable for combat tasks such as lifting battle-damaged aircraft from carrier decks, or the support of mobile construction battalions, and for vertical onboard delivery has

an internal cargo load of 13608 kg (30,000 lb).

Further capability enhancement for the mine countermeasures helicopter was explored first with a prototype, initially designated **CH/MH-53E**, which was a conversion from a pre-production CH-53E and flown for the first time on 23 December 1981. Early evaluation by the US Navy resulted in the construction of a pre-production aircraft, then designated **MH-53E** and named **Sea Dragon**, which was flown on 1 September 1983. Since then the Navy has stated its requirement for at least 57 of these aircraft and the first production example was scheduled for delivery during 1986. The MH-53E is easily identified externally by its enlarged sponsons containing additional fuel and allowing the helicopter to operate for up to six hours on station; it is also equipped with an inflight-refuelling probe and, at the hover, can refuel by hose from a surface vessel. Extended capability is provided by duplicated digital automatic flight-control systems and automatic tow couplers which allow automatic approach to and departure from the hover. Export versions of the CH-53E and MH-53E are being offered by Sikorsky under the respective designations **S-80E** and **S-80M**.

Specification: Sikorsky CH-53E Super Stallion
Origin: USA
Type: heavy-duty multi-role helicopter
Powerplant: three 3266-kW (4,380-shp) General Electric T64-GE-416 turboshaft engines
Performance: maximum speed 170 kts (315 km/h; 196 mph) at sea level; cruising speed at sea level 150 kts (278 km/h; 173 mph); initial climb rate 2,500 ft (762 m) per minute; service ceiling 18,500 ft (5640 m); unrefuelled self-ferry range 2076 km (1,290 miles)
Weights: empty 15071 kg (33,226 lb); maximum take-off, internal payload 31638 kg (69,750 lb) and external payload 33339 kg (73,500 lb)
Dimensions: main rotor diameter 24.08 m (79 ft 0 in); length, rotors turning 30.19 m (99 ft 0.5 in); height, tail rotor turning 8.66 m (28 ft 5 in); main rotor disc area 455.37 m² (4,901.68 sq ft)
Armament: none, but there are suggestions that AIM-9 Sidewinders might be provided to give a self-defence capability

A Sikorsky MH-53E Sea Dragon of the US Navy.

Sikorsky CH-53E Sea Stallion Super

Two CH-53E Super Stallions of the US Marine Corps, refuelling from a KC-130T Hercules. The CH-53E differs from earlier variants in having three engines and an uprated transmission.

This CH-53E Super Stallion serves with the US Navy's VC-5, 'Workhorse of the Fleet', a composite evaluation and general duties squadron which operates from Cubi Point, Philippines.

Sikorsky S-70B (SH-60B)

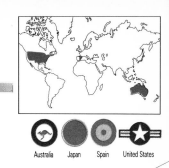

Australia   Japan   Spain   United States

The undoubted success of the US Navy's LAMPS (Light Airborne Multi-Purpose System) aircraft in the ASW/ASST/SAR roles spurred the development of more capable systems. However, the Kaman SH-2F LAMPS Mk I helicopter was considered to be unsuitable to carry more advanced equipment and a LAMPS Mk II system was abandoned pending the availability of a more suitable carrier. In 1977, about a year after the Sikorsky S-70A had been selected by the US Army to meet its UTTAS requirement, the US Navy conducted a similar fly-off and techncial evaluation of a developed version of the Boeing Vertol YUH-61A and Sikorsky YUH-60A, selecting the Sikorsky airframe for inte-gration of the LAMPS Mk III system. This last had been under development by IBM Federal Systems Division since 1974, a three-year period which perhaps emphasized better than anything the complexity and, conse-quently, the cost and capability of this advanced system.

US Navy adoption of the **Sikorsky S-70B** airframe as the **SH-60B Seahawk** LAMPS Mk III carrier resulted in the construction of five **YSH-60B** prototypes, the first of them flying initially on 12 December 1979. Almost two and a half years of development and operational tests followed before the initial production contract was authorized, the first production aircraft flying on 11 February

1983. HSL-41, based at North Island, San Diego, was the first USN squadron to be equipped, gaining initial operational capability in 1984.

The SH-60B differs in several ways from the US Army's UH-60A, including the intro-duction of more powerful and navalized engines, automatic main rotor folding, a rotor brake, tail pylon folding, buoyancy features incorporated in the airframe structure, simpli-fied landing gear, a sliding cabin door, pro-vision of a sensor operator's station, rescue hoist, and pilot/co-pilot seats without armour. Optimum mission capability is pro-vided by such features as increased fuel and hovering inflight-refuelling capability, cargo hook, RAST (Recovery, Assist, Secure and Traversing) gear to help land and hangar the helicopter in rough sea conditions, search radar, a pylon (starboard) for MAD gear, a pylon on each side for torpedoes or auxiliary fuel tanks, a sonobuoy launcher, and chin-mounted pods for ESM equipment. Secure communications are provided, plus a data-link between the helicopter and its mother ship, and the LAMPS Mk III system provides com-prehensive avionics for the expected roles. The US Navy hopes to procure a total of 204 SH-60Bs, plus an unspecified number of an **SH-60F** version under development to defend the inner zone of a carrier battle group from submarine attack.

A Sikorsky XSH-60J Seahawk of the Japan Maritime Self-Defence Force.

Sikorsky S-70B/SH-60B Seahawk

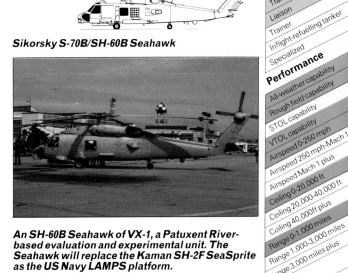

An SH-60B Seahawk of VX-1, a Patuxent River-based evaluation and experimental unit. The Seahawk will replace the Kaman SH-2F SeaSprite as the US Navy LAMPS platform.

NAS North Island is a major US Navy air base in California, with a large number of resident units, including two SH-60B squadrons, HSL-43 'Battle Cats' and HSL-41.

Specification: Sikorsky SH-60B
Origin: USA
Type: ASW/ASST/SAR helicopter
Powerplant: two 1260-kW (1,690-shp) General Electric T700-GE-401 engines
Performance: maximum speed in tropical day conditions at 5,000ft (1525m) 126kts (233km/h; 145mph); initial vertical climb rate 700ft (213m) per minute
Weights: (estimated, ASW role) empty 6191kg (13,648lb); mission take-off 9183kg (20,244lb)
Dimensions: main rotor diameter 16.36m (53ft 8in); length, rotors turning 19.76m (64ft 10in); height, rotors turning 5.18m (17ft 0in); main rotor disc area 210.14m² (2,262.04sqft)
Armament: can include two Mk 46 torpedoes

Role	
Fighter	
Close support	
Counter-insurgency	
Tactical strike	
Strategic bomber	
Tactical reconnaissance	
Strategic reconnaissance	
Maritime patrol	
Anti-ship strike	
Anti-submarine warfare	
Search and rescue	
Assault transport	
Transport	
Liaison	
Trainer	
Inflight-refuelling tanker	
Specialized	

Performance	
All-weather capability	
Rough field capability	
STOL capability	
VTOL capability	
Airspeed 0-250 mph	
Airspeed 250 mph-Mach 1	
Airspeed Mach 1 plus	
Ceiling 0-20,000 ft	
Ceiling 20,000-40,000 ft	
Ceiling 40,000ft plus	
Range 0-1,000 miles	
Range 1,000-3,000 miles	
Range 3,000 miles plus	

Weapons	
Air-to-air missiles	
Air-to-surface missiles	
Cruise missiles	
Cannon	
Trainable guns	
Naval weapons	
Nuclear-capable	
Rockets	
'Smart' weapon kit	
Weapon load 0-4,000 lb	
Weapon load 4,000-15,000 lb	
Weapon load 15,000 lb plus	

Avionics	
Electronic Counter Measures	
Electronic Support Measures	
Search radar	
Fire control radar	
Look-down/shoot-down	
Terrain-following radar	
Forward-looking infra-red	
Laser	
Television	

135

Sikorsky's Hawk Haulers

A crescendo of noise signals the arrival of the Black Hawks, disgorging troops and vital operational equipment set to engage the enemy. Such is the primary role of this highly important US Army helicopter, but it is only one among several performed by land-based models of the H-60 design.

Although the helicopter was used quite extensively during the Korean War, it was employed in that conflict principally as a SAR vehicle or for casualty evacuation, playing little or no part in the actual conduct of battle. In view of that, it is probably fair to say that the rotary-winged flying machine really came of age only a decade or more later, coincidentally in pretty much the same part of the world. Then, in South Vietnam, the helicopter played a quite major role with all four elements of the US armed forces, namely the Air Force, the Army, the Marine Corps and the Navy.

Naturally, each service had rather different operational requirements and, whilst some tasks overlapped, there were others that were the sole prerogative of just one service. Thus, whilst the Army and Marines used helicopters to move troops swiftly around the battlefield, the Navy machines were principally engaged in SAR from vessels operating in the Tonkin Gulf, whilst one role unique to the Air Force was that of recovering reconnaissance drones launched from the Lockheed DC-130 Hercules. Nevertheless, the helicopter usually seemed to be more than equal to the task, whatever the mission, and there is no doubt that the type matured rapidly as that long conflict dragged on.

As far as the Army was concerned, the ubiquitous Bell UH-1 Iroquois (more widely known as the 'Huey') was arguably the most versatile rotary-winged

craft to see action in Vietnam and, indeed, variants of this highly successful machine also served with all the other services, albeit in rather smaller quantities. Needless to say, combat experience played a major part in the Huey's evolution, larger and more capable models making their debut as the war progressed. This same experience was to play a significant part in the development of what is now viewed as the Huey's successor, namely Sikorsky's UH-60A Black Hawk, a type that is now well established in service with the US Army and one that has been much in the news recently as a result of Sikorsky's fight to secure a chunk of Westland Helicopters.

As is so often the case with modern military aircraft and helicopters, the Black Hawk was a long time coming and the process of evolution may be traced back as far as October 1965, when the US Army first began to consider the question of acquiring a new model. At that time, the requirement was rather vague and it took several years for what eventually became known as the Utility Tactical Transport Aircraft System (UTTAS) to progress from the conceptual to the constructional phase. In fact, the gestation period was remarkably long for it was not until January 1972 that the Army issued an RFP to industry, this naturally being greeted warmly by quite a few manufacturers, for it could well result in several thousand examples of the successful design being ordered by the

Role-versatility is a key factor in the UH-60's favour, with several operational configurations available. This machine carries prominent markings for its medical evacuation (medevac) role, while making full use of its external cargo hook to lift construction material.

Army.

In the event, the inevitable weeding-out process reduced the number of contenders quite significantly to a point where just two (those originating with Boeing Vertol and Sikorsky) were considered worthy of proceeding to the prototype stage. Consequently, on 30 August 1972, these two companies received contracts covering the construction of three prototypes for competitive evaluation by the Army, which would subsequently order the winning design into quantity production.

Sikorsky's contender, known by the company as the S-70, was given the service designation YUH-60A, the three prototypes covered by the Army contract taking to the air between mid-October 1974 and the end of February 1975. A ground test specimen and a fourth, company-funded, prototype were also com-

The deliberately compact dimensions of the Black Hawk allow for transport in several of the USAF's airlift aircraft, thus enabling the Army to receive its prime transport helicopter around the world to meet operational requirements in times of potential conflict.

placed at about this time. Initial flight testing proved to be a quite exhaustive and lengthy process, but eventually culminated in an eight-month GCT programme which was accomplished between March and November 1976, this resulting in the Sikorsky Black Hawk being adjudged superior.

Army orders

Formal announcement of the decision to proceed with quantity production for the Army followed a fairly brief evaluation of the GCT findings and was made just two days before Christmas 1976, an initial contract for 15 UH-60As being awarded at the same time. Of greater long-term value to Sikorsky, though, was the revelation by the Army that it planned to purchase no fewer than 1,107 Black Hawks in due course, these all being earmarked to replace the UH-1 in the utility role, a vague mission definition which actually encompasses a multitude of functions ranging from casualty evacuation through troop transport to air cavalry support.

As far as the Black Hawk itself is concerned, it naturally embodied most of the breakthrough that had occurred in helicopter technology since the Iroquois first came on the scene in the latter half of the 1950s. For a start like the Huey it is turbine-powered, employing a pair of General Electric T700-GE-700 turboshaft engines, these being quite novel in that they feature a self-contained lubrication system and a built-in inlet particle separator. Rated at 1151 kW (1,543 shp) for normal continuous operation, they bestow a top speed of 160 kts (297 km/h; 184 mph) at sea level and permit loads of 11 infantrymen or 3629 kg (8,000 lb) of externally-slung cargo to be handled with ease. Thus, the UH-60 not only flies faster than the UH-1 but it does so with more payload, a fact which lets 15 Black Hawks accomplish the same amount of work as 23 Hueys.

Perhaps more important, though, in view of the literally vast numbers of Iroquois helicopters lost as a result of battle damage sustained in combat, is the fact that the Black Hawk incorporates a

number of measures aimed at enhancing its survivability. These include a fair amount of armoured protection for the pilots, extremely tough main rotor blades (they can take hits by 23-mm HE or incendiary shells without separating) and fire-proof main fuel tanks capable of absorbing hits by anything up to 12.7-mm (0.5-in) ammunition.

In addition, a fair measure of system redundancy has been built-in to the Black Hawk, whilst vulnerable features such as electrical and hydraulic systems are duplicated and widely separated so as to reduce the chance of losing both in the event that severe battle damage is sustained. The question of battle damage was actually a key aspect of the Army's original requirement, one of the contractual obligations stipulating that the UH-60A be able to fly for 30 minutes after sustaining a hit anywhere in the undersides and lower fuselage by a 7.62-mm (0.3-in) bullet fired from a range of just 300 ft (91 m). This was successfully demonstrated during the course of the flight test programme.

Minimum maintenance

Equally important, since the UH-60A may well be called upon to deploy to austere sites lacking in sophisticated support equipment, is the ability to sustain operations with the minimum of maintenance down-time. In fact, this aspect of the specification was particularly stringent but it has resulted in a

As a forerunner to the full-scale Night Hawk programme, the USAF procured 11 Black Hawks to act as trainers and project development machines. The majority of the examples, with their distinctive camouflage scheme, are in service with the 55th ARRS.

helicopter that requires only about one-quarter of the maintenance support demanded by the previous generation of turbine-powered types. As far as figures are concerned, the specification stipulated that no more than 2.8 man hours per flight be required for organizational maintenance and that routine preventative inspection and servicing requirements be met by a ratio of one man hour to each flight hour.

This was a tough set of figures, but the Army's insistence appears to have paid dividends, the Black Hawk displaying impressive levels of reliability in situations ranging from routine operations at a major Army installation with good support infrastructure to simulated combat in a variety of climatic conditions.

Entering service with the 101st Airborne Division at Fort Campbell, Kentucky in the summer of 1979, well over 600 examples of the UH-60A have now been delivered and, with production now

The large cabin door slides back to reveal the main cabin with seating for 11 fully-equipped infantrymen or a high-density arrangement for 14 troops. The cabin 'box' was specifically designed to remain largely intact in high-impact crash-landings.

running at 10 per month, the numbers on charge continue to increase at a rapid rate. Initial deliveries were made to US-based units, but examples of the Black Hawk have also been deployed overseas, most notably to West Germany where the type now operates in conjunction with the Iroquois.

Action in Grenada

As well as those helicopters permanently based overseas, the Black Hawk has also operated in North Africa as part of the 'Bright Star' programme of military manoeuvres. Perhaps more importantly, its combat debut came in October 1983 when some UH-60As of the 82nd Airborne Division took part in the invasion of Grenada. By all accounts, the type acquitted itself well although there were a few casualties, a couple of aircraft apparently being destroyed when they collided.

Almost inevitably, the original Army model has spawned a number of derivatives, some for service with the original customer whilst others now fly with both the US Navy and US Air Force.

Looking at the Army sub-types first, this service plans to acquire a total of 77 EH-60As for communications jamming tasks, this model being fitted with specialized equipment able to locate, classify and disrupt enemy signals traffic. Development of the EH-60A began in the late 1970s under the codename 'Quick Fix II', and the type duly flew for the first time in prototype form during September 1981, being instantly recognizable by virtue of prominent dipole antennas on the aft fuselage sides and a retractable ventral whip antenna. Less visible differences concern the 816 kg (1,800 lb) of mission-related electronics located in the cabin.

Another electronic warfare version was the EH-60B 'SOTAS' (Stand-Off Target Acquisition System) which made its maiden flight in February 1981 and which was eventually abandoned later in that year. Had it gone ahead, it would have carried Motorola scanning equipment beneath the cabin, this being lowered in flight and rotated so as to provide full-hemisphere coverage. Fitment of the

antenna necessitated a revised landing gear arrangement, this being designed to retract rearwards.

As far as the US Navy is concerned, the SH-60B Seahawk is significantly different in that it is optimized for anti-submarine warfare. Accordingly, it will be examined in detail later.

The third US customer for a variant of the S-70 is the Air Force, which is to acquire a total of 90 HH-60A Night Hawks for combat SAR tasks. Deliveries are expected to get under way in 1988, this service having originally proposed the procurement of a full-system all-weather variant known as the HH-60D backed up by the less capable HH-60E.

Air force hybrid

In the event, neither model was proceeded with, the USAF instead opting for the HH-60A which made its maiden flight in February 1984 and which will feature a sophisticated avionics suite encompassing a FLIR sensor, terrain-following radar, terrain-avoidance radar and ground mapping radar. Basically a marriage of a modified UH-60A airframe with the SH-60B's more powerful T700-GE-701 engines, the HH-60A will also employ the Seahawk's transmission system, rotor brake and rescue hoist. Other changes required by the SAR mission include the addition of stub wings on which will be mounted a pair of 875-litre (231-US gal) auxiliary fuel tanks, whilst this version will also be able to refuel in flight.

Designed specifically to airlift an infantry squad into hostile territory quickly and with good survivability rates, the Black Hawk is a worthy successor to the UH-1 Huey within US Army forces worldwide. Note the deflected tailplane, keeping the fuselage at an optimum angle in the hover.

Pending delivery of its own purpose-built HH-60As, the USAF is currently operating a total of 11 UH-60As, these mainly being employed on training duties.

Despite the fact that the Iroquois found a ready market for overseas sales, the Black Hawk has thus far proved rather less popular although this may well have something to do with the fact that large numbers of surplus Hueys are readily available at far less cost. Whatever the reason, the only overseas air arms which have opted to buy the basic UH-60A are those of the Philippines and Switzerland, these nations respectively ordering two and three aircraft.

Glossary
FLIR Forward-Looking Infra-Red
GCT Government Competitive Test
RFP Request For Proposals
SAR Search and Rescue
SOTAS Stand-Off Target Acquisition System
UTTAS Utility Tactical Transport Aircraft System

After many trials and tribulations, the USAF HH-60 Night Hawk combat rescue helicopter programme is now under way, with 90 HH-60As on order. External fuel tanks and an inflight-refuelling probe increase mission radius and loiter time.

Sikorsky H-60 in service

US Army

To date, US Army contracts for the Sikorsky UH-60A Black Hawk cover 930 machines, though this figure is likely to rise to as many as 1,715 by the 1990s. Approximately 700 examples have been delivered and are in service with a large number of front-line, National Guard and Army Air Reserve units, these being deployed within the continental USA, South Korea, Hawaii, Panama and West Germany. Within the US Army in Europe (USAREUR) forces based in West Germany, approximately 150 UH-60As are in service, principal role being troop transport and medical evacuation. It is envisaged that 205 Black Hawks will be committed to USAREUR by 1992, replacing more of the large Bell UH-1H force. Typical force structure at present is 15 UH-60As in a Combat Aviation Company, within a Combat Aviation Brigade, and a single UH-60A within the brigade's Air Cavalry Squadron. Two existing Corps Aviation Companies, each with 15 Black Hawks, are set to be redesignated Combat Support Aviation Companies during 1987, their parent Combat Aviation Groups attaining brigade status. Three Attack Helicopter Battalions will be added to each brigade, their inventory including a total of nine UH-60As per brigade.

US Air Force

Though plans are well advanced for the procurement and introduction of a substantial number of HH-60A combat rescue helicopters into service during the late 1980s, current USAF operation of the H-60 models is restricted to nine UH-60A Black Hawks assigned to the 55th ARRS, 39th ARRW at Eglin AFB, Florida, primarily to serve as lead-in trainers for the HH-60 force. Two additional machines were set aside to become full scale development prototypes for the HH-60D.

Philippine Air Force

Two Sikorsky S-70A-5s are in service with the PAF, this being a tactical utility version of the UH-60A, though their current operational status is unclear.

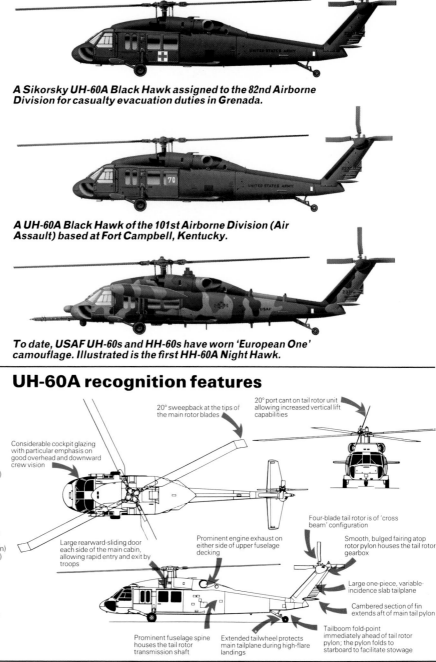

A Sikorsky UH-60A Black Hawk assigned to the 82nd Airborne Division for casualty evacuation duties in Grenada.

A UH-60A Black Hawk of the 101st Airborne Division (Air Assault) based at Fort Campbell, Kentucky.

To date, USAF UH-60s and HH-60s have worn 'European One' camouflage. Illustrated is the first HH-60A Night Hawk.

Specification: UH-60A Black Hawk

Rotors

Main rotor diameter	16.36 m	(53 ft 8 in)
Tail rotor diameter	3.35 m	(11 ft 0 in)
Main rotor disc area	210.05 m²	(2,261 sq ft)

Fuselage and tail unit

Accommodation	three-man crew plus up to 11 troops	
Length overall, rotors turning	19.76 m	(64 ft 10 in)
Length, fuselage	15.26 m	(50 ft 0.75 in)
Length, rotors and tail pylon folded	12.60 m	(41 ft 4 in)
Height overall, tail rotor turning	5.13 m	(16 ft 10 in)
Tailplane span	4.38 m	(14 ft 4.5 in)

Landing gear

Non-retractable tailwheel landing gear with single wheel on each unit

Wheelbase	8.83 m	(28 ft 11.75 in)
Wheel track	2.71 m	(8 ft 10.5 in)

Weights

Empty	4819 kg	(10,624 lb)
Maximum take-off	9185 kg	(20,250 lb)
Maximum external load (on hook)	3629 kg	(8,000 lb)
Internal fuel load	1340 litres	(354 US gal)

Powerplant

Two General Electric T700-GE-700 turboshafts		
Rating, each	1163 kW	(1,560 shp)

UH-60A recognition features

20° sweepback at the tips of the main rotor blades

20° port cant on tail rotor unit allowing increased vertical lift capabilities

Considerable cockpit glazing with particular emphasis on good overhead and downward crew vision

Four-blade tail rotor is of 'cross beam' configuration

Smooth, bulged fairing atop rotor pylon houses the tail rotor gearbox

Large one-piece, variable-incidence slab tailplane

Large rearward-sliding door each side of the main cabin, allowing rapid entry and exit by troops

Prominent engine exhaust on either side of upper fuselage decking

Cambered section of fin extends aft of main tail pylon

Tailboom fold-point immediately ahead of tail rotor pylon; the pylon folds to starboard to facilitate stowage

Prominent fuselage spine houses the tail rotor transmission shaft

Extended tailwheel protects main tailplane during high-flare landings

Sikorsky H-60 variants

UH-60A Black Hawk: initial production model for service with US Army in utility tactical transport role, being capable of carrying 11 fully-equipped troops as well as a crew of three; approximately 700 now delivered with manufacture continuing towards the planned total of 1,715; nine delivered to USAF for training duties pending availability of forthcoming HH-60A rescue version

EH-60A Black Hawk: specialized variant to perform battlefield ECM tasks with US Army, and instantly recognizable by virtue of dipole antenna array; first flown in prototype form as **YEH-60A** on 24 September 1981, current Army planning anticipating procurement of 77 production examples as part of on-going SEMA (Special Electronics Missions Aircraft) programme

HH-60A Night Hawk: combat search-and-rescue version for service with USAF, which intends to buy 90 for delivery from 1988; will possess ability to perform SAR by day or night at treetop height over a radius of 463 km (287 miles) and without recourse to inflight-refuelling or escort support

EH-60B Black Hawk: specialized version developed for Army's SOTAS (Stand-Off Target-Acquisition System) and first flown in February 1981; project terminated in September 1981

SH-60B Seahawk: anti-submarine warfare/anti-ship missile defence model now being delivered for use aboard US Navy surface combatants; present planning anticipates procurement of just over 200; features sophisticated array of sensors, sonobuoys and electronic equipment plus towed MAD (Magnetic Anomaly Detector)

SH-60C Seahawk: planned Navy model to equip carrier-borne ASW squadrons which presently use the SH-3H Sea King; deliveries are expected to begin in about 1988

HH-60D Night Hawk: initial all-weather combat SAR variant proposed for service with USAF; abandoned in favour of HH-60A

HH-60E Night Hawk: less capable version of SAR variant, originally to be operated alongside full-system HH-60D model; abandoned in favour of HH-60A

HH-60A recognition features

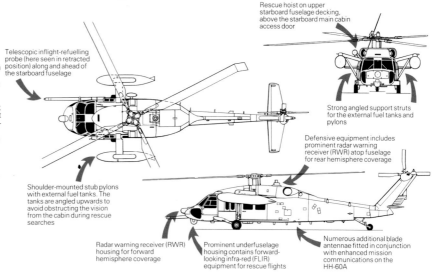

Rescue hoist on upper starboard fuselage decking, above the starboard main cabin access door

Telescopic inflight-refuelling probe (here seen in retracted position) along and ahead of the starboard fuselage

Strong angled support struts for the external fuel tanks and pylons

Defensive equipment includes prominent radar warning receiver (RWR) atop fuselage for rear hemisphere coverage

Shoulder-mounted stub pylons with external fuel tanks. The tanks are angled upwards to avoid obstructing the vision from the cabin during rescue searches

Numerous additional blade antennae fitted in conjunction with enhanced mission communications on the HH-60A

Radar warning receiver (RWR) housing for forward hemisphere coverage

Prominent underfuselage housing contains forward-looking infra-red (FLIR) equipment for rescue flights

Above: The ESSS pylons can carry four external fuel tanks, these consisting of two 870-litre (230 US-gal) tanks on the outboard pylons and two 1703-litre (450 US-gal) tanks inboard.

Above: Weapons trials with the Black Hawk and the External Stores Support System (ESSS) units have included the carriage and live firing of the Hellfire anti-armour missile, 16 of which can be carried.

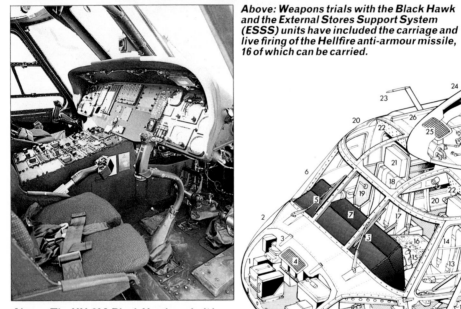

Above: The UH-60A Black Hawk cockpit is designed for two-pilot operation with full dual controls. The centre console between the pilot's armour-plated seats carries radio communication and systems controls.

Left: Another distinctive Black Hawk variant, which will not enter production, is the EH-60B, which was designed as a component within the Army's Stand-Off Target Acquisition System. The long underfuselage housing contains the antenna for the Motorola radar, with retractable landing gear.

Above: The EH-60A is easily distinguished the fuselage dipole antenna arrays and the underfuselage whip aerial, these forming p of the Quick Fix II radio jamming and ECM suite.

korsky UH-60A Black Hawk cutaway drawing key

Nose radio and electronics bay
Nose glazing

13 Sliding side window
14 Co-pilot's seat
15 Control column
16 Centre instrument console
17 Armoured seat backs
18 Pilot's seat
19 Sliding side armour panels
20 Cockpit eyebrows windows
21 Armoured headrests
22 Electrical fuse panels
23 Pitot tubes
24 Control equipment sliding access cover
25 Cooling intake grille
26 Sliding fairing guide rails
27 Control runs
28 Handrail/aerial bar
29 Gunner's sliding side windows, open
30 Cockpit step/main axle fairing
31 Port navigation light
32 Main undercarriage pivoted axle
33 Ground power supply
34 Swivelling gun mounting
35 Gunner's side facing seat
36 Port M-23D 7.62-mm machine-gun
37 Undercarriage shock absorber strut

46 Rotor blade titanium main spar
47 Bevel gearboxes
48 Starboard engine intake
49 Central main reduction gearbox
50 Rotor control swash plate
51 Rotor mast
52 Main rotor head (elastomeric non-lubricated bearings)
53 Bi-filar vibration damper
54 Rotor head fairing
55 Blade root attachments
56 Composite titanium spar/glass-fibre main rotor blades
57 Rotor blade drooped leading edge
58 Fixed trailing edge tabs
59 Blade pitch control rods
60 Port engine intake
61 Engine drive shaft
62 Aft sliding cabin door
63 Emergency door release handle
64 Cargo hook 3630-kg (8,000-lb) max capacity
65 Cabin accommodation, 11 troops plus one crew chief/gunner or four stretchers or internal cargo
66 Cabin rear bulkhead

79 Fireproof main fuel tanks, port and starboard, capacity 594 litres (157 US gal) each
80 Pressure refuelling connection
81 Fuselage frame and stringer construction
82 Tailcone joint frame
83 Engine exhaust shroud
84 APU exhaust
85 Engine/transmission rear fairing
86 Chaff dispenser
87 Anti-collision light

Radio compartment access door
Air grille
Windscreen wipers
Windscreen panels
nstrument panel shroud
Rudder pedals
Downward vision window
Boarding step
Cockpit door
Cyclic pitch control lever

67 Troop seats
68 Sliding door rail fairings
69 Engine cowlings
70 General Electric T700-GE-700 turboshaft engine
71 Exhaust cooling air fan, infra-red suppression
72 Oil cooler fan
73 Infra-red suppression oil cooler exhaust
74 Fire extinguishers
75 Formation light
76 Solar T-62T-40-1 auxiliary power unit
77 Engine exhaust pipe
78 Spring loaded maintenance steps

88 Tailcone frame and stringer construction
89 Dorsal spine fairing
90 Transmission shaft
91 Shaft bearings
92 Tail rotor control cables
93 Communications aerial
94 Tailwheel axle strut and fairing
95 Tailwheel
96 Shock absorber strut
97 Formation light
98 Bevel drive gearbox
99 Folding footrest
100 Tailcone rear fairing
101 Pull-out maintenance steps

102 Tail rotor drive shaft
103 Starboard tailplane
104 Formation light
105 Static discharge wicks
106 Fin leading edge supppressed aerial
107 Fin construction
108 Tail rotor drive gearbox
109 Canted (20-deg) tail rotor
110 Lightweight cross beam rotor hub
111 Pitch change spider
112 Graphite epoxy composite rotor blades
113 Anti-collision light

114 Tail navigation light
115 Troop commander's communications aerial
116 Cambered section fin
117 Tailplane hydraulic jack
118 Tailplane pivot fixing
119 Port tailplane construction
120 Formation light
121 Static discharge wicks

38 Port mainwheel
39 Cabin floor level
40 Folding maintenance step
41 Undercarriage mounting main frames
42 Hydraulic pump
43 Flight control mixer unit
44 Cabin heater
45 Engine driven accessory units

© Pilot Press Limited

---

erformance:

imum speed at sea level	160 kts	296 km/h (184 mph)
ice ceiling	19,000 ft	(5790 m)
ering ceiling in ground ect at 35°	9,500 ft	(2895 m)
ering ceiling out of ground ect at 35°	5,600 ft	(1705 m)
imum range at maximum weight with 30-minute erve	556 km	(345 miles)

Maximum cargo load, carried externally

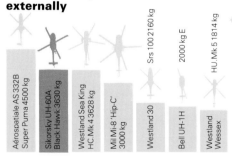

Aérospatiale AS 332B Super Puma 4500 kg
Sikorsky UH-60A Black Hawk 3630 kg
Westland Sea King HC.Mk 4 3628 kg
Mil Mi-8 'Hip-C' 3000 kg
Westland 30
Bell UH-1H
Westland Wessex
Srs 100 2160 kg
2000 kg E
HU.Mk 5 1814 kg

Maximum rate of climb

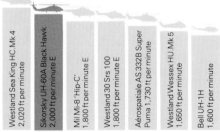

Westland Sea King HC.Mk 4 2,020 ft per minute
Sikorsky UH-60A Black Hawk 2,000 ft per minute E
Mil Mi-8 'Hip-C' 1,800 ft per minute E
Westland 30 Srs 100 1,800 ft per minute E
Aérospatiale AS 332B Super Puma 1,730 ft per minute
Westland Wessex HU.Mk 5 1,650 ft per minute
Bell UH-1H 1,600 ft per minute

aximum speed at low altitude

orsky UH-60A Black Hawk 160 kts
rospatiale AS 332B Super Puma 151 kts
estland Sea King HC.Mk 4 129 kts
estland 30 Srs 100 120 kts
Mi-8 'Hip-C' 119 kts
estland Wessex HU.Mk 5 115 kts
ll UH-1H 110 kts

Standard range maximum fuel

Aérospatiale AS 332B Super Puma 635 km
Westland Wessex HU.Mk 5 628 km
Sikorsky UH-60A Black Hawk 600 km*
Bell UH-1H 511 km
Westland Sea King HC.Mk 4 445 km*
Mil Mi-8 'Hip-C' 360 km*
Westland 30 Srs 100 352 km

(* with 30 minutes reserves)

Number of troops carried with full equipment

Westland Sea King HC.Mk 4 28
Mil Mi-8 'Hip-C' 28
Aérospatiale AS 332B Super Puma 21
Westland Wessex HU.Mk 5 16
Westland 30 Srs 100 14
Bell UH-1H 11
Sikorsky UH-60A Black Hawk 11

Vought A-7A, B, C, E and L Corsair II

A Vought EA-7L Corsair II ECM aircraft of VAQ-34.

The Vought A-7 Corsair II was designed to replace the McDonnell Douglas A-4 Skyhawk, the US Navy's standard carrierborne light attack aircraft during the late 1950s and early 1960s. The A-4, affectionately known as the 'Scooter', was fast and agile but lacked range and load-carrying capability. On 11 February 1964 it was announced that Vought had won the competition to produce a low-cost replacement, which was to have a longer range and greater payload. Whereas the A-4 had been optimized for the delivery of a single nuclear weapon, its replacement was to be the first post-war aircraft to be developed for close air support and battlefield attack targets.

America's involvement in the Vietnam war highlighted the shortcomings of the A-4, and every effort was made to get the new aircraft into service as soon as possible. It was decided at a very early stage that the new aircraft should be an adaptation of an existing design, and that it should use an existing engine. Vought's submission was based on the successful F-8 Crusader supersonic fighter, but using the Pratt & Whitney TF30 turbofan of the ill-starred F-111B.

Whereas the slim and shapely Crusader was highly supersonic, the new A-7 had a shorter, fatter fuselage, a shortened fin and a blunt nose, and was designed from the outset to be subsonic, with long range and endurance being more important priorities

than high speed. A prototype was quickly constructed, and made its maiden flight on 27 September 1965.

One hundred and ninety-nine of the initial production variant, the **A-7A**, were eventually ordered by the US Navy, the first entering service with VA-174 'Hell Razors' on 14 October 1966. Steam ingestion problems restricted the A-7A's catapult launch weight to 17236 kg (38,000 lb), but this problem was remedied in the **A-7B**, powered by the more powerful TF-30-P-8 turbofan. One hundred and ninety-six A-7Bs were built, 24 later being converted to two-seaters with the designation **TA-7C**.

The 67 **A-7C**s built were an interim variant with a new head-up display, updated bombing system and a single M61A1 Vulcan cannon with 1,000 rounds of ammunition replacing the twin Mk 12 20-mm cannon with their 680 rounds. Thirty-six were later converted to TA-7Cs. Forty-nine TA-7Cs are being rebuilt with TF41 engines, new ejection seats and automatic manoeuvring flaps.

Six of these will be the aircraft reassigned to VAQ-34 for electronic warfare duties and redesignated **EA-7L** during March 1983. The final US Navy Corsair variant was the **A-7E**, basically an A-7C with the TF41-A-2 turbofan, a development of the Rolls-Royce Spey. These modifications were similar to those specified by the US Air Force for its A-7s. Five hundred and thirty-five were built.

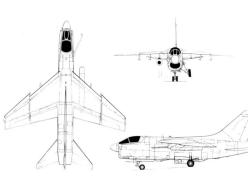

Vought A-7E Corsair II

Although many Corsair units have already re-equipped with the more versatile and more modern McDonnell Douglas F-18 Hornet, the A-7E will be in service for some years.

Many surviving US Navy A-7E Corsair IIs have been re-equipped with FLIR pods for all-weather attack duties, and some will remain in front line service until the end of the decade.

Specification: Vought A-7E Corsair II
Origin: USA
Type: single-seat tactical fighter
Powerplant: one 6804-kg (15,000-lb) thrust Allison TF41-A-2 turbofan engine
Performance: maximum speed 600 kts (1112 km/h; 691 mph) at sea level; maximum speed at 5,000 ft (1525 m) with a 2722-kg (6,000 lb) bombload 561 kts (1040 km/h; 646 mph); service ceiling 51,000ft (15545 m); ferry range on internal fuel 3669 km (2,280 miles)
Weights: empty 8676 kg (19,127 lb); maximum take-off 19051 kg (42,000 lb)
Dimensions: span 11.81 m (38 ft 9 in); length 14.06 m (46 ft 1.5 in) height 4.90 m (16 ft 0.75 in); wing area 34.84 m² (375.0 sq ft)
Armament: one M61A1 20-mm cannon with 1,000 rounds in the port lower fuselage, plus more than 6804 kg (15,000 lb) of stores on eight weapon stations.

Vought A-7D and K

United States

Although originally designed as a strike fighter for the US Navy, the Corsair soon began to attract interest from the US Air Force, who saw the aircraft as an ideal replacement for the F-100 Super Sabre and F-105 Thunderchief in the tactical strike role. Although attempts to write a common USN/USAF specification for a new attack aircraft failed, USAF interest in the A-7 Corsair was always strong, and grew steadily. A request to buy A-7s was included in the FY 1967 budget.

To meet USAF requirements a new variant, the **A-7D**, was developed. Although the first two **YA-7D** prototypes were initially powered by the standard TF-30-P-6 of the A-7B and A-7C, the other three prototypes, and all production USAF aircraft were powered by the Allison TF41-A-2 turbofan, developed from the Rolls-Royce Spey.

Other changes incorporated in the USAF aircraft included an updated and refined nav/attack system, a new head-up display, and new internal cannon armament. The twin Mk 12 20-mm cannon, with their 680 rounds of ammunition, were replaced by a single M61A1 Vulcan with 1,000 rounds. The pilot can select several different rates of fire between 4,000 to 6,000 rounds per minute.

The first YA-7D made its maiden flight on 6 April 1968, and the third TF41-A-2 powered YA-7D followed on 26 September. The first 16 A-7Ds were delivered with a US Navy style retractable inflight-refuelling probe, but later aircraft had a standard USAF refuelling receptacle on the fuselage spine. 459 A-7Ds

were built, one being converted to two-seat configuration to serve as the A-87K prototype.

Initial service deliveries were made in December 1969, to the 4525th Fighter Weapons Wing at Luke AFB, and the type was soon in service in South East Asia. By the mid-1970s the US Air Force was examining its requirements for a new attack aircraft optimized for dealing with the Soviet armoured threats. Tests were carried out with an A-7D armed with two podded underwing GAU-8/A 30 cannon, but this solution was rejected in favour of procurement of the Fairchild A-10A Thunderbolt II, which began to replace the A-7 in front line squadrons during the early 1980s.

The A-7D's career is far from over, however, since it continues to serve with the Nellis-based 4450th Tactical Training Group. and with 14 squadrons of the Air National Guard. The first ANG squadron re-equipped with the A-7 during October 1975, and a 15th unit may convert from the A-37.

All surviving A-7Ds were retro-fitted with Automatic Manoeuvring Flaps from 1977, these being fitted to the last two production aircraft 'on the line'. Thirty two-seat **A-7K**s were built, the last being delivered in September 1984. None served with the active duty air force. Forty-eight A-7Ds and six A-7Ks are currently being fitted with Low Altitude Night Attack (LANA) pods, containing a FLIR. The name Corsair II has never been formally adopted by the US Air Force.

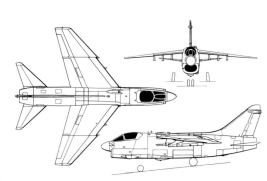

An A-7K of the 125th Tactical Fighter Squadron, Oklahoma Air National Guard.

Vought A-7D

This A-7D of the 175th TFS, South Dakota Air National Guard, was pictured during the 'Coronet Buffalo' deployment to RAF Waddington, from Joe Foss Field, Sioux Falls.

This A-7K wears the 'HA' tailcode and yellow fin stripe of the 174th TFS, Idaho Air National Guard, based at Sioux City Municipal Airport. A small bat emblem decorates the fin stripe.

Specification: Vought A-7D
Origin: USA
Type: single-seat tactical fighter
Powerplant: one 6577 kg (14,500-lb) Allison T41-A-1 non afterburning turbofan engine
Performance: maximum speed 600 kts (1112 km/h; 691 mph) at sea level; maximum speed at 5,000 ft (1525 m) with a 2722-kg (6,000 lb) bombload 561 kts (1040 km/h; 646 mph); service ceiling 51,000 ft (15545 m); ferry range on internal fuel 3669 km (2,280 miles)
Weights: empty 8676 kg (19,127 lb); maximum take-off 19051 kg (42,000 lb)
Dimensions: span 11.81 m (38 ft 9 in); length 14.06 m (46 ft 1.5 in); height 4.90 m (16 ft 75 in); wing area 34.84 m² (375.0 sq ft)
Armament: one M61A1 20-mm Vulcan cannon with 1,000 rounds in the port lower fuselage, plus more than 6804 kg (15,000 lb) of stores on eight weapons stations.

Role
Fighter
Close support
Counter-insurgency
Tactical strike
Strategic bomber
Tactical reconnaissance
Strategic reconnaissance
Maritime patrol
Anti-ship strike
Anti-submarine warfare
Search and rescue
Assault transport
Transport
Liaison
Trainer
Inflight-refuelling tanker
Specialized

Performance
All-weather capability
Rough field capability
STOL capability
VTOL capability
Airspeed 0-250 mph
Airspeed 250 mph-Mach 1
Airspeed Mach 1 plus
Ceiling 0-20,000 ft
Ceiling 20,000-40,000 ft
Ceiling 40,000 ft plus
Range 0-1,000 miles
Range 1,000-3,000 miles
Range 3,000 miles plus

Weapons
Air-to-air missiles
Air-to-surface missiles
Cruise missiles
Cannon
Trainable guns
Naval weapons
Nuclear-capable
Rockets
'Smart' weapon kit
Weapon load 0-4,000 lb
Weapon load 4,000-15,000 lb
Weapon load 15,000 lb plus

Avionics
Electronic Counter Measures
Electronic Support Measures
Search radar
Fire control radar
Look-down/shoot-down
Terrain-following radar
Forward-looking infra-red
Laser
Television

GLOSSARY

AAA	Anti-Aircraft Artillery		**MCAS**	Marine Corps Air Station
AAM	Air-to-Air Missile		**NAS**	Naval Air Station
ACM	Air Combat Manoeuvre		**NAVWAS**	NAVigation and Weapon-Aiming System
AFB	Air-Force Base		**NWDS**	Navigation and Weapons Delivery System
AFRes	Air Force Reserve		**OAS**	Offensive Avionics System
ANG	Air National Guard		**OCU**	Operational Conversion Unit
AHRS	Attitude and Heading Reference System		**OTEAF**	Operational Test and EvaluAtion Force
ALARM	Air-Launched Anti-Radiation Missile		**PGM**	Precision-Guided Munition
ALCM	Air-Launched Cruise Missile		**Photint**	Photographic intelligence
ARM	Anti-Radiation Missile		**QRA**	Quick-Reaction Alert
ASM	Air-to-Surface Missile		**RAAF**	Royal Australian Air Force
ASMP	Air-Sol Moyenne Portee (medium-range surface-to-air)		**RDT&E**	Research, Development, Test and Evaluation
AMRAAM	Advanced Medium-Range Air-to-Air Missile		**RIO**	Radio Intercept Officer
AV-MF	Soviet Naval Aviation		**RNAS**	Royal Naval Air Station
BW	Bomber Wing		**RWR**	Radar Warning Receiver
CBU	Cluster Bomb Unit		**SAC**	Strategic Air Command
CILOP	Conversion In Lieu Of Procurement		**SACEUR**	Supreme Allied Commander EURope
CITS	Central Integrated Test System		**SACLANT**	Supreme Allied Commander AtLANTic
COMED	COmbined Map and Electronic Display		**SAM**	Surface-to-Air Missile
CRT	Cathode Ray Tube		**SAR**	Search And Rescue
DARIN	Display, Attack, Ranging and Inertial Navigation		**SEAM**	Sidewinder Expanded-Acquisition Missile
DME	Distance Measuring Equipment		**SIOP**	Single Integrated Operational Plan
ECM	Electronic CounterMeasures		**SLEP**	Service Life Extension Program
Elint	Electronic Intelligence		**SNOE**	Smart Noise Operation Equipment
EMP	Electro-Magnetic Pulse		**SOR**	Specific Operational Requirement
EO	Electro-Optical		**SRAM**	Short-Range Attack Missile
ESM	Electronic Support Measures		**Tacan**	Tactical air navigation
EVS	Electro-optical Viewing System		**TAC**	Tactical Air Command
EW	Electronic Warfare		**TERCOM**	TERrain COntour Matching
FLIR	Forward-Looking Infra-Red		**TFR**	Terrain Following Radar
GP	General Purpose		**TFS**	Tactical Fighter Squadron
GSFG	Group of Soviet Forces in Germany		**TFW**	Tactical Fighter Wing
HARM	High-speed Anti-Radiation Missile		**TFX**	Tactical Fighter eXperimental
HUD	Head-Up Display		**TISL**	Target Indicator System - Laser
HUDWAS	Head-Up Display and Weapon-Aiming System		**TRAM**	Target Recognition and Attack Multi-sensor
IFF	Identification Friend or Foe		**TRIM**	Trails, Roads, Interdiction Multi-sensor
ILS	Instrument Landing System		**TTTE**	Trinational Tornado Training Establishment
INS	Inertial Navigation System		**UHF**	Ultra High Frequency
IOC	Initial Operational Capability		**VG**	Variable Geometry
IR	Infra-Red		**VHF**	Very High Frequency
IRCM	Infra-Red CounterMeasures		**VOR**	VHF Omni-directional Range
JATO	Jet-Assisted Take-Off		**VTAS**	Visual Target-Acquisition System
LID	Lift-Improvement Device		**VTOL**	Vertical Take-Off and Landing
LLLTV	Low-Light-Level TV		**V-VS**	Soviet air force
LRMTS	Laser Ranger and Marked-Target Seeker		**WAC**	Weapon-Aiming Computer
			WSO	Weapons System Officer